A. R. GURNEY
Collected Plays Volume V
1991–1995

ALSO BY A. R. GURNEY

A. R. Gurney Collected Plays Volume I: Nine Early plays

A. R. Gurney Collected Plays Volume II: 1977–1985

A. R. Gurney Collected Plays Volume III: 1984–1991

A. R. Gurney Collected Plays Volume IV: 1992–1999

A. R. GURNEY

Collected Plays Volume V
1991–1995

CONTEMPORARY PLAYWRIGHTS
SERIES

SK
A Smith and Kraus Book

A Smith and Kraus Book
Published by Smith and Kraus, Inc.
177 Lyme Road, Hanover, NH 03755
www.SmithKraus.com

Copyright © 2001 by A.R. Gurney
All rights reserved
Manufactured in the United States of America
Cover and text design by Julia Hill Gignoux, Freedom Hill Design
Cover Photo: Susan J. Coon and Christopher Wells. Photography by Ken Howard.
First Edition: August 2001
10 9 8 7 6 5 4 3 2 1

CONTENTS

PREFACE

All the plays in this volume are either adaptations or, in some way, responses to other written works. They come out of those times in my writing life when I have been seized by the feelings caused by a story or a book or another play rather than inspired by the raw material of the real world. (*The Snow Ball* is a stage adaptation of my own novel so it doesn't quite count as a response to another writer's work.) In any case, you might want to argue that these adaptations are less vibrantly original than works which are more anchored in actuality, but I'm not sure you'd be right. It's hard to know what best triggers the creative impulse; there are many ways to light a fire.

THE SNOW BALL

To Jack O'Brien and Graciela Daniele

ORIGINAL PRODUCTION

The Snow Ball was produced at the Hartford Stage Company (Mark Lamos, Artistic Director; David Haukanson, Managing Director) in Hartford, Connecticut, on February 9, 1991. It was directed by Jack O'Brien; the set design was by Douglas W. Schmidt; the costume design was by Steven Rubin; the lighting design was by David F. Segal; the sound design by Jeff Ladman; the choreographer was Graciela Daniele; the ballroom coach was Willie Rosario and the production stage manager was Barbara Reo. The cast was as follows:

COOPER JONES	James R. Winker
LUCY DUNBAR	Kandis Chappell
LIZ JONES	Katherine McGrath
VAN DAM, BALDWIN HALL	Tom Lacy
YOUNG JACK	Christopher Wells
YOUNG KITTY	Susan J. Coon
SAUL RADNER	Robert Phalen
JOAN DALEY	Deborah Taylor
JACK DALEY	Donald Wayne
KITTY PRICE	Rita Gardner

VARIOUS MEMBERS OF THE COMMUNITY
AS CHILDREN AND ADULTS . . . . . . Mary R. Barnett, Terrence Caza, Brian John Driscoll, Driscoll, Cynthia D. Hanson, Robert Phalen, Mimi Quillin, Deborah Taylor, John Thomas Waite

The Snow Ball was subsequently produced at the Old Globe Theatre in San Diego, California, on May 4, 1991, and at the Huntington Theatre in Boston, Massachusetts, on September 25, 1991, with much of the same cast. In these two productions, Douglas Pagliotti was the production stage manager. In Boston, George Deloy and Deborah May played Cooper and Lucy.

AUTHOR'S NOTE

In 1990, Jack O'Brien, the artistic director of the Old Globe Theatre, who over the years had produced or directed several of my plays, asked me to try "a larger palette." I decided to adapt a novel of mine, *The Snow Ball,* which had been published in 1984 and which I had put in novel form only because it seemed to require too large a cast and too many sets for the stage. With Jack's encouragement, I managed to confine the story to a cast of fifteen, Graciela Daniele joined us as choreographer, and we gathered an excellent cast from New York and San Diego. With the help of Mark Lamos, the artistic director of the Hartford Stage Company, we opened there first, before going on to the Old Globe, and finally to the Huntington Theatre in Boston. Along the way, we shaped and adjusted it, garnering some pretty good reviews, with the result that several New York producers became interested in "bringing it in." Our hopes were dashed by a bad review in the *Boston Globe,* but even so, I suspect that the peculiar form of the work—half play, half musical—didn't inspire total confidence in what we had done.

A couple of years later, Mark Brokaw directed a first-rate production of the play at the Studio Arena Theatre in Buffalo, but beyond that, it hasn't had much of a life. Occasionally, community theaters will take a crack at it, but I know from experience it's not easy to do. On the other hand, I remain very fond of this piece. I like its Gatsbyesque plot, and its feel for the city of Buffalo, where I spent my youth. The dance scenes always seem to pay off because they are about more than just dancing, and Cooper's middle-aged dalliance with Lucy I like to think forms an ironic counterpoint to Jack and Kitty's youthful innocence. I also am fond of several scenes in the play; particularly the ones with Kitty's husband and Jack's wife, pay off, in my humble opinion.

The Snow Ball also became a cause for me to resign from the Dramatists Guild, which during that period was seeking various concessions from the regional theaters. The controversy was complicated on both sides and in retrospect seems somewhat unnecessary, but at the time, passions were raging, and my play got caught in the crossfire. All is forgiven now, I hope, on both sides.

CHARACTERS

(Sixteen actors minimum)

Individual parts:

> COOPER JONES.
>
> LIZ, his wife.
>
> LUCY DUNBAR, his friend.
>
> JACK DALEY, as a young man.
>
> JACK DALEY, as an older man.
>
> KITTY PRICE, as a young woman.
>
> KITTY PRICE, as an older woman.

Multiple Parts:

> MR. VAN DAM and BALDWIN HALL
>
> SAUL RADNER, WORKMAN, and FRITZI KLINGER.
>
> JOAN DALEY, BARBARA FISKE, and RHODA RADNER.
>
> GINNY WATERS and TELEVISION INTERVIEWER.
>
> BILLY WICKWIRE, TELEVISION CAMERAMAN, and WAITER.
>
> CALVIN POTTER, MUSICIAN, and WAITER.
>
> HEATHER HEALY and WAITRESS.
>
> BREWSTER DUNN, MR. SMITHERS, and WORKMAN.
>
> MARY MONTESANA and others.

SETTING

The play takes place primarily in the Cotillion Room, an elegant ballroom in the old George Washington Hotel, in a large midwestern city. There is a sumptuous staircase, a good dance floor surrounded by small tables and gilt bentwood chairs, and a high palladian window looking out at a downtown skyline. Snow may be seen through the window as necessary. Props as needed. A rolling table, serving as a blueprint stand at the beginning, may become a desk, a bar, a counter, and so forth.

The play is designed to be performed to recorded music.

The time is today and yesterday.

THE SNOW BALL

ACT ONE

At rise: A spotlight isolates a young couple, Jack Daley and Kitty Price, danc-
ing elegantly, spinning, turning, dipping, with a wonderful casual ease to the
sounds of a lovely old tune played by a brisk society band. Behind them, through
the window, we can see large snowflakes slowly drifting down.
   Cooper Jones, a middle-aged man in a raincoat, enters down the stair-
case, watches them, and then speaks to the audience.

COOPER: Jack Daley and Kitty Price were the best dancers in town. There is
   absolutely no doubt about that. It took your breath away to watch them.
   A kind of special space would emerge around them on the dance floor,
   as the rest of us would step back to give them room and then stand around
   and watch them dance. *(He watches them for a moment.)* Of course, they
   weren't quite so good when they were dancing with someone else. *(Billy*
   Wickwire cuts in on Kitty.) Kitty would be light on her feet and follow
   fairly well, but she'd always get a little lazy and run into trouble on the
   turns . . . *(We see this. Heather Healy comes on to dance with Jack.)* And
   the girls used to say, when they danced with Jack, that he was always looking over their shoulders, looking for Kitty, yearning for a time to dance
   with her again . . . *(We see this, too. Then they change partners so that Jack*
   is once again dancing with Kitty. The other couple disappears.) But together
   Jack and Kitty were unbeatable. For a few years there, in the center of
   the century, they ruled the roost. They were by far the best at dancing
   school, the main attraction at all the other parties, and topped even themselves at the Snow Ball . . . *(The light fades on the dancers. The music fades*
   into the sound of hammering and power tools as the lights come up on the
   Cotillion Room. We see ladders, a worktable with blueprints, as Two Workmen
   finish up for the day. Through the window, upstage, we see the lights from
   other downtown buildings, glassy and modern. It is late afternoon, late fall.
   Lucy Dunbar, also middle-aged, also in an overcoat, hurries in.)
LUCY: *(Breathlessly.)* Sorry I'm late. Our sweet little bookstore has just been
   bought out by what is called "a chain." Which means they chain us to
   the checkout counters. I had to plead temporary insanity to get away.
COOPER: I've been looking around.
LUCY: I knew you would . . . Doesn't it ring a wonderful old bell?
COOPER: A bell, at least.

LUCY: Dancing school?

COOPER: Jack and Kitty . . .

LUCY: The Snow Ball?

COOPER: Jack and Kitty dancing at the Snow Ball . . . *(A glimpse of Jack and Kitty, dancing in the shadows.)*

LUCY: We're making the room exactly the way it was, Cooper. Floor, furniture, everything. We had it legally landmarked.

COOPER: I can see.

LUCY: The rest of this hotel, the rest of downtown, the rest of the WORLD can be redeveloped to DEATH for all I care, but this room stays exactly the same.

COOPER: Good work.

LUCY: I thought you, of all people, should see.

COOPER: What's that supposed to mean?

LUCY: Well I mean you sold the building.

COOPER: The bank sold it.

LUCY: You made the DEAL, Cooper. You were the real estate broker for the whole operation.

COOPER: It's what I do, Lucy.

LUCY: Oh yes. And you did it. I just hope you made a huge pile of money.

COOPER: I made almost enough to keep two kids in college another term.

LUCY: Well, the point is, a few of us managed to save this room.

COOPER: I'm glad you did. *(A Workman passes by, putting on his coat.)*

WORKMAN: Night, Mrs. Dunbar.

LUCY: Goodnight, Eddie.

ANOTHER WORKMAN: *(Indicating the window.)* Starting to snow. *(They leave.)*

LUCY: *(Calling after them.)* Drive carefully! *(Pause. They look at each other.)*

COOPER: I'd better get home, too. *(Starts out.)*

LUCY: I'm thinking of bringing it back, Cooper.

COOPER: Bringing what back?

LUCY: The Snow Ball. This Christmas. To reopen this room.

COOPER: Oh come on . . .

LUCY: And I want you to help me organize it.

COOPER: Why me?

LUCY: I need your clout. You're a civic leader around here.

COOPER: Not these days, Lucy.

LUCY: You ran the Symphony Drive. You did that work for the Zoo . . .

COOPER: I don't do dances.

LUCY: You owe it to me, Cooper.

COOPER: OWE it to you?

LUCY: And to yourself.

COOPER: Oh please.

LUCY: You sold your heritage.

COOPER: Oh for Chrissake!

LUCY: Your grandfather BUILT this building! Your father kept it going. And you let the whole thing slip through your fingers!

COOPER: Times change!

LUCY: If we let them.

COOPER: Life goes on, Lucy.

LUCY: Life? Is that life out there? In those great, glass buildings? Or in that lonely walk-up I go home to these days? Is that LIFE? Or was this life, right here, in this lovely old room?

COOPER: *Was* is the operative word.

LUCY: And could be again. At least for one night.

COOPER: It would never work without Jack and Kitty. *(Jack and Kitty glide through the shadows upstage.)*

LUCY: Then we'll bring them back, too!

COOPER: You're a hopeless romantic, Lucy.

LUCY: *(Touching his arm.)* Me? What about you? I KNOW you, Cooper Jones. I used to dance with you, remember? *(He goes to look out the window.)*

COOPER: It's early for snow.

LUCY: See? It's a good omen.

COOPER: Or a warning.

LUCY: Oh please, Cooper. Let's do it. Let's put our best foot forward, one last time.

COOPER: Better get home.

LUCY: And I've got to get back to the chain gang. We're doing inventory, God help us. Everything over six months old gets immediately remaindered. Even the Bible will be fifty percent off. *(Starts off.)*

COOPER: Need a ride?

LUCY: No thanks. Gordon at least left me a car . . . Will you do it, Cooper?

COOPER: Liz would laugh in my face.

LUCY: Well if she won't dance with you, I will.

COOPER: I haven't danced in twenty years.

LUCY: It'll all come back, I promise . . . *(She hurries off. The lights focus in on Cooper. Behind, in a dim light, the Cotillion Room begins to emerge as it once looked. Off to one side, a group of boys gathers in the shadows. They wear white shirts and dark blue suits and shined shoes.)*

BREWSTER DANN: *(Calling to Cooper.)* Come on, Cooper! You can't get out of it!

BILLY WICKWIRE: No one gets out of dancing school!

FRITZI KLINGER: Unless you get the mumps.

BREWSTER: *(Clutching his groin.)* Aagh! Which is almost worth it. *(On the other side, a group of girls begins to gather, all in formal dresses with white gloves and black patent leather shoes. They primp and giggle.)*

BARBARA FISKE: Is it true you hate girls, Cooper?

GINNY WATERS: Or are you just shy?

HEATHER HEALY: He's cute when he blushes.

LIZ: *(As a young girl.)* Boys never know what to say.

BARBARA: That's why they have to go to dancing school.

COOPER: *(Becoming a boy.)* I'll never go to dancing school. Ever. If they send me, I'll walk right out and go to the movies.

BREWSTER: Five bucks says you don't.

COOPER: Shake. *(They shake hands. The handshake turns into Indian wrestling, which degenerates into a chaotic wrestling match on the floor, as the boys cheer and the girls squeal and shriek. Mr. Van Dam, the dancing master, a portly man in tails, appears from the shadows. He taps his walking stick on the floor for order. The boys quickly break up their fight and scamper to their seats on one side of the room. The girls hurry to the other. Cooper gets caught in the center without a chair, has to find one. When things are settled, Van Dam slowly parades in front of the class, inspecting it. Lucy, now in a formal dress, has by now joined the girls.)*

VAN DAM: Posture! Posture! Show the world a straight back! *(He moves up the line.)* I am looking at feet, I am looking at hands, I am looking at fingernails.

BREWSTER: *(To himself.)* Oh Christ, I forgot to pee.

BARBARA: *(To herself.)* I'm getting a pimple on my nose. It feels like Mount Monadnock!

VAN DAM: The young ladies, while seated, will keep their heels, and knees, together, with their hands folded delicately, palms upward, in their laps. *(The girls do this.)*

FRITZI: *(To himself.)* What a waste of time! I could be organizing my comic books.

LIZ: *(To herself.)* I hate being new at places. Everybody knows everybody and nobody knows me.

VAN DAM: The young gentlemen, on the other hand, will keep their legs somewhat apart, with each hand resting lightly on each knee, palms downward, in a manly fashion. *(The boys do this. They begin to communicate with each other.)*

CALVIN: *(To his neighbor.)* I wanted to bring my dog, but my parents wouldn't let me.

BREWSTER: *(Indicating the row of girls.)* There's plenty of dogs right here. *(Van Dam is now taking a furtive slug from a silver flask.)*

HEATHER: *(Whispering to her neighbor.)* Do you realize we're missing the entire *Hit Parade*?

MARY: My little brother's making a list of the songs.

BILLY: *(To Cooper.)* Why do we have to come here, anyway?

COOPER: My mother says it will make us better husbands.

FRITZI: My father says it will make us better lovers. *(The others look at him; he shrugs.)*

LUCY: *(To another girl.)* I just read *Peyton Place.*

MARY: I hear that's a dirty book.

LUCY: Oh, it is! They even take a shower together.

LIZ: *(To Barbara.)* My name's Liz. My mother sent me here to make friends.

BARBARA: I have too many friends. But I could squeeze you in on Saturday mornings.

COOPER: *(To Brewster.)* This afternoon, we saw Rita Hayworth in *Gilda.*

BREWSTER: Boiingg! *(Van Dam notices Billy.)*

VAN DAM: Mr. Wickwire, we do not wear white socks to dancing school.

BILLY: I was playing hockey, sir. I hardly had time to change my pants. *(Giggles from all.)*

VAN DAM: Gentlemen bathe, Mr. Wickwire. Gentlemen change their stockings and their linen. And gentlemen say "trousers" instead of "pants."

BILLY: Yes, sir.

VAN DAM: Mr. Cromeier, may I review the music? *(He exits.)*

BARBARA: I hate boys. I hate their guts.

HEATHER: I wish they weren't so basically grubby.

MARY: You're cheating, Lucy. You're wearing a bra!

LUCY: This is just Kleenex. It doesn't count.

BREWSTER: Who farted? Somebody cut the cheese around here. *(Van Dam comes back, tapping his stick.)*

VAN DAM: The young gentlemen will now ask the young ladies to dance. *(The boys reluctantly cross the floor, jockeying for position. Liz goes up to Van Dam. Whispers in his ear.)* What? . . . Again? . . . Oh go on. *(Liz scurries out.)* The young gentlemen will bow. *(The boys bow awkwardly.)* The young ladies will rise and curtsy. *(The girls do.)* Handkerchiefs out . . . Positions, please . . . One, two, three . . . *(The boys take handkerchiefs out of their pockets and put them in their right hands, so as not to soil the girls' dresses.)* One, two, three, four . . . *(They assume the dancing position. Van Dam taps his stick again.)* We will now review the Schottische . . . Music, Mr. Cromeier, if you please. *(The music begins: some simple two-step, played very slowly. The couples move stiffly, as Van Dam, with his stick, moves among them.)* Small steps, please . . . And one and two and . . . Gently, please . . . If you young ladies and gentlemen can't learn the simple Schottische, how do you ever expect to dance at the Snow Ball?

LUCY: *(To Cooper, as they dance.)* Isn't this fun?

COOPER: *(Sullenly.)* Oh yeah. Sure. Goodie goodie gumdrop.

LUCY: No, but just think. Last week, you chased me home from school. And now you're *dancing* with me.

COOPER: I plan to get out, you know. Errol Flynn got out of Nazi Germany, and so will I.

LUCY: But why? Dancing can be a wonderful way of getting to know people.

COOPER: Stop talking, please. I'm planning my escape.

(They dance. Liz, now in modern clothes, stands at a table. She combs her hair in a "mirror." The music continues under.)

LIZ: *(Calling to Cooper as he dances.)* What's this I hear about reviving the Snow Ball?

COOPER: *(Coming out of the dance.)* What? There's talk of it. Yes.

(The dancers dance off.)

LIZ: From Lucy Dunbar, I'll bet.

COOPER: *(Going through the mail on the table.)* Lucy is exploring the idea, yes.

LIZ: Ever since her divorce, she's had a bug up her ass.

COOPER: Jesus, Liz.

LIZ: Well she has. And I didn't like that kiss she gave you the other night.

COOPER: She was wishing me a happy birthday.

LIZ: Oh is that what she was wishing?

COOPER: She's recovering from a rough marriage, Liz. They say that guy used to beat her up.

LIZ: And how does the Snow Ball solve that?

COOPER: I imagine she wants to be treated like a lady again.

LIZ: I imagine she wants to meet another man. *(She gets her bag.)*

COOPER: Where're you going?

LIZ: I've got a meeting. Down at the office.

COOPER: At seven in the evening?

LIZ: It's the only time we could all meet. There's that macaroni stuff in the freezer.

COOPER: Sounds delicious. *(Reads his mail.)* What's this "Lab supplies" for Teddy? I thought he hated science.

LIZ: That's a film course. It's called Film Lab. They make films.

COOPER: 225 bucks! What's he making? *Ten Commandments Two?*

LIZ: Now, now.

COOPER: No science, no foreign language, no history. Next term he at least has to take a history course. Agreed?

LIZ: Agreed.

COOPER: He who ignores the past is doomed to repeat it.

LIZ: I said I agreed. *(Pause.)*

COOPER: But you don't like the idea of the Snow Ball.

LIZ: I think it sucks.

COOPER: Liz, hey, your language. You've been working with street people too long.

LIZ: *(Putting on lipstick.)* Well at least I'm not Lucy Dunbar, digging up dead dogs.

COOPER: She got them to refurbish the Cotillion Room. That's a good thing.

LIZ: I guess.

COOPER: You *guess?* We met in that room. We had our wedding reception there.

LIZ: It was a lovely room . . .

COOPER: Why not reopen it with a splash?

LIZ: Because no one *dances* that way any more, Cooper. Kids don't know how to, and grown-ups don't want to.

COOPER: I want to.

LIZ: Oh come on.

COOPER: *(Trying to dance with her.)* I remember a time when you wanted to.

LIZ: *(Breaking away.)* Cooper, I am late. It's a meeting on homelessness, and I happen to be running it.

COOPER: *(Watching her get ready.)* There's even talk of bringing back Jack and Kitty.

(Upstage Young Jack and Kitty are seen dancing.)

LIZ: Jack and Kitty haven't even *seen* each other in several centuries.

COOPER: Still, there's talk.

LIZ: Don't tell me you're personally involved in all this.

COOPER: I'm thinking about it.

LIZ: Oh Lord, Cooper. You always go overboard on these things. First it was the philharmonic. Then the zoo . . .

COOPER: I happen to care about endangered species.

LIZ: Well I'm sorry, but I can't get wound up over some dumb dance while this city disintegrates around us.

COOPER: Maybe you'd like to turn the Cotillion Room into a shelter.

LIZ: Better than having a bunch of old Wasps waddle the dance floor!

COOPER: Don't knock your roots all the time, Liz!

LIZ: The hell with roots! Roots hold you down!

COOPER: They also keep you alive.

LIZ: You can't turn back the clock, Cooper!

COOPER: So I'm left to turn on the microwave.

LIZ: Cooper, it's snowing like mad and I'm already late!
    (She starts out.)

COOPER: *(Calling after her.)* Homelessness begins at home, Liz! *(Picks up telephone, starts to dial.)*

LIZ: *(Returning.)* You made me forget my briefcase — Who're you calling?

COOPER: A friend.

LIZ: Oh.

COOPER: An old friend.

LIZ: Oh.

COOPER: Someone who stays at home at the end of the day.

LIZ: Oh, Cooper.

COOPER: Why? Do you care?

LIZ: *(Kissing him.)* Sweetheart, I care about being late at the moment! *(Starts out again.)* Oh, and if you go to bed before I'm back, don't forget to turn down the furnace! *(She's out.)*

COOPER: *(Calling after her.)* It's already down, toots! I'm worried about the pipes freezing! *(He starts to dial, then turns to the audience.)* I mean, Jesus, how do you like that woman? Everyone says she's bloomed since the kids left home, and she got this job — "Liz has bloomed," everybody says. O.K. O.K., she's bloomed, she's a flower, she's a goddam gardenia, but what about me? No. Wrong. What about us? When do we talk, when do we make love, when to we EAT, for chrissake? *(He starts to dial, then turns to the audience again.)* She wants to move out of this house, you know. Oh sure. She wants to sell this fine old house and move. Downtown! To some waterfront condo where she can be quote in the thick of things unquote. What about the garden? What about my grandmother's furniture? What about the goddam dog? "Time to move on," Liz says. "Time to grow." Well maybe it's time to remember who we are. *(He picks up the phone again.)* My mother says it's roots that count. That's why Liz and I have lasted so long. That's why the kids have turned out so well. Roots, says my mother. Similar backgrounds. Birds of a feather. All that shit. *(Piano music. The ghostly dancers begin to return.)* Well, maybe so. Liz and I sure knew the steps for a while. With each other. With the kids. Maybe that's why I'm hung up on this goddam dance. I want to glide through the world with a woman again, at least for one night! *(Into telephone.)* Lucy? Hi . . . It's me . . . Hey, on this Snow Ball thing, I think it's one hell of a good idea.

(The dancers return, dancing better than before. Van Dam pounds out the beat with his stick.)

VAN DAM: And one and two and one and two and . . . *(Liz reappears in her formal dress. She sits in a chair on the sidelines and then calls to Cooper furtively.)*

LIZ: Pssst . . . Hey you! . . . Are you Cooper Jones?

COOPER: What's it to you?

LIZ: You're supposed to dance with me.

COOPER: Says who?

LIZ: Says your mother. I'm new in town, and your mother told my mother you'd ask me to dance.

COOPER: News to me. *(Starts to walk away.)*

LIZ: Oh come on. It's like going to the dentist. It prevents problems later on. *(Cooper reluctantly goes to Liz, bows in front of her. Liz gets up from her chair, curtsys to him, and then they join the circle of dancers, dancing stiffly around the room.)* Thank you.

COOPER: *(Grumpily.)* You're not welcome.

VAN DAM: And one and two, and small steps two, and one and two and . . .

LIZ: I hear this town is going rapidly downhill.

COOPER: Wrong!

LIZ: My father says we've climbed aboard a sinking ship.

COOPER: For your information, we're the thirteenth largest city in the United States. And our zoo is internationally famous.

LIZ: All I know is, there are bad slums. Next summer I'm going to be a junior counselor for slum kids.

COOPER: Goodie for you.

LIZ: Want to help? They need boys.

COOPER: No thanks. I'm going to a tennis camp.

LIZ: You're kind of superficial, aren't you?

COOPER: At least I'm not a do-gooder.

LIZ: At least I care about other people.

COOPER: At least I — are you wearing perfume?

LIZ: Sure. Smell. *(She offers her neck.)* I swiped it from my mother. *(Cooper furtively sniffs her neck.)* Like it?

COOPER: At least you don't have BO.

(They dance closer. Van Dam notices.)

VAN DAM: Mr. Jones: just what do you think you're doing?

COOPER: Making quiet conversation, sir.

VAN DAM: Come to the center of the circle, please!

COOPER: *(To Liz; under his breath.)* Thanks a bunch.

LIZ: I didn't do anything.

COOPER: You seduced me.

VAN DAM: We're waiting, Mr. Jones! The rest of you may take your seats. *(Cooper goes to the center. The other boys and girls sit down.)* Please demonstrate the box step to the assembled multitude, Mr. Jones.

(Cooper dances awkwardly by himself as Van Dam jerks him around or pokes him with his stick.)

COOPER: *(To audience, in rhythm as he dances.)* How could I have done this? How could I have done this? Week by week, year by year? Was this me, then? Was this really me, then?

(Van Dam pokes him.)

VAN DAM: And how do we hold our hands?

(Cooper holds his hands out appropriately.)

COOPER: Is this what my roots are? This degrading ritual? Week by week, year by year? *(Breaks out of the rhythm.)* Why didn't I protest against this drunken old fascist? My own sons would have taken one look and headed for the hills! Why didn't I rebel — like Stewart Granger in *SCARA-MOUCHE?*

(Suddenly grabs Van Dam's stick, pretends to run him through, stands over him triumphantly. The others clap. But Van Dam bounces to his feet.)

VAN DAM: One together, two together . . .

COOPER: Oh, but not me. Oh no! Me, I volunteered to be a galley slave, like Ben Hur on a bad day. Why did I accept it? Why did I keep going?

(Lucy enters on the side, carrying a book, talking furtively on the telephone.)

LUCY: I can only talk a minute! They're watching me like hawks. But I've managed to call all the old gang, and they say they'll come out of the woodwork for the Snow Ball!

COOPER: *(Still in dancing school.)* We'd look like fools without Jack and Kitty.

LUCY: Slowly, Cooper! Gently! One step at a time, remember? *(She goes off.)*

VAN DAM: *(Simultaneously.)* . . . One step at a time, remember? *(Kitty Price*

*enters on the staircase, in a shining white dress. She is young and gorgeous
— and is to be cast young, the only woman in the dancing class who is close
to her stage age. Van Dam sees her, raps his stick angrily on the ground. The
music stops. Everyone looks at Kitty.)*

KITTY: Ooops. Sorry I'm late.

VAN DAM: Indeed you are, Miss Price. It is becoming a habit with you.

KITTY: I guess I lost track of the time.

COOPER: *(Aside to Fritzi.)* Watch this. He won't dare get mad at her.

FRITZI: Why not?

COOPER: She's the richest girl in town. If she quit, so would everybody else.

VAN DAM: We will overlook it this time, Miss Price. *(Cooper and Fritzi shake
hands knowingly.)* The young gentlemen may now ask the young ladies
to dance. *(All the boys dash across the floor and slide to a stop in front of
Kitty, who beams proudly.)* STOP! *(The boys do.)* Go back! *(The boys return
to their places.)* The young gentlemen will ask the young ladies to dance.
*(This time the boys move more slowly across the floor, elbowing each other
out of the way. Cooper gets to Kitty first. In the process, Fritzi gets a nosebleed.)*

BARBARA: Mr. Van Dam! Fritzi has a nosebleed!

VAN DAM: Oh please. *(He shoos them off.)* Handkerchiefs out! A waltz please,
Mr. Cromeier! *(The piano plays a slow waltz. Lucy and Liz dance together.)*
Now the waltz is one two three, one two three . . .

LUCY: *(To Liz.)* Don't you wish you were Kitty Price?

LIZ: Sometimes.

LUCY: I mean, she's both rich and beautiful.

LIZ: I know. But she's kind of lazy.

LUCY: What makes you say that?

LIZ: I sit next to her in arithmetic. She hardly knows how to divide.

LUCY: She doesn't need to divide. When you're that rich, all you have to do is
multiply.

(Cooper dances with Kitty.)

COOPER: Will you come to Smithers drugstore afterwards? I'll buy you a soda.

KITTY: No thank you. I'm being driven straight home so no one will kidnap me.

COOPER: O.K. I'll meet you next Monday after school. I'll show you the zoo.

KITTY: No thanks. I find the monkey house generally embarrassing.

COOPER: Tell you what, then. You can watch me play hockey next Saturday
afternoon.

KITTY: I can't. I'm going skiing with my father.

COOPER: Then when CAN I see you?

KITTY: *(As he steps on her toe.)* Ouch, Cooper! . . . Maybe when you become a better dancer.

VAN DAM: That is the waltz . . . We will now take our seats for a slight collation. *(Jack enters, a young busboy in a white jacket, carrying glasses of pink punch on a silver tray. The boys and girls follow him off. Van Dam exits as well, sneaking a furtive snort from his silver flask. Downstage, Saul Radner enters as if into his office. He is a real estate developer and wears a business suit. He calls Cooper off the dance floor.)*

SAUL: Come on in, Coop. When do we start up our winter squash series?

COOPER: When you learn how to handle my serve.

SAUL: I've handled it for ten years, pal. I think you're scared of my corner shot.

COOPER: That does it! The clash of the Titans resumes next Tuesday! . . . Hey. Dig the new decor. Hard to believe this office once belonged to my old man. *(Picks up a fancy telephone.)* Gimme Donald Trump! Gimme Barbra Streisand!

SAUL: Come work for us, and we'll put one of those in your car.

COOPER: No thanks, pal. No more downtown deals for me. I'll settle for selling houses to my people as they retreat to the suburbs.

SAUL: That's a good one — your *people.*

COOPER: Sure. We're kind of the lost tribe these days, Saul.

SAUL: Bullshit.

COOPER: I'm serious. I feel like an exile. This isn't my territory any more. All these new buildings. Even the old George Washington hotel is different.

SAUL: Except for one room.

COOPER: Except for one room.

SAUL: Your "people" on the Landmark Commission cost us a small fortune on that one.

COOPER: Actually that's why I'm here.

SAUL: I figured. *(Reads a letter on his desk.)* Ms Lucy Dunbar . . . wants to put on a . . . "Snow Ball."

COOPER: She said you turned her down.

SAUL: I didn't turn her DOWN, Coop. I asked her to broaden her base.

COOPER: Broaden her base?

SAUL: When you reopen a public facility, Coop, particularly when federal funds are involved, it's a good idea to kick things off a little more well, democratically.

COOPER: Hey. The Snow Ball is open to anyone who wants to come.

SAUL: *(Referring to letter.)* Anyone in formal attire holding a two-hundred buck ticket.

COOPER: That's for a New York orchestra and open bar and special decorations and —

SAUL: Forgive me, Coop, but some of our minority citizens might see it simply as the Old Guard doing their old number at taxpayers' expense.

COOPER: Oh come on . . .

SAUL: Open it up, Coop. Reflect the ethnic diversity in town. Less liquor, more food. Tacos, pizzas, egg rolls. Throw in a folk singer, maybe a rock group for the kids.

COOPER: That room was designed for ballroom dancing, Saul.

SAUL: I know that.

COOPER: My grandfather had that dance floor imported specially from Austria.

SAUL: I know, I know.

COOPER: Grover Cleveland danced in that room. Irene Castle danced there. Charles Van Dam taught dancing school there for almost fifty years.

SAUL: Coop, the Landmarks Committee gave us the whole history lesson.

COOPER: Well what's wrong with a little history now and then? Continuity? Tradition? You, of all people, should understand that. I'll bet if this were a fundraiser for Israel, you'd be cheering us on.

SAUL: Now wait a minute.

COOPER: I want this, Saul. I want it. I put you up for the Tennis Club. I wrote that recommendation for your son to Williams. Now, please. You do this for me. *(Pause.)*

SAUL: Give your party, Coop.

COOPER: Thanks, Saul.

SAUL: Give your party.

COOPER: Now I assume you'll send us a good, healthy bill for the use of the room. We may be a lost tribe these days, but we still pay our own way.

SAUL: You sure? I hear your office lost out on that new mall.

COOPER: We're doing O.K.

SAUL: Seriously, Coop. Come work with me. Together we could get this burg back on its feet. And squeeze in some squash at lunch.

COOPER: Let's talk about it after the first of the year.

SAUL: You mean you're postponing a major career decision because of some party?

COOPER: Not a party, Saul. A dance. There's a big difference. This may even involve Jack and Kitty.

SAUL: Who and who?

COOPER: You and Rhoda come see. You're in for a big surprise.

SAUL: Sorry, Coop. We're booked that night. Flying over to Jerusalem for a major dinner party at the Wailing Wall.

(Saul goes off, as the boys and girls re-enter with Van Dam.)

VAN DAM: Concentrate on your conversations, ladies and gentlemen. *(Jack comes down to Cooper with a tray of punch.)*

JACK: Want some punch?

COOPER: Thanks.

JACK: *(Confidentially.)* Say, could I speak to you privately a minute?

COOPER: Sure. *(They come downstage.)*

JACK: How do I get into this dancing school?

COOPER: Huh?

JACK: I've been watching from the kitchen. I already learned the steps. *(He gives a demonstration; he is good.)*

COOPER: If you know already, why do you want to get in?

JACK: Personal reasons.

(Kitty comes down to Van Dam.)

KITTY: Mr. Van Dam. I have to leave.

VAN DAM: The class is not over, Miss Price.

KITTY: *(With a quick curtsy.)* I know, but I think I've had enough for one evening. *(She bounces up the staircase.)* Thanks! *(She goes out.)*

JACK: That's the reason.

COOPER: Kitty?

JACK: I want to dance with her.

COOPER: You and the rest of the Free World.

JACK: So how do I get in?

COOPER: I don't know exactly. My mother has some list. You have to know people.

JACK: I know you.

COOPER: I don't know you.

JACK: I'm Jack Daley.

COOPER: Cooper Jones . . . Hiya, Jack. *(They shake hands.)* And I think you have to pay three hundred dollars.

JACK: I can come up with that.

COOPER: You can come up with three hundred *dollars?*

JACK: I saved it. Working here.

COOPER: Do you have a dark suit?

JACK: I'll get one.

COOPER: Then you definitely should get in. I mean, are we a democracy, or what? I'll ask my mother.

VAN DAM: *(Tapping his stick, with great distaste.)* We will now undergo a lindy-hop. *(Everyone cheers; Van Dam drinks.)* Music, Mr. Cromeier, if you please. *(Music begins, a lively lindy.)*

JACK: *(Dancing off with his tray.)* Tell your mother I want to start next Saturday.

COOPER: *(Dancing with Liz.)* O.K., Jack Daley. *(To Liz.)* Stop leading. I'm the boy.

LIZ: Then lead, please.

COOPER: I'm trying to. But you keep going your own way.

LIZ: Why do you keep dancing with me, then?

COOPER: I'm practicing for the wrestling team.

VAN DAM: Change partners! *(Cooper switches to Lucy.)*

LUCY: You dance beautifully, Cooper.

COOPER: Thanks.

LUCY: I'm serious. I can put myself completely into your hands.

COOPER: Thanks.

LUCY: And you'd be even better if you took that thing out of your pocket.

COOPER: What thing? Oh. Gosh. Sorry. *(Lucy dances off with the others as a waiter sets up a table with two coffee cups. Cooper calls off as he moves toward it.)* Joe! If my secretary calls, tell her I'll be back in ten minutes. *(Lucy comes back on, in contemporary clothes. They settle at the table.)*

LUCY: I've tracked them down.

COOPER: Jack and Kitty?

LUCY: Both. Since you seem to feel they're so essential.

COOPER: Yep. I do. They're the heart of the matter.

LUCY: *(Checking her notebook.)* Jack is living in Indianapolis with wife and children.

COOPER: I knew that. He sends me a Christmas card every year.

LUCY: I'll bet you didn't know he's running for governor.

COOPER: Governor!

LUCY: According to my cousin, who lives there . . . *(Reads from her notes.)* He's assistant district attorney now, and he's being seriously mentioned as the Republican candidate for Governor of Indiana!

COOPER: Good old Jack. Still moving on up . . .

LUCY: *(Consulting her notes.)* And Kitty . . .

COOPER: Ah, Kitty . . .

LUCY: Kitty has married again.

COOPER: Again?

LUCY: Number three. A retired banker named Baldwin Hall. They live in this posh resort down in Florida.

COOPER: Oh boy. We've got our work cut out for us.

LUCY: Exactly. I think we should start by writing them both letters, just to break the ice.

COOPER: O.K. I'll write Jack. You write Kitty.

LUCY: Fine.

COOPER: And tell Kitty I have the music.

LUCY: The music?

COOPER: The musical arrangements. From the Snow Ball. Jack gave them to me when they split up. *(Calls as if for bill.)* Joe!

LUCY: And you kept them? All these years? I knew you were a closet romantic, Cooper Jones. *(She pokes him with her pencil.)*

COOPER: Tell Kitty I'll Xerox them and send them on.

(They get up from the table; Cooper leaves money.)

LUCY: We should work out a budget.

COOPER: Yes.

LUCY: I'm hopeless at budgets. Gordon did all that.

COOPER: Oh budgets aren't so difficult.

LUCY: Then stop by tonight and show me, step by step.

COOPER: Can't. It's Liz's birthday.

LUCY: Oh. Well. Far be it from me to intrude on THAT . . .

(The music and lights come up as the class reenters. Again the dancing has improved. Jack dances downstage with Barbara Fiske.)

BARBARA: Don't you love dancing cheek to cheek, Jack?

JACK: I don't know. It gets a little sweaty, maybe.

BARBARA: I like that. I think it's sexy.

JACK: I dunno. I think I'm getting a rash.

(Cooper and Lucy are back in by now. Kitty enters down the stairs. Van Dam sees her and once again raps for order. The music stops.)

KITTY: I know, I know. I'm late again. *(She looks around.)* Gulp.

VAN DAM: I believe everyone has found a partner, Miss Price.

KITTY: Then I'll just sit this one out. *(She sits.)*

VAN DAM: Miss Price! *(He approaches her.)* Perhaps you would like to dance with *me.*

KITTY: You?

VAN DAM: *(He bows to her.)* May I have this dance?

(Kitty does not rise and curtsy.)

LIZ: *(Aside to Heather.)* The old letch.

HEATHER: What will she DO?

VAN DAM: *(He holds out his arms to Kitty.)* Music, Mr. Cromeier, if you pl —

JACK: *(Suddenly.)* I'll dance with her.

VAN DAM: I believe you already have a partner, Mr . . . ah . . . Mr. . . .

JACK: Daley.

VAN DAM: I believe you are already dancing with Miss Fiske.

JACK: No offense, but she doesn't get the beat. She can't follow me at all. *(Barbara bursts into tears, and runs to the other girls, who comfort her.)* Tell you what: you dance with Miss Fiske. I'll dance with Miss Price. *(General uproar. Van Dam gets order by pounding on the floor with his stick.)*

VAN DAM: No. I'll tell you what, Mr. . . . ah . . . Daley. You will dance with Miss Price. And the rest of us will take our seats and watch.

JACK: O.K.

VAN DAM: And let me add, Mr. Daley, that you had better be very, very good!

KITTY: *(To the other girls.)* Eeeek.

VAN DAM: Mr. Cromeier, if you please . . . a rumba.

KITTY: A RUMBA? Hey, no fair! We haven't even learned that one!

VAN DAM: Ah, but Mr. Daley will teach you.

KITTY: Yipes.

VAN DAM: Be seated, everyone. . . . Music, Mr. Cromeier, if you please. *(Music: a rumba. Jack gives Kitty a beautiful, deep bow. Kitty responds with a dramatic, ironic parody of a curtsy. The handkerchief comes out, and then they dance. They dance tentatively at first, finding the beat, Jack taking the lead, Kitty following, always with a wry little shrug and always a little bit late. They learn as they go along, and as they learn they get trickier, trying this and that, and the music seems to respond and take fire from what they do. The boys and girls cheer them on, so that Van Dam has to tap his stick and yell, "Settle down! Settle down!" Soon Jack and Kitty are looking pretty good, building finally to an elaborate coda, where he spins her off in a lovely flourish and ends the dance with a deep theatrical bow. Everyone applauds. The boys all gather enthusiastically around Jack and bring him downstage as the girls gather around Kitty and propel her off. Mr. Smithers, a druggist in a white jacket, sets up a counter downstage as Van Dam exits, taking a nip from his flask. The boys do a lot of whooping and cheering and backslapping as they settle in around the table.)*

COOPER: I'm paying for Jack. I got a dollar for shoveling snow.

BILLY: That's not all you shovel, Cooper. *(Roars of laughter.)*

SMITHERS: What'll it be, boys?

COOPER: You got that new chocolate-chip ice cream?

CALVIN: You got cherry phosphates?

FRITZI: You got Prince Albert in the can? If so, let him out!

(More roars of laughter.)

BILLY: When we heard the sirens and saw the patrols, We knew it was Smithers for whom the bell tolls.

(*Laughter.*)

CALVIN: Hey, Mr. Smithers! Have you got that new paperback, *The Tiger's Revenge*, by Claude Balls? (*Laughter.*)

SMITHERS: All right, boys. Settle down, settle down.

(*He goes off.*)

COOPER: Say, you're a terrific dancer, Jack!

(*Other boys echo approval: Fred Astaire! Gene Kelly.*)

JACK: Thanks for getting me into dancing school.

BILLY: Thanks? You said thanks? You mean you wanted to go?

COOPER: He wanted to dance with Kitty.

CALVIN: I dunno. I don't think even Kitty is worth going to dancing school for.

JACK: I had another reason, too. I figure dancing school will be good for my future.

FRITZI: Your future!

JACK: Sure. You learn things in dancing school. You learn manners. You learn clothes. You learn how to talk to people when you don't give a shit.

FRITZI: That's true . . .

JACK: Sure. And you meet people. Getting to know you people will help me succeed in life. I figure it's worth three hundred dollars.

BILLY: You mean you're PAYING for it? With your OWN money?

JACK: Sure. I saved it for my college education, but I decided this was an equally important investment. (*Smithers returns.*)

SMITHERS: Who here is Jack Daley? (*Everyone: Ta-da, pointing out Jack.*)

JACK: Me. Why?

SMITHERS: There's a fellow in a uniform asking to see you.

FRITZI: Jiggers. The cops.

CALVIN: You rob a bank for that three hundred, Jack?

COOPER: (*Looking out.*) That's no cop! That's a chauffeur . . . And Kitty's father's sitting in the back of the car.

ALL: Uh oh.

SMITHERS: He wants to meet you, son.

JACK: O.K! (*Runs off jauntily.*) So long, suckers!

CALVIN: (*Looking out.*) This I gotta see!

BILLY: It's one of those new Lincoln Continentals!

COOPER: They're shaking hands!

BILLY: He's getting in!

COOPER: They're driving off!

FRITZI: *(Producing a schoolbook, with a brown paper cover.)* Hey! Jack forgot his book.

COOPER: What book?

FRITZI: This book he studies on the bus.

COOPER: *(Taking it, reading the cover.)* Tenth Grade Civics. Holy Angels Collegiate Institute. *(Reads inside.)* How Democracy Works.

BILLY: *(Looking after Jack.)* It sure is working for him.

(The boys go off, leaving Cooper. Restaurant music comes up. The lights become more romantic. A Waiter brings on a table with a cloth and a candlestick. Liz comes in, breathlessly late, wearing an overcoat. She kisses him.)

LIZ: Sorry, sweetheart . . . What with a late meeting, and the snow, and . . .

COOPER: *(Helping with her coat, which the Waiter takes.)* Happy birthday . . . *(He gives her a warm kiss.)*

LIZ: Thanks. *(She settles in.)* Susie called as I was going out the door. She wants to stay at college over Thanksgiving and put her travel money toward a used car.

COOPER: No.

LIZ: That's exactly what I said. No.

COOPER: The children come home, Thanksgiving and Christmas. That's absolutely nonnegotiable.

LIZ: I couldn't agree more.

COOPER: Can you imagine you and me, all by ourselves, eyeing each other over a Thanksgiving turkey?

LIZ: I suppose we'll have to face that some day.

COOPER: Not if I can help it. *(Waiter reappears.)*

WAITER: A cocktail, madam?

LIZ: Just club soda, please.

COOPER: *(Indicating his own drink.)* You won't join me?

LIZ: No thanks.

COOPER: How about champagne? On your birthday?

LIZ: Champagne gives me a headache. *(To Waiter.)* Just club soda, please. *(Waiter goes off.)*

COOPER: I've decided on your present.

LIZ: Oh yes?

COOPER: You've got to pick it out.

LIZ: I hope it's not jewelry, Cooper. I can't wander around town, dripping with jewels while people are sleeping in the streets.

COOPER: It's not jewelry . . . It's a new dress.

LIZ: Cooper, I'm not sure I need a . . .

COOPER: A long dress. For the Snow Ball.

LIZ: Oh.

COOPER: I checked out Berger's. I saw a great dress there. The salesgirl held it up. You'd look sensational in it.

LIZ: Describe it.

COOPER: Well, it has a . . . and a little . . . Oh hell, it's dark green. You'll have to go see.

LIZ: How much?

COOPER: Never mind.

LIZ: How MUCH, Cooper?

COOPER: Four hundred smackeroos.

LIZ: Four hundred dollars?

COOPER: Including tax.

LIZ: That is outrageous! To pay four hundred dollars for some dumb dress, when the library closes three days a week! *(The Waiter shows up with the seltzer.)* Nope. Sorry. I'll wear some old rag, thanks . . . I suppose we should order. *(She looks at the menu.)*

COOPER: I've already ordered. Something special.

LIZ: What.

COOPER: Rack of lamb.

LIZ: Lamb?

COOPER: And fresh asparagus.

LIZ: Sweetheart, lamb is saturated with fat.

COOPER: It is not.

LIZ: Darling, it's oozing with it. And do you know what they do to these baby lambs in order to —

COOPER: Oh Liz . . .

LIZ: *(To Waiter.)* Could I just have the . . . I don't know . . . scrod, broiled, no butter, and a small green salad with dressing on the side.

WAITER: Certainly, madam.

COOPER: I'll have the goddam lamb.

WAITER: *(To Cooper.)* What about the soufflé, sir?

COOPER: *(To Liz.)* I ordered the grand marnier soufflé for dessert.

LIZ: Oh that sounds wonderful! *(To Waiter.)* I'll have a taste of his.

WAITER: A single soufflé then?

COOPER: A single soufflé.

LIZ: And herb tea, for me.

COOPER: Not even decaf?

LIZ: Do you know what those coffee companies pay their peasants in Peru?

COOPER: Help. *(The Waiter goes off.)*

LIZ: The reason I was late was we had this knock-down, drag-out meeting at the office. They want to give the holiday party down at the Community Center the Saturday after Christmas.

COOPER: But that's the night of the Snow Ball!

LIZ: I KNOW, darling. I fought it tooth and nail. But it's the best date for everyone else.

COOPER: So what gives? You're not coming to the Snow Ball?

LIZ: I'll just have to make a showing at both.

COOPER: Say you've got a previous engagement. You've done it before.

LIZ: I can't this time, sweetheart . . . I've been promoted.

COOPER: No kidding! When?

LIZ: Last week.

COOPER: Why didn't you tell me?

LIZ: Because I was nervous about what you'd say.

COOPER: What I'd say?

LIZ: It'll take much more time.

COOPER: Will you come home Thanksgiving and Christmas?

LIZ: See? That's what I was nervous about.

COOPER: No, seriously. Congratulations! *(Kisses her.)* What's your title?

LIZ: I am now known as a Family Interventionist. I intervene, when necessary.

COOPER: You'll be great at that.

LIZ: Well, we could use the dough, sweetie. With the kids in college and all.

COOPER: Right. So. For your birthday, what would you like? Is there an Interventionist's Handbook? Or how about a four-volume history of the Marshall Plan? Name it. It's yours.

LIZ: No, listen, here's what I'd really like. Computer lessons. To learn how to work one of those things. I could use it in the office, and maybe get one for home, and I could get twice as much done in half the time . . .

(The lights fade on Liz, as she talks, and come up on Lucy, across the stage, sitting at a bar, with two glasses of white wine in front of her. She hails Cooper.)

LUCY: Hey! Yoo-hoo! Over here! *(Cooper crosses to her.)*

COOPER: *(Glancing around.)* Hey, how'd you find this joint? The Half Moon Bar and Grille?

LUCY: Where else should we meet? Your precious club? With everyone breathing down our necks? No thanks. It's time you branched out a little, Cooper Jones. *(Indicating the wine.)* And I've already ordered you a drink.

COOPER: In the middle of the day?

LUCY: Absolutely. I think you and I should spend this entire snowy afternoon stuffing our faces with greasy chicken wings and getting pleasantly polluted.

COOPER: *(Sitting beside her.)* What's the trouble?

LUCY: My job, for one thing. They just chewed me out for talking to the customers. They say I flirt with the men.

COOPER: *(Mock horror.)* What? You? I don't believe it.

LUCY: I like men. I like talking about books. I don't know why I can't combine the two.

COOPER: Why don't you quit?

LUCY: Money, Cooper. Believe it or not, there are some people in the world who need it. Besides, it's a place to go. Anyway, look what finally arrived from Kitty.

COOPER: Better late than never.

LUCY: Not when you read what she says.

COOPER: *(Reading.)* "I couldn't possibly drag Baldwin north in the dead of winter."

LUCY: Baldwin's her husband.

COOPER: "And we're expecting a houseful of children and stepchildren and grandchildren over Christmas vacation."

LUCY: See?

COOPER: Shit.

LUCY: And, to make things worse, Jane Babcock tells me she just ran into her at the Mayo Clinic. She was having tests — Jane didn't dare bring up the Snow Ball.

COOPER: Hell.

LUCY: So that's that . . . Anything new from Jack?

COOPER: Just what I told you. I wrote two letters and got two polite put-downs from some assistant in his office.

LUCY: So where are we?

COOPER: Nowhere. *(He stares at Kitty's note.)*

LUCY: So. Let's talk about books. What have you read lately? *The Decline of the Wasp?*

COOPER: *(Rereading Kitty's note.)* Hey!

LUCY: What?

COOPER: Did you read this last sentence?

LUCY: What?

COOPER: *(Reading.)* ". . . Just think. Another Snow Ball. Jeez Louise. My heart automatically goes thumpety-thump . . ."

LUCY: Typical Kitty.

COOPER: She's giving us an opening, Lucy.

LUCY: The size of a pinhole.

COOPER: She is beckoning to us. She is calling. She's saying tell me more.

LUCY: Oh Cooper . . .

COOPER: I sense it. I feel it in my bones.

LUCY: So what do we do?

COOPER: We telephone them both. Immediately.

LUCY: You mean just . . .

COOPER: Call them up. Person to person. Tell each one that the other is on the fence.

LUCY: But that wouldn't be —

COOPER: All's fair in love and dancing! I'll call Jack, you call Kitty.

LUCY: Heavens, Cooper. You certainly are taking the bit in your teeth.

COOPER: Faint heart never won fair lady.

LUCY: But if she's sick?

COOPER: If she says so, we'll back right off. *(Gets up.)* Come on. We'll go over to my office and telephone.

LUCY: Could we make it my place?

COOPER: Why?

LUCY: I'm expecting a call. From Minneapolis. From this man. Well I mean, he's a welcome change from that prick who held me hostage for twenty years. *(Pause.)* He keeps wanting to marry me.

COOPER: And why don't you?

LUCY: Because he's not . . . I mean, he wouldn't . . . I mean, something like the Snow Ball is totally out of his league.

COOPER: Ah hah.

LUCY: So. Let's go to my place. If Minneapolis calls, I'll say I'm otherwise engaged. *(Pause.)*

COOPER: I have to show a house this afternoon.

LUCY: Oh well. A house . . .

COOPER: Money, Lucy. Remember? I haven't been holding my end up at the office lately.

LUCY: Oh well. I wouldn't want to take bread from the mouths of your children. We'll call separately. *(Cooper puts down money.)* No, no. My turn. *(Lucy puts her money on top of his; their hands touch and stay touching.)* After all, we're both in this thing together.

COOPER: *(Bowing and offering his arm.)* Shall we dance?

LUCY: *(Curtsying.)* You must have gone to dancing school, sir. Which is more than I can say for my man from Minneapolis. *(She goes off. Cooper turns to the audience.)*

COOPER: *(To audience.)* It wasn't that great, actually. Not at the start. Maybe because it really wasn't about us. It was all about Jack and Kitty. They were on our minds that afternoon, and those other afternoons when we met again. It was as if we were just the subplot, two minor characters marking time until the stars were ready to come on and play their big scene. *(Lucy comes on dressed informally.)*

LUCY: I just thought you should know: Ruthie Curtis saw Kitty at Bergdorf's in New York. Buying an evening dress!

COOPER: For the Snow Ball?

LUCY: She wouldn't say. But it was not the sort of thing you'd wear to some golf club in Florida! *(They kiss.)*

COOPER: I finally got through to Jack. He said he hasn't danced in thirty years.

LUCY: Did you tell him it will come back?

COOPER: I said it was like riding a bicycle.

LUCY: Exactly. Like that, or other things. *(They kiss more passionately; then Lucy breaks away.)* Hey! Slow down. I'm right in the middle of a good book.

COOPER: What book?

LUCY: *Lady Chatterley's Lover.* *(She goes off invitingly. Cooper turns to the audience again.)*

COOPER: So things got better as we got closer to the Snow Ball. Jack and Kitty were still on the fence, but we began to feel that by making love, we could copulate them into commitment. In our more lurid moments, we even joked about it; We called it "Snowballing" *(Saul Radner crosses the stage, in shirtsleeves, carrying a squash racquet, drying his hair with a towel.)*

SAUL: Good game, Coop. You're hotter than a pistol these days.

COOPER: Thanks, Saul.

SAUL: You been exercising on the sly?

COOPER: No, no. Just generally keeping fit.

SAUL: No, it's more than that. You seem like a guy who's got a girl somewhere. *(Cooper laughs nervously as Saul goes off passing Liz on the way in.)*

LIZ: *(Holding a little pink note.)* Look what I got in the mail!

COOPER: What?

LIZ: An anonymous note. "Interventionist: intervene thyself."

COOPER: Some crank. Some weirdo from your work.

LIZ: On pink writing paper? With that little face at the end? It's someone we know.

COOPER: But the grammar's wrong. Intervene is an intransitive verb. It should be "intervene on thyself." Or "with thyself." It's some uneducated kook.

LIZ: At least it has a Biblical ring . . . I'll look it up in Bartlett's . . . *(She goes off.)*

COOPER: *(Looking after her; then to audience.)* Oh God, what a shit I am! What a shit! Because I love her! I love her even when I argue with her. I love her even because I argue with her. She keeps life interesting every minute of the day. As for Lucy, do I love her, too? Or are we just hung up on the Snow Ball? Am I another one of those menopausal men, desperately trying to turn back the clock before the last alarm goes off? *(Lucy comes out, in a negligee.)*

LUCY: Where've you been?

COOPER: Kitty's husband called me at the office.

LUCY: And?

JACK: She's in the hospital. For an operation.

LUCY: Oh no.

COOPER: I telephoned Jack, and he immediately backed off.

LUCY: Oh no!

COOPER: I wonder if we should back off, too.

LUCY: I know what you mean.

COOPER: I keep thinking of Liz.

LUCY: And the man from Minneapolis.

COOPER: The Snow Ball should keep rolling, of course.

LUCY: Of course. We'll just have to go through the motions.

COOPER: Well. I ought to get back. One of our kids is home for the weekend.

LUCY: Oh then definitely you should go.

COOPER: So long, then, Lucy. *(Kisses her on the cheek.)*

LUCY: Good-bye, Cooper. *(He starts out.)* Cooper . . . will you still dance with me at the Snow Ball?

COOPER: Of course I will, Lucy.

LUCY: I mean, we may not be Jack and Kitty, but I'd hate to think we spent all those years dancing for nothing.

COOPER: Oh something will come of this. I'm sure of that. *(They go off either way, as the music comes up, bouncily, and plays continuously. Decorations swing into place. We are now at a series of parties, spanning several years. The boys are now in tuxedos, the girls in long dresses. A couple dances by; the girl is in a strapless dress.)*

BREWSTER: How come they call this a coming-out party?

HEATHER: *(Hoisting up her front.)* Wait till the conga, and you'll see.
(Jack and Kitty dance by, beautifully. Another couple watches.)

GINNY: I hear Jack Daley quit that Holy Angels Parochial School and is now going to Country Day.

BILLY: That's right. Kitty's father got him a full scholarship.

GINNY: My Lord! Is he doing well?

BILLY: Straight A's! And Co-captain on the football team!

GINNY: *(Suddenly kissing him.)* Oh, that Jack! He makes me proud to be an American.

(Jack and Kitty dance by again; people applaud as they dance off. Two boys, with drinks, cross.)

CALVIN: *(Confidentially.)* I saw Jack last Friday night out with another girl.

FRITZI: Probably Terri Tolentino, his old girl from Holy Angels.

CALVIN: I thought Jack stayed in, Fridays, to do his homework.

FRITZI: *(Lewdly.)* He stays in Fridays, all right. He stays in all night long. *(Quickly; as Jack dances on with Lucy.)* Hi, Jack.

JACK: Guys. *(Jack and Lucy dance.)*

LUCY: You're a beautiful dancer, Jack.

JACK: Thanks, Lucy.

LUCY: No, you are. You're fabulous.

JACK: Thanks a lot.

(Cooper cuts in on Jack and Lucy. Jack goes off. Music continues. Cooper dances with Lucy.)

LUCY: You're a beautiful dancer, Cooper.

COOPER: Thank you, Lucy.

LUCY: I hear Liz doesn't like you to dance with me.

COOPER: She thinks I'm a pushover for your line.

LUCY: Line? What line? I don't have a line. *(Calvin cuts in.)*

COOPER: That's what I told her. *(He goes off.)*

LUCY: *(To Calvin, who dances terribly.)* You're a beautiful dancer, by the way.

CALVIN: Hey, thanks.

(They dance off. Jack joins Cooper in the men's room. Cooper stands at the "urinal." Jack combs his hair in a "mirror.")

JACK: Look at you, Cooper. You're a slob. Your pants don't even fit.

COOPER: That's because this tux belonged to my grandfather.

JACK: I got mine tailor-made. It cost a mint, but I'm buying it on time.

COOPER: Hey, I could have lent you my older brother's.

JACK: No thanks. A man's clothes should fit. If your clothes fit, you feel fit. And if you feel fit, you dance well.

COOPER: And if you dance well? What then?

JACK: Oh well, my God, then the sky's the limit! *(They go off either way. Kitty, Heather, and Ginny come into the ladies room. Kitty adjusts her dress.)*

HEATHER: *(From "stall.")* There's a boy here from Princeton who says he loves me.

KITTY: Don't believe him.

GINNY: *(From next "stall.")* And this guy from Amherst wants to pin me.

KITTY: Watch it. He'll pin you to the ground.

HEATHER: *(As they wash their hands.)* Oh God! How do you tell if a man's sincere?

KITTY: Dance with him. Let him lead. You can tell immediately.
(She goes off; the girls look at each other and go off the opposite way. Jack dances with Liz.)

LIZ: Congratulations, Jack. I hear you got into Harvard.

JACK: Right. And they gave me this great scholarship. Instead of waiting on tables, they want me to dance with Kitty at Alumni functions.

LIZ: That's terrific!

JACK: We'll be what the Whiffenpoofs are for Yale!

LIZ: What about Kitty? Where does she stand in all this?

JACK: Oh she's with me all the way. She's found a college near Harvard which gives lab credit for dancing. *(They dance off. Brewster and Heather dance by.)*

BOY: Do you think Jack and Kitty are sleeping with each other?

GIRL: I don't think it's any of our business.

BOY: I hear they spent all last weekend down at Niagara Falls in the Maid of the Mist Motel.

GIRL: Honestly, Charlie! May we change the subject, please?

BOY: Sure. Go ahead.

GIRL: All right. Now. Here's the thing. I think I'm pregnant.
(They dance. Cooper and Kitty dance by.)

COOPER: When we were little kids, I was in love with you.

KITTY: You were not.

COOPER: I was! I thought you were the cat's ass.

KITTY: I love that expression!

COOPER: I still dream about you sometimes.

KITTY: That's because we're such good old friends.

COOPER: Say, how about coming skiing with me over New Year's?

KITTY: Can't, sweetie. I'll be with Jack.

COOPER: Thank God. I've already invited Liz.

KITTY: What would you have done if I'd said yes?

COOPER: Asked Lucy Dunbar to join us. *(Both laugh.)* Do you love Jack, Kitty?

KITTY: Oh Cooper, I don't know.

COOPER: He's good for you, Kitty. He's given you something to go for.

KITTY: I know. *(She does a little spin.)* But it's hard WORK being Ginger Rogers.

COOPER: *(Imitating.)* It's no cinch being Jimmy Stewart, either. *(Ginny and*

Mary come downstage to settle at a table. They have white ballots, white envelopes, and white pencils.)

GINNY: This is agony . . . who are you going to vote for, for Snow Queen?

MARY: I think I'll vote for Kitty.

GINNY: But she's so antisocial. She's spent almost the entire vacation down in her rumpus room, alone with Jack.

MARY: Maybe she should just be Maid of Honor. *(Barbara joins them.)*

BARBARA: I'm voting for Agnes Underhill.

GINNY: But Agnes has that gimpy leg. And that horrible skin problem.

BARBARA: I know, but she deserves a sympathy vote. Besides, her cat just died.
(They vote carefully, hiding their ballots from each other.)

GINNY: Oh God. These decisions. I'm just not sure democracy's worth it. *(They go out. Cooper crosses with Liz.)*

COOPER: I voted for you for Snow Queen.

LIZ: You sure you didn't sneak one in for Lucy Dunbar?

COOPER: No, I swear. You're Queen to me, all the way.

LIZ: Whatever that means.

COOPER: I guess it means I'm asking you to go steady.

LIZ: Cooper — Gosh. Let me think about that.

COOPER: Let me know at the Snow Ball. *(She goes off as he turns to the audience.)* Because it all came down to the Snow Ball. This was the only party you had to pay for, but the profits went to some good cause, and besides, you could always stick your grandmother for the bill. Balls are balls, as my father says, but the climax of this one, like the parading of the Virgin in an Italian street festival, was the presentation of the Snow Queen to the assembled multitude. *(A fanfare. Van Dam comes down the staircase with a mike on a cord.)*

VAN DAM: Ladies and gentlemen: it is my great pleasure to present to you . . . this year's queen and her court. The beautiful Miss Kitty Price and her two lovely maids of honor. *(A drum roll. A spotlight on an entrance upstage, as Kitty is wheeled on in an elaborate sleigh. She wears a crown and holds flowers. Liz and Lucy sit below her, as maids of honor. Cooper and three other boys pull the sleigh around, as the band plays a swing version of a Christmas song, and everyone applauds. Over the mike.)* Prance, gentlemen! Prance! You're supposed to be reindeer! *(The sleigh finally lurches to a stop in the center of the floor. More applause.)*

KITTY: *(Holds up her hand to speak.)* I just want everyone to know this thing is held up primarily by faith in God and Bergdorf Goodman. *(Laughter.)*

VAN DAM: *(Holding up his hand.)* Ladies and gentlemen: I'd also like a word, please. It has long been observed, by people wiser than myself, that every American city requires two things to keep it civilized: it must have a park, and it must have a dancing school. For forty-six years, I have been somewhat involved in the latter. *(Laughter and applause.)* This year, however, will be my last. *(Genial protests.)* No, no. My last. Because during the course of this year, I have enjoyed the rare pleasure of seeing my labors bear fruit. I have seen the dancing of Mr. Jack Daley and Miss Kitty Price. *(Cheers and applause.)* The escorts will now ask the queen and her court to dance. *(Cooper goes up, bows to Liz, helps her out of the sleigh.)*

COOPER: So? Are we going steady?

LIZ: Yes, Cooper. If you mean it seriously.

COOPER: Of course I do.

LIZ: Well let's hope.

(Another boy escorts Lucy. Kitty remains seated in the sleigh.)

GINNY: Kitty doesn't have a partner!

BILLY: Where's Jack?

BARBARA: Who knows?

FRITZI: Maybe he's over at Terry Tolentino's.

HEATHER: This is embarrassing. Kitty'll have to dance with her father.

VAN DAM: *(On mike.)* I notice our lovely queen remains unattended. Perhaps, for my last Snow Ball, I might finally have the pleasure of dancing with her myself.

LIZ: *(To someone.)* He's still an old letch. *(General confusion. Van Dam goes to bow to Kitty in the sled.)* May I have this dance, Miss Price?

KITTY: Um . . . *(And everyone freezes.)*

COOPER: *(To audience.)* Jack, of course, had arranged this whole moment. He wanted the suspense. He had ordered music specially arranged in New York and dug up some guy who did the lighting for Ringling Brothers, and now he was waiting offstage, ready to make his move.

BILLY: There's Jack. In the orchestra.

MARY: Thank God!

GINNY: He's handing out sheet music.

(Jack comes on. He nods as if to the orchestra. A long drum roll. He signals to the flies. The lights dim except for two gorgeous pink spotlights, which hit him and Kitty. The drum roll continues. The other dancers back off. Jack goes to the sleigh, bows to Kitty, holds out his hand, helping her out. She steps down and gives her bemused curtsy. Jack signals to two boys, who ease the sleigh out of the way. Then Jack gestures again toward the orchestra.)

JACK: Hit it, Eddie! *(The band strikes up a snappy arrangement of dance tunes, and Jack and Kitty launch into a terrific number. They have obviously worked on it carefully, and both the lights and the musical arrangements support what they do.)*

BILLY: *(On the sidelines.)* No fair. That's cheating. They've been practicing to their own music.

GINNY: So that's what they were doing down in Kitty's Rumpus Room.

LIZ: *(To Cooper.)* I still think she's lazy. Notice how she's always a little late.

COOPER: At least she follows him.

LIZ: That's because he knows where he wants to go.

(The dance modulates into a slower tempo. Cooper and Lucy exit unobtrusively.)

FRITZI: *(Watching the dancers.)* Poetry in motion, that's what it is. Poetry in motion.

GINNY: If they wore skates, they could be in the Olympics.

FRITZI: They make the hair stand up on the back of my neck.

CALVIN: You said that yesterday about the new Thunderbird.

(Jack and Kitty's dance builds. They might dance up the staircase and freeze on the balustrade. Cooper and Lucy, both now in contemporary overcoats, enter from either side downstage. They meet somewhere in the center, isolated in light.)

COOPER: I got your message.

LUCY: Kitty telephoned. She's out of the hospital and now wants to come more than ever!

COOPER: I'll call Jack immediately! We've done it, haven't we?

LUCY: We're bringing it all back home.

COOPER: Lucy, I want to sleep with you all night long!

LUCY: What about Liz?

COOPER: I'll tell her I got stuck in the snow. *(They kiss passionately and go up the stairs as Jack and Kitty dance down, building their dance to a rousing climax. At the end, everyone gathers in on them, applauding, including Cooper and Lucy, who have had time to reenter as their young selves.)*

END OF ACT ONE

ACT TWO

The Cotillion Room is bustling with preparations for the revival of the Snow Ball. Someone is setting up tables, Lucy and others are on stepladders in work clothes, stringing up a large sign: WELCOME BACK, KITTY AND JACK! Downstage, Cooper addresses the audience.

COOPER: *(To audience.)* And so the day arrived. There were articles in the paper, interviews on TV, and a special exhibit at the historical society with pictures of Jack and Kitty and taped interviews of people who had seen them dance . . .
(Brewster, who has been working on the decorations, calls to another.)
BREWSTER: Question for a fellow sports fan.
BILLY: Yo.
BREWSTER: How many times did Jack and Kitty dance, during their final season together?
BILLY: Are we talking home, or away?
BREWSTER: Both, naturally.
BILLY: Twenty-seven times, according to the latest statistics.
BREWSTER: Wrong. Twenty-nine. They danced twice in Toronto.
BILLY: Canada? We're counting Canada now? Since when do we count Canada?
COOPER: *(To audience.)* We became the hottest ticket in town . . .
(Saul comes up to him.)
SAUL: Hey, Coop, can you do me a favor? I need two tickets tonight for me and Rhoda.
COOPER: We're sold out, pal. Sorry.
SAUL: Couldn't you squeeze us in? I'll pay for it. Extra.
COOPER: Tell you what, Saul. We're setting up bleachers in back. Give your name to Mrs. Klinger.
SAUL: Bleachers? For Rhoda? You must be mad.
COOPER: Or . . .
SAUL: Or what?
COOPER: You could help underwrite a sponsor's table.
SAUL: That's blackmail, Coop. But I'll call you. *(He goes out.)*
COOPER: *(To audience.)* I wish I could say the day dawned bright and clear. But it didn't. It dawned damp and gray. And we all knew, without knowing we knew, that we were in for a major snowstorm . . .
(Liz comes on, in parka and boots, carrying Cooper's tuxedo in a plastic bag.)
LIZ: Here's your stuff, Cooper. Tux, shirt, studs, everything.

COOPER: Thanks. I'll change in the men's room.

LIZ: That tuxedo cost a small fortune to repair, by the way. It was riddled with moth holes.

COOPER: Just as long as it fits.

LIZ: It never did, remember?

COOPER: What's it like outside?

LIZ: Beginning to snow. I wonder if they'll make it.

COOPER: They'll make it. What's a little snow between friends?

LIZ: See you later, then. *(She starts off then stops, calls up to Lucy, who's still on ladder.)* Hey, is that sign fireproof?

LUCY: Of course, Liz.

LIZ: Are you sure? These manufacturers get away with murder these days.

COOPER: It's O.K., Liz.

LIZ: Well I'm worried about people who smoke. I think you should rope them off, at the far end of the room.

LUCY: We're not going to do that, Liz.

COOPER: It's O.K., Lucy.

LUCY: Anyway, why do you care, Liz? I hear you have another party on your agenda tonight.

LIZ: Right. Over at the Community Center. *(Rhythmically.)*
    Tell Jack and Kitty to forget this fuss,
    For some free-style rap dancing over with us.
    (She executes a step, and goes out.)

LUCY: *(Coming down off the ladder.)* She hates me, doesn't she?

COOPER: Naw.

LUCY: She wouldn't look at me.

COOPER: She's got a lot on her mind.

LUCY: She's got us on her mind.

COOPER: I wish she did.

LUCY: What does that mean?

COOPER: Skip it.

LUCY: Tell her, Cooper.

COOPER: Tell her what?

LUCY: Everything. That we love each other and want to get married.

COOPER: I will.

LUCY: You keep saying that, but you don't.

COOPER: I'm waiting for the right time.

LUCY: Tell her tonight.

COOPER: Tonight?

LUCY: After the Snow Ball. To clear the air.

COOPER: I can't just take my wife home after a festive occasion and tell her I'm leaving.

LUCY: Cooper, I am out on a limb here! I just got fired because of this goddamn festive occasion!

COOPER: What?

LUCY: They noticed the telephone bill . . . all those long distance calls to Kitty.

COOPER: Oh boy.

LUCY: Oh well. I can still call Minneapolis.

COOPER: Hey look . . .

LUCY: I'm serious, Cooper. Tonight's the night. Now bite the bullet. Or get off the pot. *(She goes out.)*

COOPER: *(To audience.)* Oh God! Can a man be in love with two women at the same time? Which way do I turn? Lucy, with her satin nightgowns, and agreeable ways, and spectacular behavior in bed — Oh Lucy, I'm young again when I'm with you! She's found this cozy little carriage house off in the woods and is already thumbing through the Laura Ashley catalogue. Why shouldn't I settle there and listen to good old songs and read good old books and watch *Masterpiece Theater* on Sunday nights? What's wrong with that? . . . Of course, there's Liz. Impossible Liz. Fighting her past, fighting the world, fighting ME, all the way to the finish. Only after we're dead will I get off the hook. Then I can relax. In hell, with all the other adulterers. While Liz goes straight to heaven. Of course once she's there, I'm sure she'll spend most of her time getting God to register as a Democrat. *(A Musician comes up to Cooper. He carries a clarinet.)*

MUSICIAN: Mr. Jones, we're ready to rehearse in the back room.

COOPER: *(Getting a stack of music; to Musician.)* Could you start by running through these arrangements? Because of the snow, the dancers might be a little late.

MUSICIAN: *(Looking them over.)* Hey, this is great stuff! Where'd you dig it up?

COOPER: It's a long story . . .

MUSICIAN: I think the boys will get a kick of these . . .

(He goes off. . . Jack appears, carrying an identical stack of musical arrangements. He wears informal clothes: a sweater, gray flannels, white bucks.)

JACK: *(As if on telephone.)* Coop, I got to talk to you. Can you meet me at Smithers'? *(Mr. Smithers begins to set up the drugstore counter.)*

COOPER: I'll be there.

(Cooper and Jack meet at the counter.)

JACK: *(Tossing Cooper the arrangements.)* Here's a souvenir for you.

COOPER: What's this?

JACK: Our music. Take it. It's worth over three hundred bucks.

COOPER: Hey, simmer down. What's the matter?

JACK: We're breaking up.

COOPER: You and Kitty?

JACK: Her parents are packing her off to Europe. They won't even let her go back for the second semester. Off she goes, the day after tomorrow.

COOPER: Why?

JACK: Because of that goddam Snow Ball.

COOPER: You were spectacular at the Snow Ball.

JACK: Tell that to her parents. They thought it was vulgar.

COOPER: Vulgar?

JACK: That's what her mother said. Cheap and vulgar. Hollywood stuff. That's what she said.

COOPER: Oh for chrissake!

JACK: And it didn't help when this agent called. From New York.

COOPER: A New York agent!

JACK: He saw us in Boston and saw us again here and offered us two hundred and fifty dollars a week, each, plus expenses, to work at a nightclub in Toledo!

COOPER: That's a lot of dough!

JACK: And we'd get second billing. We'd go on right after Henny Youngman!

COOPER: Oh hey, wow!

JACK: I know. Just think. Dance with Kitty eight times a week and get paid for it!

COOPER: Did Kitty go along with it?

JACK: Sure! She was raring to go! Hell, maybe we would have ended up in the movies!

COOPER: You still could, Jack.

JACK: That's what her folks were scared of. So they lowered the boom. We all had this big scene. Her mother starts to scream, Kitty starts to cry, the old man kicks me out of the house. Then Kitty calls today and says she's off to Europe.

COOPER: I thought her father liked you.

JACK: He did, until the Snow Ball. Now he thinks I'm just an Irishman on the make.

COOPER: Well you are a little, Jack.

JACK: I know I am. But that's not all I am.

COOPER: She'll be back, Jack.

JACK: That's what she says. But it'll be too late, Coop! I know her! She's lazy. Some guy will give her a big rush, and I won't be there to dance her out of it. *(Upstage, on the opposite side, Kitty comes out in a wedding dress, carrying two glasses of champagne, being congratulated by well-wishers.)* So here: take the music. They can play it when you marry Liz.

COOPER: *(Taking the arrangements.)* I'll keep it for you, Jack. You'll be dancing with Kitty again, I swear.

JACK: Oh Coop. Grow up! You're just a dreamer, like everyone else around here!

(Jack goes off as Kitty calls to Cooper from across the stage. There is dance music in the background.)

KITTY: Cooper! *(Cooper crosses to her.)* You haven't kissed the bride yet. *(Cooper gives her a perfunctory kiss.)* Oh Cooper, don't be mad. Please. He's a wonderful guy.

COOPER: He's not Jack.

KITTY: He's more my type, Cooper. Really. His family knows my family, and he skiis like a dream. We had the most fabulous time in Switzerland.

COOPER: Does he dance?

KITTY: *(Defiantly.)* Yes. Very well. He dances very well.

COOPER: I saw you dance with him out there. He could hardly move.

KITTY: That's because he hurt his ankle.

COOPER: Oh, Kitty.

KITTY: He has a bad ankle, Cooper. From Lacrosse. At Princeton.

COOPER: Bullshit, Kitty. That's bullshit, and you know it.

KITTY: Oh stop, Cooper. Please. Just stop.

COOPER: Jack's here, by the way.

KITTY: I know that. Why wouldn't I know that? I invited him. We've had a long talk. Everything's fine. He's got a scholarship for Law School and made big plans.

COOPER: I notice you wouldn't dance with him.

KITTY: I don't know what you mean.

COOPER: I saw him cut in on you, and you sat right down.

KITTY: I was tired, Cooper.

COOPER: You were scared, Kitty.

KITTY: That's ridiculous.

COOPER: You were scared he'd dance you right out the door!

KITTY: *(Starting to cry.)* Don't, Cooper. Please. I can't stand it.

COOPER: *(Touching her.)* Why'd you do it, Kitty?

KITTY: There's more to life than hanging around nightclubs.

COOPER: That's your mother talking.

KITTY: There's more to life than dancing, then.

COOPER: You were lazy, Kitty. You made a lazy choice. It was just easier to slide downhill.

KITTY: You can't always marry the perfect person, Cooper! No one does!

COOPER: You can try.

KITTY: Anyway, Jack's found someone, Cooper! He says he's almost engaged! He says she types his papers, and is terribly well organized, and will be a big help in his career. *(The sounds of an airport. Joan Daley appears. She is neat and well dressed. She looks around impatiently.)* She'll be much better for him than I'd ever be!

(Kitty runs off in tears as a Waitress sets up a cocktail table. Lucy joins Cooper, indicates Joan.)

LUCY: She must be the one. *(They cross to Joan.)*

JOAN: Oh hi. I'm terribly sorry to drag you two all the way out to the airport, but I was between planes, and I thought I'd just give you a jingle. I'm Joan Daley.

COOPER: Hiya.

LUCY: Hello.

(Everyone shakes hands. They settle at the table. Joan gestures imperiously to the Waitress.)

JOAN: I just spent the weekend at Andover visiting the boys, and I have to be back for a major fundraiser in Indianapolis tonight, but I thought I ought to stop by and say hello. *(She briskly removes her gloves.)* And, frankly, I thought we should lay our cards on the table. Before this Snow Ball thing gets completely out of hand.

LUCY: Out of hand?

JOAN: *(To Waitress.)* Pina colada, please . . .

LUCY: White wine . . .

COOPER: Light beer. *(The Waitress goes off angrily.)*

JOAN: *(Pulling a pack of cigarettes out of her purse; looking around.)* Do you suppose Jack will lose the election if I sneak one tiny little Menthol Light? I mean, wives have to be so careful in politics . . . *(She offers them to Cooper and Lucy who shake their heads.)* No? How disgustingly healthy. *(She lights up and takes a deep draw.)* Well. Tell me. How serious is it? This . . . Snow Ball?

COOPER: Sort of serious.

LUCY: Very serious.

JOAN: You mean you seriously want Jack to dance, My Jack? Republican

Candidate for Governor Jack Daley? You want him to dance around some room with some old flame?

LUCY: That's what we want.

JOAN: The kids think it's an absolute hoot. We all roared about it when he told us.

COOPER: Jack was a great dancer.

JOAN: So he says. He's out in the garage, every chance he gets, practicing to some tape. I mean, who are we kidding?

LUCY: You're in for a big surprise.

JOAN: Let's be a tad more specific. Will the media be there? Photographers? Television? Any of that?

COOPER: Oh sure. It's a story, after all. Downtown renewal, the hotel fixed up . . .

JOAN: So it will be on TV.

COOPER: Local TV, certainly.

JOAN: *Our* TV, too, I should think. Candidate returns to roots, all that . . .

LUCY: Actually, there's talk of national TV. *Entertainment Tonight* has made some inquiries.

JOAN: Don't count on it, folks.

LUCY: Well I mean, it's a story, after all. Two old friends come home to dance . . .

JOAN: It's a local story, here and back home.

COOPER: Probably. Yes.

JOAN: Suppose I danced with him.

COOPER: I hope you will.

JOAN: No, I mean instead of her.

LUCY: Mrs. Daley —

JOAN: Joan.

LUCY: All right, Joan.

JOAN: Actually, we have danced a little. We've — we've done the Twist. We were — quite good.

COOPER: Well you can dance the Twist again, if you'd like, Mrs. Daley.

JOAN: Joan.

COOPER: We're hoping, Joan, that Jack will dance the main dance with Kitty.

JOAN: I'm the Main Dance, Mister.

LUCY: Well we know you are, but —

JOAN: I'm his WIFE.

LUCY: Oh well . . .

JOAN: He can dance, O.K. He can even do a number, off camera, with this Kitty. But when it comes to magic time, he dances with me.

COOPER: It's just for old times sake —

LUCY: Exactly. It's just a fun thing.

JOAN: Just a fun thing? You tell that to the unemployed steelworkers in Cary watching it on TV. You tell that to the farmers downstate up to their ass in debt. You tell that to me, ME, who shook all those sweaty hands and sat through all those lousy speeches for twenty years. "Just a fun thing!" You think I'm going to sit on the sidelines and watch my husband throw away a chance to be governor, just so he can bounce around with some society broad? No sirree, gang. Sorry. He dances with me, or he doesn't dance at all.

COOPER: Does Jack go along with that?

JOAN: He better. *(She puts on her gloves.)* Otherwise I won't come with him. Which will look bad. And I might not be there when he gets back. Which will look worse. Now where the fuck is the ladies room? *(Gets up.)*

LUCY: I think it's —

JOAN: *(Extending her hand.)* Thank you very much. What a lovely city. What a lovely airport. What a pleasant way to break up my trip. *(She goes out.)*

LUCY: *(To Cooper.)* Maybe I can still butter her up.

COOPER: I'm amazed she got through security. *(Lucy hurries off after Joan.)*

LUCY: Wait, Mrs. Daley . . . Joan . . . Wait . . . *(Meanwhile, on the opposite side of the stage, Baldwin Hall, a tanned, white-haired, elderly man in resort clothes, has come on with a telephone.)*

BALDWIN: *(On telephone.)* Cooper Jones?

COOPER: *(As if on the telephone.)* Who's this?

BALDWIN: It's Baldwin Hall. Kitty's husband.

COOPER: Ah.

BALDWIN: I wonder if I might talk to you about this Snow Ball business.

COOPER: Shoot.

BALDWIN: *(Putting on a jacket and tie.)* I prefer it to be face to face. My plane gets in at forty-five.

COOPER: I'll be there. *(A white-jacketed Waiter sets up a table and chairs. Cooper and Baldwin meet centerstage and shake hands.)* I thought we'd go to the club.

BALDWIN: Any place where it's quiet. *(They cross to the table and order from the Waiter as they settle in.)* I'll have a gin martini on the rocks with a twist, please.

COOPER: Light beer, Martin.

BALDWIN: *(Looking around.)* Nice club. Did Kitty ever dance here?

COOPER: Every spring. In the courtyard.

BALDWIN: She's a lovely dancer.

COOPER: I'll say.

BALDWIN: Even with an old fool like me. We dance very well together. Every Thursday night we go to the Golf Club down at Ocean Reef and dance under the stars.

COOPER: Sounds great. *(The Waiter brings drinks.)*

BALDWIN: Well. Now. This Snow Ball thing. How definite is it?

COOPER: Pretty definite.

BALDWIN: Sometimes these things don't materialize.

COOPER: The invitations are out. The band's all signed up.

BALDWIN: Then the die is cast.

COOPER: I'm afraid it is. Some problem?

BALDWIN: *(Drinking.)* Kitty's not very well . . . Actually, she's . . . in serious difficulty. She's got . . . During the operation, they discovered . . . They say I could lose her. *(He starts to cry.)*

COOPER: Oh hey, please. Would you like to go somewhere? We have a lounge here. We have a library which is never used . . .

BALDWIN: *(Shaking his head.)* I'm all right. I'm fine now. *(Taps his glass.)* I'd like another of these, if I may. *(Cooper signals the waiter.)* She refuses to do anything about it until after the party. She's heard you can lose your hair . . .

COOPER: Boy. *(To Waiter.)* More of the same for Mr. Hall, Martin. And I might shift to scotch.

BALDWIN: She wants to risk her life, come up here in the dead of winter, dance with some fellow she hasn't seen for thirty years. I can't get over it. I can't make it out. *(Waiter brings more drinks.)*

COOPER: Do you want me to find some way to call it off?

BALDWIN: She'd never forgive me.

COOPER: Well then look. All she needs to do is a few steps, really. Just a bow and a spin. Then we'll put her right back on the plane.

BALDWIN: No. She wants to do the whole thing. She took the music you sent her and found some fella who plays the piano, and she's been working on her steps ever since. She's very serious about it.

COOPER: Oh, boy.

BALDWIN: This man. Jack Daley. Is he serious, too?

COOPER: I think he is.

BALDWIN: Is he practicing, too?

COOPER: I hear he is.

BALDWIN: Good. Because she wants this to work. It's terribly important to her.

(Downs his drink, gets up.) And therefore to me. Now, if you'll return me to the airport . . .

COOPER: Won't you have some dinner?

BALDWIN: No thank you. I can just get back for a late supper with Kitty.

COOPER: Tell her I hope she feels better.

BALDWIN: I'll tell her nothing at all. She thinks I'm playing golf in Fort Lauderdale.

COOPER: I'll tell Jack to go easy.

BALDWIN: Sir: we have just had a drink at your club. I assume everything we discussed was strictly confidential. You may simply tell him to dance as well as he possibly can. *(He goes off as the Waiter clears the table. The lights come up on the Cotillion Room, now all prepared and decorated for the Snow Ball. Lucy comes on, carrying some decoration.)*

LUCY: Cooper! We just heard on the radio. The storm's worse. The airport has closed down.

COOPER: Oh God.

LUCY: I called the airlines. Jack's plane never took off, and Kitty's stacked up somewhere over Albany.

COOPER: Shit.

LUCY: So what do we do?

COOPER: Do? We do what we always do in times of trouble: we change our clothes. *(He goes off.)*

LUCY: *(Calling after him.)* And then we change our LIVES, Cooper Jones!
(No answer. Lucy throws up her hands, goes off another way. Music. Lights. Decorations drop into place. Guests enter down the staircase in their evening clothes and overcoats; among them are Saul and Rhoda Radner.)

CALVIN: *(Brushing off his shoulders.)* God! What weather!

MARY: Who cares? Look at this!

RHODA: Let it snow, let it snow, let it snow!

A MAN: Dig the music!

RHODA: It's like walking into the Piazza San Marco when the band strikes up!

SAUL: Rhoda never got over our trip to Venice.

HEATHER: Let's hope those Arthur Murray brush-ups pay off!
(She starts a tentative tango with Brewster.)

CALVIN: *(To his wife.)* What say, Mary? Think we can still cut a rug?

MARY: Go easy, Calvin. I've had a hip replacement.

SAUL: Look at the floor, Rhoda. Notice the workmanship!

RHODA: They should've gotten Johnson's Wax to underwrite this thing. *(Looking at tango dancers.)* Olé! *(Downstage, Older Jack enters, in an overcoat. He carries a Valpac bag over his shoulder. He is ruddy-faced, gray-haired, and looks at least fifty. He watches the dancing for a moment then speaks to a Waiter.)*

OLDER JACK: Would you find Mr. Cooper Jones and tell him I'm here?

WAITER: Who shall I say it is, sir?

OLDER JACK: He'll know. *(The Waiter goes off. Jack looks around.)*

BREWSTER: *(To Heather as they tango.)* My grandmother danced on this floor!

HEATHER: We should've brought her! We should've dragged her out of that nursing home!

RHODA: *(Removing her coat.)* Oh but the lights, the music! I feel like Madame Bovary!

SAUL: Just don't act like Madame Bovary! *(Cooper comes out, now in his tuxedo.)*

COOPER: *(To Jack.)* May I help you?

JACK: I certainly hope so.

COOPER: *(Peering at him.)* Jack?

JACK: *(Holding out his hand.)* Hiya, guy.

COOPER: Jack! My God. Jack . . . *(They embrace.)* You look . . . great, Jack.

JACK: I look old, Coop. And so do you. *(Indicating the others.)* So does everyone. It's been thirty years.

COOPER: *(Looking at the others.)* Right. I never noticed . . . But hey! How did you get here? Your flight was cancelled.

JACK: I took an earlier one.

COOPER: I would've met you, Jack.

JACK: Naaa. I needed to get my bearings. Things sure have changed, haven't they? Smithers is now a video store.

COOPER: Right. But hey, but you're here! *(Calls toward the dancers.)* Hey, gang! Look who's —

JACK: *(Shushing him.)* Hold it. Where is she?

COOPER: Hasn't shown up yet.

JACK: Knew it! She chickened out, didn't she?

COOPER: The STORM, Jack. Remember?

JACK: Oh. Right.

COOPER: Let's hope she's just . . . late.

JACK: *(Nervously laughing.)* Where have we heard that one before? *(The other guests have drifted out.)*

COOPER: We never thought we'd get through to you, Jack! All those letters, those telephone calls! But here you are! And you get the VIP treatment, buddy. We're giving you the Executive Suite, free of charge, with a telephone in the john!

JACK: Thanks, but I'll stay with my mother.

COOPER: *(Carefully.)* Your wife isn't with you?

JACK: She . . . couldn't make it.

COOPER: That's too bad.

JACK: Yes. That is. That is too bad. Well. I better get into my monkey suit, huh?

COOPER: Come on. You can still use the suite for that. *(They go off. Police sirens. Baldwin comes on with Lucy; both are in evening clothes.)*

BALDWIN: Well we're here. And it's been hell getting here. And I'm not sure why we're here. But we're here.

LUCY: I'm sorry, but I'm hopelessly confused. Where is Kitty?

BALDWIN: Getting dressed, of course. I engaged a room.

LUCY: But what were those sirens? And who were all those policemen?

BALDWIN: It's very simple, really. We had to land in Syracuse, so Kitty insisted on renting a car. And insisted on driving at an unconscionable speed. Naturally she ploughed into a snowbank. The troopers dug us out, and Kitty charmed her way into a police escort right to the front door.

LUCY: The gods are with us!

BALDWIN: Then do you suppose the gods could provide us with a good, stiff drink?

LUCY: *(Taking his arm.)* That you shall have, sir. That you shall have. *(They go off. More music. Liz comes on, in an overcoat. She looks around. Cooper comes on.)*

COOPER: Well, well. You're early.

LIZ: The kids wanted the car. They dropped me off.

COOPER: Aren't they coming? I reserved them seats in the bleachers.

LIZ: They decided on the movies instead.

COOPER: Son of a BITCH!

LIZ: They said you and I don't show up for the Grateful Dead. Why should they for Jack and Kitty?

COOPER: You should have made them stay.

LIZ: We can't MAKE them do things any more, Cooper. They're too old. And so are we.

COOPER: Let me take your coat. *(He takes off Liz's coat.)* Hey! *(She's wearing a lovely green dress.)*

LIZ: What's the matter?

COOPER: The green dress from Berger's.

LIZ: They had it on sale.

COOPER: You look good.

LIZ: I don't know . . .

COOPER: You look gorgeous.

LIZ: I must say, getting into these duds gets all the old juices going.

COOPER: What did I tell you? *(He starts dancing with her.)*

LIZ: *(As they dance.)* Smell the perfume?

COOPER: Do I ever. What's it called?

LIZ: Some dumb name. I borrowed it from mother.

COOPER: *(Stopping dancing.)* Liz, before the preliminaries, I want to ask you something important.

LIZ: Ask away.

COOPER: Are you happy?

LIZ: Happy?

COOPER: Here. With me. Tonight.

LIZ: You want me to speak frankly?

COOPER: Yes I do, Liz. I really do.

LIZ: All right then, Cooper. Yes and no.

COOPER: Give me the yes first.

LIZ: O.K. Yes, I like getting gussied up occasionally. I like being with you, dressed or undressed. I even like it when we fight. We keep each other honest, and I like that a lot. So yes, yes, yes, to all of that.

COOPER: And now the no.

LIZ: I don't think you've thought about the morning after.

COOPER: Which means . . .?

LIZ: Which mean that after every party, somebody has to clean up the crap.

COOPER: Watch your language, lady.

LIZ: This is no lady. This is your wife. *(Lucy, Baldwin, and the others come on.)*

BALDWIN: There is much to be said for a good drink with good company when you're a poor traveler on a snowy night.

COOPER: *(Handing champagne around.)* Anybody need champagne?

LUCY: Notice the decorations, everyone. We're having the champagne cooled in real snow. *(Jack comes in, now resplendent in tails.)*

COOPER: Ah hah! Here he is. Jack, let me introduce you to —

JACK: *(Arm around Baldwin.)* That's all right. We met in the corridor, didn't we, Baldwin?

BALDWIN: We did indeed. And cemented our friendship in the bar.

LUCY: *(Low to Cooper.)* They seem to get along.

COOPER: They seem to like each other.

BALDWIN: *(Raising his glass; pointedly.)* Ladies and gentlemen, I would like to propose a toast. To Kitty.

JACK: To Kitty.

COOPER: To all of us.

LIZ: To a better world.

LUCY: *(Low; to Cooper.)* To you and me, tomorrow. *(Cooper winces.)*

JACK: Still no Kitty?

EVERYONE: She's getting dressed, Jack.

LUCY: For a while we thought we'd lost her.

LIZ: Oh well, then you could have gone on in her place.

LUCY: What kind of a fool do you think I am?

LIZ: I've never been quite sure.

LUCY: *(Grabbing Cooper by the arm.)* Did you hear that? I'm going to tell her myself!

COOPER: Lucy —

(A TV Crew enters. A Woman Reporter speaks into a recorder.)

REPORTER: We are now coming into the Cotillion Room of the old George Washington Hotel, as guests gather to celebrate the homecoming of two special friends *(She finds Jack, shoves a microphone in his face.)* Mr. Daley: How does it feel to come home and dance with an old flame?

JACK: I think you'd do better to call us young sparks . . . is there an ambulance waiting in the wings?

(Laughter from the group.)

REPORTER: As a candidate for governor, are you concerned about the lack of any minority representation at this party?

JACK: Oh these folks are a minority. They just don't know it yet.

(Laughter from crowd.)

COOPER: *(Low to Jack.)* I see you're still light on your feet, Jack.

REPORTER: It's hard to believe you'd remember all your old steps.

JACK: I've got a memory like an elephant. I'll probably dance like one, too.

(More laughter. The crowd moves upstage for more interviews, as Cooper steps forward.)

COOPER: *(To audience.)* What have I done? says Alec Guinness, as he surveys *The Bridge on the River Kwai?* What in God's name have I done. Why are we here in this tacky old room? Everyone's trying much too hard, and no one's having a good time. Jack is obviously in bad trouble at home and seems to have been drinking since noon. Poor Kitty is probably crumped out on some couch. And me? What about me? My job is in shambles — I haven't sold anything in weeks. I've had to borrow money, just to buy Christmas presents. And my marriage? Have I messed it up permanently? Is Liz thinking about divorce? Will I end up with Lucy, living on sex and nostalgia? Oh, what have I done, Guinness asks himself, before he throws himself on the plunger and blows the whole damn thing to smithereens! *(A cry of delight from the staircase. Everyone looks toward it in anticipation.)* And then Kitty arrived and it all made perfect sense! *(The older Kitty enters as she once entered in dancing school. She wears a lovely dress, but like Jack, she is now much older.)*

KITTY: Ooops! I guess I'm late. *(Applause from the crowd. The television camera moves in, and the television lights come on. She blinks.)* What do I do now? Say *cheese* or what?

BALDWIN: *(Going to her.)* You're home, darling. *(He helps her with her coat, gives her his arm, and walks her downstairs. Squeals and hugs as she greets her old friends. Finally Baldwin brings her through the crowd to Jack. More applause. Jack bows to Kitty, as if it were the old days.)*

KITTY: Oh well, why not? Let's do it from soup to nuts. *(She responds with a deep curtsy. Applause again from the crowd. They kiss.)*

JACK: You look great, Kitty.

KITTY: I feel like an old Studebaker, trotted out for an antique show.

JACK: No, no. You look terrific.

KITTY: Thank you, Jack. So do you.

MARY: Come on, you two! Dance!

LUCY: But everyone's not here yet.

BALDWIN: It might be good to get started.

KITTY: *(To Jack.)* Do you suppose we could sneak out and practice a little? *(The Crowd calls out: "No! No! Do it now!")* Hey, come on! Give us a break.

JACK: Looks like there isn't time, Kitty. We'll just have to hope for the best.

KITTY: I tried going through it on my own. Some of it came back, some of it didn't.

JACK: Ditto with me. It's hard to dance alone.

KITTY: At least tell the band to go slow. Say we're no spring chickens.

JACK: You're young as a girl.

KITTY: Still. Tell them. *(Jack goes off; Kitty glances around.)* Cooper Jones, is that you? Where have you been hiding? Crawl from there, you bad boy! You should be ashamed of yourself, putting me on the spot this way.

COOPER: *(Coming to her.)* Oh Kitty, you'll come through with flying colors. *(They hug.)*

KITTY: Well, flying or not, get me a glass of water, and all will be forgiven. *(Baldwin brings her a pill; Cooper produces a glass of water. Kitty downs the pill quickly and smiles.)*

COOPER: Are you all right?

KITTY: Fine. Never better.

LUCY: Surprise, surprise! *(Out comes the old Snowball sleigh, drawn by two men.)* Prance, gentlemen, prance!

EVERYONE: You're supposed to be reindeer!

KITTY: Where'd you find that? In the ruins of Pompeii?

COOPER: *(Leading Kitty to it.)* Sit in it, Kitty . . . and Lucy . . . and Liz, sit beside her.

LIZ: You're not going to get me into that thing!

COOPER: Do it, Liz. Please. Once, without arguing.

LIZ: All right. But under protest. *(Liz joins Kitty and Lucy in the sleigh. The TV people focus in. Everyone applauds, then freezes.)*

COOPER: *(To audience.)* Oh my God, you see? You see? This is it! This is what I've wanted all along! Woman, in all her glory! *(Indicating Kitty.)* Goddess . . . *(Indicating Liz.)* Wife and mother . . . *(Indicating Lucy.)* And finally, lover! Oh, if I could only have all three forever!

LIZ: Cooper, you're in the way! *(The freeze breaks.)*

JACK: *(Returning.)* The orchestra's all set. *(He sees Kitty and her court; stands enrapt.)* Holy Cow.

KITTY: Let's get at it. I think I'm sitting on a nail. *(Jack lifts her out of the sleigh, as before. Lucy tells others to remove it, shoos the TV people out of the way. Jack and Kitty assume their old starting position.)* Well then. It's all a question of faith, isn't it? I mean, we'll just have to hold our noses and jump.

JACK: That's it. *(The crowd back off settles into chairs or stands along the wall. Jack signals. The orchestra sounds a drumroll.)*

KITTY: *(Holding up her hand.)* Hold it. *(The drumroll stops.)* I don't know . . . Jack and I have come so far . . . and all these people have managed to brave the storm . . . Shouldn't we join hands and pray, or sing the "Star Spangled Banner," or something? *(General laughter. Then the number begins. Jack and Kitty dance their old Snow Ball number, to the same music, but because they're older now, and out of shape, and out of practice, they make many mistakes. Some of it works beautifully, and the crowd supports them with oh's and ah's and occasional applause. As the dancers continue, the younger Jack and Kitty join them, swirling and dipping around them, until soon we are seeing the number from several simultaneous perspectives — a complicated, intricate, shifting quartet, sometimes gloriously nostalgic, sometimes precariously out of date. Finally, as the music moves to its conclusion, the younger couple disappears, and the older Jack and Kitty manage a good enough finish to bring on a round of decent applause. At the end, people cluster around them, congratulating them. Others begin to drift off.)*

MARY: *(To Heather.)* How can you leave after seeing something like that? They make me want to dance all night!

HEATHER: I have to get up early tomorrow for a root canal. *(She goes off.)*

CALVIN: Well, we've seen it. Now I can die happily.

MARY: Oh Calvin . . .

CALVIN: No, I mean it. I've seen the Parthenon, I've seen the Taj Mahal, I've seen Jack and Kitty. It's all downhill from here.

MARY: Can't we at least take a peek at the Grand Canyon?

(They go off. Cooper, Liz, and Lucy are in the crowd of well-wishers.)

COOPER: Champagne for Jack and Kitty! *(Cheers.)*

KITTY: No thank you, Cooper. *(She glances at Baldwin.)* I think it's time I was in bed.

BALDWIN: I agree. *(He slips her another pill, which she swallows surreptitiously.)*

LUCY: Now you and Baldwin are staying with me, Kitty.

KITTY: We can't, Lucy. We decided to stay right here in this hotel. That way we can be off bright and early.

BALDWIN: The policeman said the airport would be clear tomorrow.

KITTY: Yes, all this snow is supposed just to melt away.

LUCY: But we have a luncheon planned. And a tour of all the old sights.

KITTY: Don't dare, love. I'd probably never leave. *(She starts kissing people good-bye, as Baldwin follows her, shaking hands.)* Good-bye, good-bye . . . Lovely to see you again . . . Hey, don't everybody stop dancing! Good-bye . . . such fun . . . Come to Florida . . . Come see us . . . Good-bye. *(Cooper and Lucy accompany them towards an exit. Kitty turns to them.)* So long, you two. Thank you for asking me back. *(She kisses Lucy, then Cooper.)*

COOPER: Kitty, you were great.

KITTY: Well, at least it ties things up, Cooper. I had to do that.

JACK: *(Agonizingly.)* Kitty!

KITTY: Did you think I'd forget you? Come here, you sweet man, so I can say a special goodbye.

JACK: We did O.K., didn't we, Kitty?

KITTY: Well, we tried our damnedest.

JACK: We could try again.

KITTY: Oh Jack . . .

JACK: I mean, just dancing occasionally.

KITTY: Wouldn't that be fun?

JACK: I could visit in Florida. Or you could . . .

KITTY: Oh heavens no, Jack. As Shakespeare says . . . *(She gives him a quick kiss on the cheek.)* Enough is enough.

BALDWIN: *(Taking her arm.)* Come on, dear.

KITTY: Good-bye, Jack darling. And thank you.

JACK: Good-bye, Kitty. *(Kitty and Baldwin go. More people also leave.)*

COOPER: Champagne, Jack?

JACK: *(Looking after Kitty.)* What? Oh no thanks.

COOPER: Scotch, then? Something. We haven't really caught up.

JACK: Actually, Coop. Now I'm back, I'd better go all the way. The clarinet player is an old pal from Holy Angels. He wants to go out and hoist a few brews.

COOPER: I'll pick you up tomorrow, then. Show you around.

JACK: No thanks, friend. It's breakfast with me dear old Mum, then off to face the music.

COOPER: The campaign?

JACK: No, no. Actually, there won't be a campaign this year, Coop. Marriage troubles. Things are kind of messy.

COOPER: Oh Jack, I'm sorry.

JACK: Naaa. Would've happened anyway. This just brought doings to a boil.

COOPER: Then come home, Jack. Work here. Run for office if you want. I'll help. Look, I feel responsible. I stirred this up.

JACK: I'm glad you did, buddy. *(Looks toward where Kitty has gone.)* It was worth it, even after thirty years. *(Pause.)* Well. Onward and upward.

COOPER: So what's next, Jack?

JACK: You know me. I guess I'll land on my feet. *(He does his old dance step from dancing school.)*

COOPER: I'm sure you will, Jack.

JACK: So long then, pal.

(They hug, and he goes off. Saul comes in, now in his overcoat.)

SAUL: Rhoda's in the car, Coop. She overdid the champagne.

COOPER: I'm sorry, Saul.

SAUL: But I wanted to say thanks. It reminded me of those dances we saw on our cruise to the South Pacific. I mean, it told some story, even if we didn't know what it was.

COOPER: Thanks, Saul.

SAUL: Call me Monday. We'll talk business.

COOPER: Maybe, Saul. Thanks. *(Saul goes off. The TV crew is packing up. Lucy sits down forlornly at one of the tables. Liz comes up to Cooper.)*

LIZ: I'll change for the community shindig.

COOPER: I'd better do a little cleaning up.

LIZ: *(Glancing at Lucy.)* Yes. You'd better. *(Liz goes off Cooper takes off his jacket, crosses to Lucy. Others continue to drift off.)*

COOPER: The snow's stopping.

LUCY: I know . . . *(Pause.)* I didn't tell you this, but I was asked out to Minneapolis for New Year's. *(Looks at him.)* Think I should go?

COOPER: I think you should.

LUCY: I think I should, too. *(Getting up.)* He's very different, you know. He was born in Bulgaria, for God's sake. He sells wall-to-wall carpeting and wants me to help him in his work. It'll be a whole new thing.

COOPER: Maybe that's good.

LUCY: Maybe it is . . . I wonder what we thought we were doing.

COOPER: Putting a little romance back into the world.

LUCY: Oh is that what it was?

COOPER: I thought they were spectacular!

LUCY: *(Kissing him on the cheek.)* Oh, Cooper! You're more romantic than any of us!

(She goes out. He watches her go. The lights dim on the room. The Reporter and Cameraman are puttering with their equipment.)

COOPER: Did you get it, people?

CAMERAMAN: What's to get? Some fat guy pushing an old broad around the room.

COOPER: I don't believe I heard you correctly.

CAMERAMAN: Hey. You get better dancing every day on MTV.

COOPER: You have no idea what you're talking about.

CAMERAMAN: You speaking to me, buddy?

REPORTER: Let's split, Eddie. O.K.?

COOPER: *(Coming up to the Cameraman.)* I'll tell you what you saw tonight. You saw a class act. You saw a man and a woman dance beautifully together. You saw the man lead and the woman follow — no, that's wrong, you saw her choose to follow, of her own accord. You saw grace and charm and harmony between the sexes. You saw an image of civilization up there tonight, that's what you fucking well saw!
(He shoves him.)

CAMERAMAN: Want to make something of it, buddy?

REPORTER: Forget it, Eddie. He's drunk.

COOPER: Sure I want to make something of it. *(More shoving and suddenly both are punching and wrestling on the floor.)*

REPORTER: Break it up, fellas! Hey! Break it up!
(Liz comes on, now in slacks and parka, sees the fight.)

LIZ: Oh Good Lord! (*She grabs the silver container for the champagne and pours it over the wrestlers drenching them in snow.*) The interventionist hereby intervenes! (*They pull apart, sputtering.*)

REPORTER: (*Helping the Cameraman up.*) Come on, Eddie. We can still catch the end of the basketball game.

CAMERAMAN: (*As they go.*) If you ruined my utility belt, I'll sue your ass off!

LIZ: Bug off! Or I'll have you arrested under Title Five!

(*The TV crew goes. Liz helps Cooper up.*)

COOPER: What's Title Five?

LIZ: I have no idea . . . What happened?

COOPER: (*Putting on his jacket.*) I was defending western civilization.

LIZ: Tell me about it in the car. Where's your overcoat?

COOPER: In the check room.

LIZ: Wait here. I'll get it. (*She goes out. Cooper looks at the empty Cotillion Room, which is now almost in darkness. The music comes up eerily.*)

COOPER: (*To audience.*) Kitty died in June, holding on longer than anyone expected. Good old Kitty, late at the last. Baldwin brought her back here for burial, and we had a small service down at the club. As for Jack, he made a very gentlemanly speech withdrawing from the election and left Indiana permanently. We now hear he's running a chain of liquor stores in Phoenix, Arizona, and from all reports, doing reasonably well.

(*Liz comes back on, hands Cooper his overcoat.*)

LIZ: Put this on before you catch cold.

COOPER: Thanks.

LIZ: Now give me the parking ticket. I'll bring the car around.

(*He does; she goes off. Cooper puts on his overcoat.*)

COOPER: (*To audience.*) No one ever again tried to revive the Snow Ball. It was over, done with, kaput. But as time went on, it was quite the thing to say you'd been there, at the last one, when Jack Daley danced with Kitty Price for the last time. (*The older Jack and Kitty dance upstage.*) O.K., O.K., maybe it was just a fat guy pushing an old broad around the room, but the older we got, the more we remembered a stalwart young man and a classy young woman, he proudly deliberate, she deliciously late, dancing together, on into the night . . . (*Younger Jack and Kitty take over. Liz comes back on.*)

LIZ: O.K. All set with the car.

COOPER: Do we have to go to the Community Center?

LIZ: Nope. Let's go home. The snow's almost stopped, by the way.

COOPER: Hand me the keys. I'll drive.

LIZ: I'd just as soon drive, Cooper.

COOPER: Come on. It'll still be slippery out there.

LIZ: Which is exactly why I should drive. *(They go off arguing as the lights fade on the young Jack and Kitty dancing beautifully downstage in a spot, as they did at the beginning.)*

THE END

THE FOURTH WALL

To David Saint

ORIGINAL PRODUCTION

The Fourth Wall was first produced at Westport Country Playhouse (James B. McKenzie, Executive Director; Eric Friedheim, Associate Producer), in Westport, Connecticut, opening on August 3, 1992, continuing on to the Cape Playhouse, in Dennis, Massachusetts, on August 17, 1992, and then to the Hasty Pudding Theater, in Cambridge, Massachusetts, in September 1992 (Andreas Teuber, Producer). It was directed by David Saint; the set design was by Richard Ellis; the costume design was by David Murin; the lighting design was by Susan Roth; the Cole Porter songs used were arranged by Jonathan Sheffer and the stage manager was Ira Mont. The cast was as follows:

ROGER	Tony Roberts
JULIA	Kelly Bishop
PEGGY	E. Katherine Kerr
FLOYD	Jack Gilpin

The Fourth Wall was subsequently produced by Norman Rubenstein's Feenix Productions, in conjunction with James B. McKenzie and Ralph Roseman, at the Briar Street Theatre in Chicago, Illinois, in April 1993. The set design was by Richard Ellis; the costume design was by Gayland Spaulding; the lighting design was by J. R. Lederle; and the production stage manager was Rebecca Green. The director was again David Saint. The cast was as follows:

ROGER	George Segal
JULIA	Jean de Baer
PEGGY	Betty Buckley
FLOYD	Mark Nelson

The Fourth Wall's most recent professional production was at the Pasadena Playhouse, in Pasadena, California, opening on March 20, 1994, and continuing on to the Poway Center for the Performing Arts in San Diego, California. The set design was by Scott Heineman; the costume design was by Zoe Dufour; the lighting design was by Martin Aronstein; musical arrangement was by Ron Abel; and the production stage manager was Daniel Munson. David Saint once again directed. The cast was as follows:

ROGER	Sam Freed
JULIA	Jean de Baer
PEGGY	Barrie Youngfellow
FLOYD	Jim Fyfe

AUTHOR'S NOTE

This is one of my favorite plays. It never landed in New York and hit a few bumps on its various venues out of town, but I got a kick out of writing it, a bigger kick out of seeing it performed, and still find it fairly funny when I read it now. It opened at the Westport Country Playhouse the summer of the 1992 presidential election and in that early version made a few cracks about George and Barbara Bush. Westport can be, I discovered, rather aggressively Republican, and I can remember the theater doors slamming and engines gunning in the parking lot as departing subscribers expressed their partisan displeasure.

If *The Fourth Wall* irritated Westport, it went on to amuse Dennis on Cape Cod and at least interest audiences in Cambridge, until it was thoroughly slammed by the *Boston Globe*. It was revived in Chicago the following winter with a different cast, and this time fared better. Yet another production opened and played at the Pasadena Playhouse, ending with a short tour that left it stranded in Santa Barbara, unable to open because the theater had closed down.

When I wrote *The Fourth Wall*, I thought I had made a very New Yorky play, theatrically sophisticated, condescending toward the provinces, liberal, and "in." It's also relatively inexpensive to produce, and it offers four good parts for actors. But New York producers never gave it a second glance. The play has had a few productions in colleges and community theaters since its initial runs, but I can't say it has ever found its true audience, if there is one besides me. I suspect that most people who go to the theater don't want to play the kind of esthetic games *The Fourth Wall* asks them to play. Oh yes: since every play in this book is an adaptation of some sort, you could say, if you had to, that *The Fourth Wall* is a sly adaptation of Bernard Shaw's *Saint Joan*.

CHARACTERS

(In order of appearance)

> JULIA
> ROGER
> PEGGY
> FLOYD

The first three are middle-aged. Floyd is somewhat younger.

SETTING

The living room of a suburban house near Buffalo. It looks pleasant, comfortable, and lived-in. Upstage is an inviting fireplace. Also upstage, a picture window through which one can see the pleasant greenery of a suburban backyard. Downstage, there are a couch, chairs, and tables, all somewhat artificially placed to face front. Down right, a working bar. Down left, a telephone, below the entrance to a front hall. On the walls are several good, rather conventional paintings. On the piano, a number of family photographs. On the mantelpiece, several knick-knacks.

(Note: This description applies to a proscenium theater. I hope a good designer could attain a similar effect on a more open stage.)

TIME

The time is the present, beginning in late afternoon and continuing on into the evening.

Special note on music by Cole Porter: Rights to present *The Fourth Wall* include permission to use the following music by Cole Porter. All programs must carry the following credits. *I'm In Love Again* Copyright 1925 (renewed), Warner Bros. Inc.; *Why Shouldn't I?* Copyright 1925 (renewed), Warner Bros. Inc.; *Big Town* Copyright 1980, Robert H. Montgomery, Jr. as Trustee; *After You, Who?* Copyright 1932 (renewed) Warner Bros. Inc.; *Let's Be Buddies* Copyright 1940, by Chappell & Co., Inc.

THE FOURTH WALL

ACT ONE

At rise: there is no one onstage. Through the windows comes late afternoon light. After a moment, Roger and Julia enter from the hall. Roger wears a business suit. Julia wears the latest thing in New York fashion.

ROGER: *(Indicating the proscenium "wall.")* You see?

JULIA: I do.

ROGER: I thought you should see.

JULIA: I certainly do. *(She looks at the "wall" carefully.)*

ROGER: This wall . . .

JULIA: Yes, this blank wall. *(She looks around.)* The other walls are quite attractive.

ROGER: I agree.

JULIA: I like the looks of these other walls.

ROGER: Thank you very much.

JULIA: *(Returning to the proscenium.)* It's just — this one.

ROGER: This fourth one.

JULIA: This is the one that throws me for a loop.

ROGER: I figured it might.

JULIA: I mean, it's just — there, Roger. This great, blank, undecorated — wall.

ROGER: I thought you should see it firsthand.

JULIA: Yes. I'm glad I flew up. Otherwise I wouldn't have believed it. *(She ponders it.)*

ROGER: Now Julia, living in New York, you must be familiar with a variety of private residences.

JULIA: Too familiar, according to my last husband.

ROGER: Well I imagine they've been decorated in many different ways.

JULIA: You'd be amazed what New Yorkers do to adorn their dens. It's their way of warding off evil.

ROGER: All right, then. Tell me frankly: Have you ever, in all your experience, seen a room done quite like this?

JULIA: You mean, with this . . . wall?

ROGER: With this wall.

JULIA: Only . . . But no.

ROGER: You were going to say?

JULIA: Roger. Do you remember those plays that used to begin with an attractive woman and a charming man coming in and talking?

ROGER: I do.

JULIA: This reminds me of those rooms they talked in.

ROGER: All right. Now keep that thought in mind and tell me something else. Do you like it?

JULIA: This wall?

ROGER: This wall.

JULIA: Roger, I've been in New York long enough never to pass judgment on how people live. We have the *New York Times* to do that.

ROGER: No, now come on, Julia. We grew up together here in Buffalo. I remember once, in third grade, you took me aside and told me you could see my underpants.

JULIA: Did I do that?

ROGER: You did. And I corrected the problem immediately. It saved me considerable embarrassment during recess.

JULIA: All right. Then I'll speak out again. Do I like this room? No, I do not. But maybe it's just how things are placed.

ROGER: Placed?

JULIA: The furniture. I mean, if this wall were behind you, you might be able to live with it. You could ignore it. Or simply glance at it occasionally. Over your shoulder. Like this. *(She demonstrates.)* See? It could be a kind of conversation piece. But with your furniture facing it, you're forced to confront it, almost head on, whenever you're in the room.

ROGER: That's the thing, isn't it.

JULIA: That's the thing. I'll go one step farther, Roger. Your decorator should be shot at sunrise.

ROGER: No decorator is responsible for this wall, Julia.

JULIA: No decorator? Then who?

ROGER: Peggy.

JULIA: Peggy? Your wife Peggy? My old friend Peggy? Who was known in the past for her quiet, good taste?

ROGER: This is the way she wants this room.

JULIA: But is she serious?

ROGER: She's never been more serious in her life.

JULIA: But what if you proved to her that she's made a serious mistake? What, for example, if you took this couch and unobtrusively eased it around to face that cozy fireplace?

ROGER: Peggy would unobtrusively ease it right back.

JULIA: And if you focused things on that pleasant greenery?

ROGER: Peggy would refocus them, the first chance she got.

JULIA: To face that blank wall?

ROGER: To face that blank wall.

JULIA: But why is Peggy behaving so strangely?

ROGER: I wish I knew.

JULIA: I keep thinking of plays.

ROGER: I asked you to keep them in mind.

JULIA: Doesn't this room make you feel, the minute you walk in , as if you were *acting* in one?

ROGER: It does, Julia! And perhaps you've noticed, since we've been here, we've begun to talk in an artificial and stagey sort of way.

JULIA: I *have* noticed that! And it's hard work! I mean, not only do I have to think about what to say, but I have to think how best to say it!

ROGER: Me, too! . . . I mean, I also.

JULIA: It's exhausting, Roger.

ROGER: Of course it is. And remember, you're just a visitor. This is my living room. I have to live here.

JULIA: But couldn't you retreat to another room? There must be a den somewhere.

ROGER: I escape to it when I can. But Peggy keeps coming in here, and since I like being with her, I follow along. And that's when the trouble starts.

JULIA: Trouble?

ROGER: The minute we get in here, she becomes restless and impatient. And I feel obligated to keep her interested. The result is, more and more, I find myself performing like a trained seal in front of this goddamn *wall,* trying to ignore it, trying *not* to ignore it, constantly aware that I'm very much on the line as a husband, as a man, and as an actor.

JULIA: Have you had any stage experience?

ROGER: None at all! I'm a businessman, Julia! I run a small factory here in Buffalo. We manufacture spherical distributors.

JULIA: Spherical distributors . . . Now don't tell me. They go in the engines of automobiles.

ROGER: No, no. They're those plastic balls that go in roll-on deodorants.

JULIA: How postindustrial! I imagine, in these anxious times, you're doing very well.

ROGER: Success means nothing, Julia, when, at the end of the day, I'm forced to confront this great blank wall. Have you ever read Melville's *Bartleby?*

JULIA: Of course not.

ROGER: Well I have. It's about — Oh hell. Skip it. Have a drink, Julia.

JULIA: Oh I don't know. No one drinks much in New York any more. At least in public.

ROGER: Just a glass of champagne?

JULIA: *(Looks at her watch.)* Actually, I should catch a plane back. I'm meeting someone tonight for some safe sex. *(She starts out.)* I'll send you a bill for my consulting fee.

ROGER: Don't go, Julia. Please. It's hell being left alone in this room. You feel compelled to have something to do.

JULIA: It's also a hard room to leave. I keep thinking I need a better exit line.

ROGER: Then have some champagne as an excuse to stay.

JULIA: All right. Just a glass. For old time's sake.

ROGER: Good. *(He goes to the bar, gets out a bottle of champagne and two glasses. Julia sits self-consciously on the couch.)*

JULIA: I must say, I am amazed by what I've seen, Roger. From the looks of your annual Christmas card, I would have said that Peggy was primarily interested in children and dogs.

ROGER: She used to be. She also had a strong commitment to community service. It was only after our last child went off to college, and our Dalmatian died, and the funds for the downtown community center dried up, that she started rearranging our furniture. *(He pops the champagne and pours.)* But welcome back to Buffalo. *(They clink glasses and drink.)* Do you like this champagne, by the way?

JULIA: May I be frank again?

ROGER: I wish you would be.

JULIA: Then no, I don't.

ROGER: That's because it's *stage* champagne, Julia! It's basically ginger ale. I don't dare serve alcoholic beverages in this room, for fear we'll slur our words, or say something stupid in front of that goddamn fourth wall! *(Peggy's voice is heard off offstage.)*

PEGGY'S VOICE: Hello!

ROGER: But there's Peggy now. You should see for yourself. *(Calls off.)* We're in here, darling.

JULIA: Quickly. How should I behave?

ROGER: Try to be natural.

JULIA: I can't! I haven't been natural in years! I'll be theatrical. The situation seems to call for it.

(Peggy comes in. She wears simple, comfortable clothes.)

PEGGY: *(To Roger.)* Hello, dear. *(Kisses Roger.)*

ROGER: Look who flew up from New York, darling. Our old friend Julia.

JULIA: *(Dramatically; holding out her arms in greeting.)* Peggy!

PEGGY: Why, Julia! Hello!

   (They kiss.)

JULIA: It's both cheeks in New York, darling. Like alternate parking.

   (Peggy kisses the other cheek.)

ROGER: Where've you been, dear?

PEGGY: Oh, out and around.

JULIA: I hear you're a do-gooder, Peggy. Have you been helping the homeless and stuff?

PEGGY: I wish I could. *(She sits and looks at the wall.)* Have you noticed my wall?

JULIA: I have to admit the subject came up, Peggy.

PEGGY: What does it do to you?

JULIA: Well, Peggy, it — raises a number of fascinating questions.

ROGER: I've been trying to answer them, darling.

JULIA: In the theater I think they call it exposition.

PEGGY: Is that where they go over old ground?

JULIA: Exactly, Peggy!

PEGGY: *(Getting up.)* There's too much exposition in the world! *(She starts out.)* I have to make a telephone call.

ROGER: Who to, dear?

PEGGY: Oh I'll think of someone. *(She exits. Pause.)*

ROGER: We lost her.

JULIA: I'm furious, Roger. She treated me as if I were simply an extra! We hardly made eye contact!

ROGER: She does it a lot.

JULIA: But we grew up together, I haven't seen her in years, and now she trumps up an excuse to walk off.

ROGER: Don't take it personally, Julia. The other night I organized a small dinner party, and she did the same thing.

JULIA: Dinner party? Why didn't you invite me? I shine at dinner parties.

ROGER: Oh it was just a little thing: a few folks who happened to be in town. Governor Cuomo . . . Cornelius Bennett, of the Buffalo Bills . . . Kitty Carlisle Hart . . . That crowd.

JULIA: I would have flown up immediately. I've been dying to sleep with all three of them.

ROGER: When you hear what happened, you'll be glad you didn't come. Like a fool, I served everybody cocktails made with real alcohol. As a result, the conversation became somewhat random. So Peggy got impatient and left the room.

JULIA: I hope she had a better exit line.

ROGER: It was worse. She announced she wanted to take a bath.

JULIA: Good Lord! Did she need one?

ROGER: Not at all. But she spent the rest of the evening in the tub, reading *The New Republic.*

JULIA: What did you do?

ROGER: I tried to keep things going, but it wasn't easy, with my wife splashing around offstage. And singing.

JULIA: Singing what?

ROGER: "If I Had a Hammer."

JULIA: How horrible! Something has got to be done!

ROGER: That's why I asked you to fly up. I thought you might get a handle on all this, being a woman and a New Yorker.

JULIA: I'm very glad I'm both. *(Pacing and thinking.)* Now let me think . . . I am reviewing in my mind what I have read recently in the Living Section of the *New York Times* . . . *(More thinking.)* Yes . . . Mmmmm . . . Yes . . . Roger, I've got it! . . . This room . . . these strange entrances and exits . . . Peggy, in her middle years, has come to see her life as some sort of play.

ROGER: You think that's it?

JULIA: Of course! It happens a lot with suburban women. The empty nest, all that. Most of them learn to accept the situation and settle for a supporting role.

ROGER: But not Peggy?

JULIA: Peggy seems to be warming up for a major part. Which is outrageous, when you think about it. I mean, she's had no New York experience.

ROGER: But to her, we're all in some play?

JULIA: Exactly. And apparently she wants us to act it out. I must say it might be fun, as long as we keep it regional and not-for-profit.

ROGER: But it's not fair! I mean, here I am, rich and free, kids educated, ready to celebrate not only my own success but the success of capitalism in general, when suddenly my wife wants me to perform some unknown play in front of some stupid fourth wall!

JULIA: Now, now.

ROGER: But I hate it, Julia! I'm beginning to see the whole world as simply a stage, and all of us men and women simply actors strutting around on it.

JULIA: Others have said that before, Roger. And said it better.

ROGER: That's because I'm no good at making up *lines,* Julia! Goddammit, it's no fair!

JULIA: Now Roger, get a hold of yourself. If Peggy wants a play, surely she must have a plot. What do you think her plot is?

ROGER: I don't know, I don't know, I don't KNOW! And I don't think she does either! I'm trying to be a good sport about things, but I'm totally unclear about what I'm supposed to be doing.

(Peggy's voice is heard offstage.)

PEGGY'S VOICE: I'm coming back!

ROGER: She's coming back. Tell me what to do.

JULIA: Try making a speech.

ROGER: A speech?

JULIA: Give her something to react to.

ROGER: But —

(Peggy re-enters.)

PEGGY: Have I missed anything?

ROGER: We've missed *you,* darling.

PEGGY: What's been going on?

JULIA: Oh well. We've been drinking champagne and doing light dialogue, Peggy.

PEGGY: Is that all? I was hoping there might be more.

JULIA: I agree with you, Peggy. *(Low to Roger.)* There's your cue.

ROGER: *(Taking a deep breath.)* Peggy, darling, let me remind you of something. This is our *living* room, dear. This is where you and I have *lived* for over twenty years.

PEGGY: I know that.

ROGER: *(Indicates the pictures on the piano.)* No but see? Here is our family, dear, arranged happily on the piano . . . Our children. Teddy in Little League, Elsie graduating from High School . . .

JULIA: How sweet.

ROGER: And our parents, Peggy . . . Mine on that trip to Italy. Yours when they came for Thanksgiving . . .

PEGGY: *(To Julia.)* They fought all during dessert.

ROGER: No, but look, love. Our hearth. Our mantelpiece. Your community service award, nestled alongside my Buffalo Better Business medal *(Indicates a vase on the table.)* And here is the lovely vase our friends gave us . . .

PEGGY: For our fifteenth anniversary . . .

ROGER: Right! And there on the rug is where the dog peed . . . And that spot on the wall, from when you threw your drink at Madge Baxter during the Vietnam war . . .

PEGGY: She wanted to assassinate Jane Fonda.

ROGER: *(Goes to the window.)* And look out the window, sweetie. Look out in the yard. There's the sandbox I made for the kids, before the cat started using it . . . And the stump which was home plate during the whiffle-ball games . . . and the maple tree, which is now as high as the house . . .

JULIA: This is a lovely speech he's giving, Peggy. It's too long, but it's lovely.

PEGGY: I know it is.

ROGER: Then come on, sweetie, look this way, face this way, not at some dumb blank wall.

PEGGY: I can't.

ROGER: Why the hell NOT?

PEGGY: It's not enough.

ROGER: Not enough? Our life together has not been enough?

PEGGY: There should be more. *(She looks dreamingly at the wall.)*

JULIA: I think she wants you to get deeper, Roger.

ROGER: Deeper?

JULIA: Isn't that it, Peggy? You want it deeper.

PEGGY: Maybe. . .

JULIA: *(To Roger.)* Try the speech again, but this time make it deeper. And shorter.

ROGER: O.K. *(Clears his throat, starts again.)* Peg, sweetheart, this is our life. Here on the piano — Goddammmit! I can't do this, Peg!

PEGGY: I know you can't.

JULIA: What we really need is a plot, Peggy.

PEGGY: Maybe that's it.

JULIA: I think it is. You don't have one up your sleeve, do you? Just to get us all going.

PEGGY: No I don't. I really don't. *(She gets up.)* But I do have the sense we're missing something.

(She goes off. Pause.)

JULIA: I'll tell you one thing, Roger. Those sudden exits are becoming irritating. She needs a good director.

ROGER: Maybe if you talked to her alone . . .

JULIA: I don't think I can . . .

ROGER: Now come on, Julia. I paid your fare. With what the airlines charge these days, it's the least you can do.

JULIA: I'm just not sure I'm up to it, Roger.

ROGER: Come on. You're a woman, after all.

JULIA: That's exactly why I can't.

ROGER: What do you mean?

JULIA: Roger: Any scene I had with Peggy would be doomed to fail.

ROGER: Why?

JULIA: Because I want it to fail.

ROGER: You want it to fail?

JULIA: I suddenly find myself wanting Peggy to continue down this strange theatrical road. I also want you to become so frustrated with her that you'll turn elsewhere for solace and sex.

ROGER: Elsewhere?

JULIA: Namely to me.

ROGER: Uh oh.

JULIA: I'm sorry, but that's what I want.

ROGER: I'm amazed, Julia.

JULIA: So am I. But what can we do? We've got to have a plot, and this is the only one I can come up with.

ROGER: But surely, living in New York, you have other sexual commitments. Lovers, a new husband, various lesbian affiliations . . .

JULIA: Of course! I'm supposed to be meeting one of the above this evening.

ROGER: I remember you mentioned an appointment.

JULIA: But now I have no intention of keeping it. I now feel feelings I haven't felt since I saw your underpants in third grade.

ROGER: Oh, hey.

JULIA: I'm here, Roger, and I'm available, and I'm famished for love. And so it's cruel of you to ask me to play a scene which goes so much against my own sexual objectives.

ROGER: Oh boy. This is a tough one.

JULIA: There it is.

ROGER: Have more champagne while we think about it.

JULIA: Better not. Given the mood I'm in, even fake champagne might make me more aggressive.

ROGER: So. Gosh. Wow. I mean, I fly you up to help me get my wife back, and now you say you want to become lovers.

JULIA: At least it's a plot, Roger.

ROGER: It is. It is definitely a plot. *(He thinks.)* Well, look. I'm an amateur here — I'm perfectly willing to admit it. But it seems to me that the theatre is riddled with scenes of self sacrifice. If you played out such a scene with Peggy, you'd be working to repair a marriage which your own sexual appetites are tempting you to destroy. I may be wrong, but I think the stuff of real drama might lie in a scene like that.

JULIA: You think so?

ROGER: I do. In fact, it sounds like a star turn to me. If there were critics beyond that wall, Julia, they might be convinced by that scene that you belonged above the title, and ahead of all the rest of us, even out of alphabetical order.

JULIA: Then I'll do it.

ROGER: *(Kissing her.)* Oh thanks, Julia.

JULIA: You shouldn't have kissed me, Roger. It whets my sexual appetite.

ROGER: That's why I did it.

JULIA: You're a ruthless man.

ROGER: I'm learning you have to be ruthless in the theater. *(He calls off.)* I think we're getting somewhere, Peggy!

(Peggy's voice is heard offstage.)

PEGGY'S VOICE: I'll be right in!

JULIA: Does she listen offstage?

ROGER: Of course not.

JULIA: Are you sure? It might affect how I play the scene.

ROGER: My wife is no eavesdropper, Julia!

JULIA: But she's so much on cue.

ROGER: That's this *room* again! It makes everything seem contrived and mechanical! That's why I need your help! Now I'll duck out, so you two women can have what the French call a "tit a tit."

JULIA: I find that remark offensive, Roger!

ROGER: I do, too, goddammit! See? See what's happening? Now I'm going for cheap laughs which ridicule women! Oh help me, Julia. Please!

JULIA: I'll do what I can to cope with an impossible situation. No New Yorker can do better than that.

(Peggy re-enters.)

PEGGY: Here I am.

ROGER: I'll go watch the ball game in the den.

PEGGY: You're not staying?

ROGER: Sorry. I've been working my ass off since square one. I need some time on the bench.

(He goes off.)

PEGGY: *(To Julia.)* He's upset.

JULIA: *(Going to the couch.)* That's what I want to talk to you about.

(She sits.)

PEGGY: Shoot.

JULIA: *(Patting a place for Peggy on the couch.)* Peggy, dear: Normally, in New York, when we talk to our friends, and we suspect the conversation might become confrontational, we try to ease into the issue with a few pleasant preliminaries. We refer to the weather, we touch on current events, we recall moments in the past which may have been mutually agreeable. Only after these diversionary overtures have been thoroughly played out do we gingerly step across the border into the area of controversy.

PEGGY: Sounds like a complicated way to keep friends, Julia.

JULIA: Well, it works. But in your case, the issue is so compelling I plan to rush right to the point. Peggy: What's the story on this fucking fourth wall?

PEGGY: I wish I knew.

JULIA: I won't accept that as an answer, Peggy.

PEGGY: It's always been there, you know. That wall. I'm just calling attention to it.

JULIA: But it makes people self-conscious, Peggy. It forces them to perform.

PEGGY: That might be a step in the right direction.

JULIA: WHAT direction? We have no idea where you're taking us, Peggy. With this wall.

PEGGY: What if we could break through it, Julia?

JULIA: Break *through* it?

PEGGY: What if something wonderful lies beyond it?

JULIA: I'll tell you what lies beyond it, Peggy. Your dining room lies beyond it. So if you broke through it, you'd end up in an entirely different play.

PEGGY: What if you're wrong, Julia? What if there were people beyond that wall? What if these people had paid money to be there? What if they had given up reading a book, or watching television, or going to some game, and were now there, sitting there, waiting for us to reach them?

JULIA: Oh now Peggy . . .

PEGGY: No, what if it were true? And what if this audience were really democratic, Julia? What if there were poor people there, as well as rich? And what if they were ethnically diverse? What, for example, if there were a decent number of African-Americans out there?

JULIA: They'd HATE this thing, Peggy. They'd rush right off to August Wilson.

PEGGY: But maybe they've *stayed*, Julia. And maybe Asians and Latinos are there too, and maybe they've all come hoping we'll break through and reach them where they live.

JULIA: *(Looking out, uneasily.)* If any people are out there at all, Peggy, I suspect they're primarily Jewish. The poor things have kept the theater going almost single-handedly for the last thirty years.

PEGGY: Then we should reach them, too.

JULIA: Neil Simon already does that, dear.

PEGGY: And we should connect to the Arab community.

JULIA: You just blew it, dear.

PEGGY: I don't care. And we should reach gays and lesbians and —

JULIA: Lesbians have been mentioned, Peggy. The word definitely came up in my scene with Roger.

PEGGY: But that wall is still there. And I'd give my eyeteeth to get beyond it.

JULIA: Peggy darling, try to remember that walls were put on this earth for two purposes: to hold up ceilings and keep people from killing each other. I'm all for them, and so I believe are most architects.

PEGGY: I don't agree, Julia. My entire life has been devoted to the breaching of walls. I broke through the wall between childhood and adolescence. I broke through the wall between single life and marriage. Then Roger and I built our own cozy wall around home and family, but I broke through that when I got a job. And then I only saw more walls — walls upon walls, everywhere I looked. I see a wall between you and me, Julia.

JULIA: I hope there is, Peggy. At school, they made us memorize Robert Frost.

PEGGY: I know, I know. "Stone walls make good neighbors." But maybe we're too hung up on these ramparts we watch. Maybe this wall — this last wall, this fourth wall — is just an illusion. All I know is I'll never be happy — never, Julia! — until I've at least *tried* to see beyond it, and get through it, and leave it behind me forever! *(Pause.)*

JULIA: Peggy, darling. Look: I've only been here . . . *(Checks her watch.)* twenty minutes, and already I feel this pressing need to take some sort of action. It's as if someone were constantly whispering in my ear, saying, "Move it, lady. Get to the plot!"

PEGGY: I hear something else . . .

JULIA: Such as what?

PEGGY: I don't know . . . something very different . . . something calling from beyond that wall . . .

JULIA: Saying?

PEGGY: I'm not sure . . . Something like "Come on in. The water's fine."

JULIA: I'm not interested in playing Esther Williams, Peggy. Now stop trying to be avant-garde, Peggy, and start thinking about your marriage.

PEGGY: Did Roger talk about that?

JULIA: I never reveal my sources.

PEGGY: I'm hoping this wall will improve our marriage, Julia. I'm hoping one of these days, he and I will sit down in front of it and be forced to talk seriously about important things. How many married couples ever do that? How many talk at all? Most of them simply eye each other at meals and fight when they get in the car.

JULIA: You might lose him, Peggy.

PEGGY: Why do you think that?

JULIA: I sense he's being pulled in another direction.

PEGGY: I sense that, too.

JULIA: Then turn away from this wall, darling! And turn your furniture away from it. Stand up right now and turn your back to it!

PEGGY: No thanks. I've been turning my back on things for too long. That wall is there, and even if there's nothing beyond it, I have to behave as if people were there.

JULIA: Even if you don't know where you're going?

PEGGY: Even so.

JULIA: Even if your behavior forces your husband into the arms of another — well, I won't give away the only plot we have.

PEGGY: I'm sorry. Here I stand.

JULIA: Then we'll have to play things out, each in her own way.

PEGGY: I'm afraid so.

JULIA: It seems to me our scene is virtually over.

PEGGY: I think it is . . . And now I'd better go do something about dinner. *(Starts off, then stops.)* You're welcome to stay, by the way. We normally eat in the kitchen, and things get more cozy and informal in there.

JULIA: I might, Peggy. It depends on what happens in my next scene.

PEGGY: Fair enough.

JULIA: So would you send Roger in as you pass by the den? I want to tell him something.

PEGGY: O.K.

JULIA: And please ask him to make it snappy. I'd hate to be stuck out here alone — doing clichéd stage business like thumbing through a magazine or fussing with my hair . . . I'd hate that, Peggy, fourth wall or not.

PEGGY: Why don't you play the piano?

JULIA: Because I don't know how.

PEGGY: Don't worry. It plays itself. It's one of those player pianos made by the old Wurlitzer Company, in Niagara Falls. *(She goes out.)*

JULIA: *(Calling after her.)* I'm not interested in provincial nostalgia, Peggy. I left all that behind back here in Buffalo. *(She soon is thumbing through a magazine, and combing her hair. But then she is drawn to the piano. She goes to it, stands by it, tentatively hits a key. It immediately starts to play an introduction to a song. She is surprised for a second, then listens. Then the piano plays a single note, as if sounding her key. She sings the note. Singing.)* Ah. *(To herself)* Too high. *(The piano sounds another note. Julia tries it.)* Better. *(The piano finds her key.)* Good. *(She begins to sing along. Singing.)*

> I'm in love again,
> And the spring is comin'
> I'm in love again,
> Hear my heart strings strummin'
> I'm in love again,
> And the hymn I'm hummin'
> Is the "Huddle Up, Cuddle Up Blues!"

(She gets up, begins to "perform" the song as the piano continues to accompany her.)

> I'm in love again,
> And I can't rise above it, I'm in love again,
> And I love, love, love it: I'm in love again,
> And I'm darn glad of it,
> Good news!

(Roger enters, as the music continues under. He now wears a sweater.)

ROGER: I see you've discovered our player piano.

JULIA: Yes.

ROGER: I programmed it strictly for Cole Porter.

JULIA: I noticed that. *(They now sing together.)*

BOTH: *(Singing.)*

> I'm in love again,
> And I love, love, love it:
> I'm in love again,
> And I'm darn glad of it,
> Good news!

(They end with a good finish.)

ROGER: Well?

JULIA: Do you think we could squeeze out one more reprise?

ROGER: I'm concerned about Peggy. She said you had something to say.

JULIA: Oh. Right. I do. Brace yourself, Roger. I've decided your wife is insane.

ROGER: Oh now . . .

JULIA: Nuts. Totally. Mad as a hatter.

ROGER: Are you sure?

JULIA: Look, if it were just a question of play-acting in this room, I'd say, fine, let's keep it up. As you know, I'm beginning to enjoy it. But she wants to break *through,* Roger.

ROGER: To where?

JULIA: To some other *side.* To *reach* people. Of different *backgrounds.* I wouldn't be surprised if she wanted to *touch* them. It's the Sixties without the Beatles!

ROGER: Good Lord.

JULIA: And she has no PLOT, Roger! Not even a subplot. Nothing but some vague desire to make connections.

ROGER: You make her sound like an unemployed telephone operator.

JULIA: *(Moving toward him.)* At least I have a plot.

ROGER: Did you tell her that?

JULIA: I broadly hinted at it.

ROGER: What did she say?

JULIA: Nothing.

ROGER: She didn't care?

JULIA: All she cares about is that stupid wall. Now I've done what I can as a concerned friend of the family. It's time to ship her off to the funny farm, toot sweet.

ROGER: Oh well, gee, Julia . . .

JULIA: No, I'm serious. The poor soul needs help. Call the men in white, and get her out of here!

ROGER: But Peggy and I have been married so long. To see her grappled to the ground, forced into a straight jacket . . .

JULIA: They did it to Blanche Du Bois in *Streetcar.* It was profoundly moving.

ROGER: But we're talking about my wife . . . the mother of my children . . .

JULIA: No, now be strong, Roger . . . Stride to that telephone and dial manfully!

ROGER: But I don't know the number of the insane asylum.

JULIA: 976-NUTS. I saw it advertised at the airport.

ROGER: *(Jiggling the phone.)* Our phone's out of order.

JULIA: I don't believe that.

ROGER: *(Listening.)* One of our kids is on the extension.

JULIA: Your children are not here, Roger. You're becoming totally implausible. Now telephone. Or I will. *(He dials reluctantly. A car door is heard slamming offstage.)* What's that?

ROGER: A car door slamming.

JULIA: Don't tell me the ambulance has arrived already? That's awfully fast work, even for the theater.

ROGER: *(Hanging up the phone.)* This may be someone else, Julia. Peggy will let him in.

JULIA: Let who in? You obviously know who it is.

ROGER: I do, Julia. Sit down, and I'll try to tell you.

JULIA: *(Sitting.)* I sense a twist that I'm unprepared for.

ROGER: Have some champagne, Julia.

JULIA: I've already told you, no. Now stop stalling, and tell me what's going on.

ROGER: All right, Julia . . . While you were having your scene with Peggy, I went, as I said I would, to watch the ballgame. When I got there, however, I found I couldn't concentrate. Not only did I find myself torn between two women, but also I felt trapped in a play not of my own making.

JULIA: I can understand your confusion.

ROGER: Finally, out of desperation, I made a telephone call.

JULIA: A telephone call?

ROGER: To the State University Department of Drama. I thought if anyone could resolve this dilemma, someone who has committed his life to the study of drama might be able to do so.

JULIA: So you dialed SUNY-Buffalo?

ROGER: I did. I braved their new touchtone centrex answering system. I defied the rudeness of the students who kept putting me on hold. But finally I found myself speaking to a member of the drama faculty named Professor Loesser.

JULIA: Professor Loesser . . .

ROGER: Naturally he prefers that we call him simply by his first name, Floyd.

JULIA: Rather than Professor Loesser. Yes. All that makes sense.

ROGER: I explained to him our problem and asked him to stop by. Like most academics, he had nothing else to do. I strongly suspect, therefore, that this now may be Floyd, arriving at our front door. *(Door chimes are heard offstage. Roger calls off.)* Would you get the door, darling?

JULIA: I must say, Roger, I'm a little hurt. You ask for my advice, and now you're suddenly calling in a second opinion.

ROGER: I had to, Julia. We need the cool, dispassionate eye of academia to examine our situation and advise what steps to take next.

JULIA: I've never much liked university professors. I've had affairs with several, and they all seem obsessed with tenure . . . No, no. I'm worried about this Floyd person already.

(Peggy comes in with Floyd, who is younger, wears jeans and a corduroy jacket, and carries a battered briefcase.)

PEGGY: We have a guest! *(Turning on a light.)* This is Floyd, people. He's an

Assistant Professor of Dramatic Literature, specializing in modern American drama.

FLOYD: Eugene O'Neill through David Mamet, actually. Though I also do a broad survey of world theater.

PEGGY: Floyd, this is my husband Roger, a successful American businessman.

ROGER: *(Shaking hands.)* Hello, Floyd.

PEGGY: And this is Julia, who purports to be a friend of the family.

JULIA: *(Shaking hands.)* Hello, Floyd. Do you have tenure?

FLOYD: Not yet.

JULIA: Thank God.

FLOYD: Enough chit-chat, gang. Everybody please sit down. *(They all do, like students in a course.)* I suppose I should say at the start that you will be judged as much by your comments along the way as by what you may write on the exam.

ROGER: Exam? Do you give exams?

FLOYD: I do indeed. I think it's important to pull things together at the end. I normally ask people to write an essay of eight to ten pages.

ROGER: Single or double spaced?

FLOYD: Double. But in this case, we might settle for oral examinations.

JULIA: *(Low to Roger.)* He sounds like a dentist.

FLOYD: Who said that? *(Pause.)* I'm waiting. *(Pause.)* We will simply stand here, wasting valuable stage time, until the person who made that remark has the courage to admit it.

JULIA: *(Finally.)* I said it.

FLOYD: Why?

JULIA: Because I thought it was funny.

FLOYD: And was it?

JULIA: It didn't get quite the laugh I thought it would.

FLOYD: Exactly, Julia. And I'll tell you why. Because it wasn't serious. Comedy, people, is a serious business. And now we've learned that, let's move on. *(Peggy raises her hand.)* Yes, Peggy.

PEGGY: I'm worried about something on the stove. May I be excused?

FLOYD: You may.

PEGGY: All of you should feel free to talk about me when I'm gone. *(She goes.)*

FLOYD: *(Looking after her.)* Now that was a sweet exit! "Talk about me when I'm gone." I liked that remark. Of course most of theatre is about that.

JULIA: Most of life is about that.

FLOYD: Wrong. Another half-baked remark. Beware of comparing life and the theater, gang. Life is sprawling and unpredictable. Theatre is confined and artificial. There is no comparison, unless your own life happens to be confined and artificial as well. Is it, Julia?

JULIA: Um, ah . . .

FLOYD: Well, we'll find out soon enough, won't we? No, people, life is action, theater is talk. Or rather, in the theater, talk is action. In any case, the best theater is primarily the best talk. Which is why I become immediately impatient . . . *(Looking at Julia.)* with characters who talk before they think.

ROGER: *(Saving the day.)* Uh, could we talk about Peggy? Now she's gone?

FLOYD: Raise your hand please, Roger.

ROGER: *(Raising his hand.)* Did you have a chance to observe my wife?

FLOYD: I did.

ROGER: Do you have any thoughts, based on your observations?

FLOYD: I'd say she was a mighty attractive woman.

ROGER: Thanks. I agree.

JULIA: We think she's nuts. Do you?

FLOYD: Hand, please.

JULIA: Do you think she might have psychological difficulties?

FLOYD: Not necessarily. I'll simply say that she seems like a woman waiting.

ROGER: A woman waiting . . .

FLOYD: Yes, she's waiting for something — some scene, some action, some plot — which will enable her to play a meaningful role. Out there, she was like an actress waiting to come on. In here, she was like an actress waiting to go off. Note now that she is preparing dinner. I suspect, when it is done, she will serve it to us — *wait* on us, so to speak. Waiting. Always waiting. I am reminded of Samuel Beckett.

ROGER: Is that good?

FLOYD: That is very good. My compliments to your wife, sir.

ROGER: Thank you, Floyd.

JULIA: But she hasn't got a plot!

FLOYD: I'll bet you have a plot, don't you, Julia?

JULIA: As a matter of fact, I do. Yes.

FLOYD: I'll bet you do. And I'll bet it's one of those cheap second rate triangle things, leading from adultery to divorce.

JULIA: At least it keeps things moving.

FLOYD: Better Beckett than that.

JULIA: Yes, well, we'll see.

FLOYD: I hope we do, Julia. I hope your clichéd little plot collapses before the evening is half over.

JULIA: I like to think —

ROGER: Hey, guys. Jesus. We're getting all hung up on plot here. I'm worried about my WIFE!

FLOYD: You're right, Roger. We've gotten ahead of ourselves. It's always better to begin by discussing the set. *(He looks around.)* So this is the sacred space, eh?

ROGER: This is it.

FLOYD: This is the grove of Dionysus.

ROGER: I guess.

FLOYD: *(Indicating.)* And this, I assume, is the infamous fourth wall.

ROGER: Right.

JULIA: Note how all the furniture faces it.

FLOYD: I am familiar with the requirements of realistic drama, madam. You forget I teach the stuff.

JULIA: *(Under her breath.)* Well hoity-toity to you.

FLOYD: I'll consider that a "stage whisper" and ignore it. *(Poking around like a detective.)* Now. Yes. Hmmm. The set is pretty much as you described it, Roger. You did a fine job on the telephone, and if this were a course in the visual arts, I'd give you a straight A.

ROGER: Thanks, Floyd.

FLOYD: That's the good news. The bad news is it's ridiculously old-fashioned. I am amazed, I am truly amazed, that in this day and age, someone would bother to design a set like this.

JULIA: I personally think, with the right adjustments, it could be a lovely room.

FLOYD: In 1925, perhaps. In 1938, at a stretch. Possibly in Britain, for a brief nostalgic period after World War II. *(He picks up the vase indicated earlier by Roger and looks at it.)* But not in America at the tail end of the twentieth century! *(He hurls the vase into the fireplace.)* No. I'm sorry, people. Bourgeois domestic comedy is dead! And I, for one, am glad to see it go! *(Roger and Julia jump up.)*

JULIA: That lovely little vase!

ROGER: *(Gazing to the fireplace.)* It symbolized our marriage!
(He picks up a shard, looks at it lovingly.)

FLOYD: Consider it just a prop, Roger. *(He begins to mix himself a drink at the bar.)* Let it symbolize your last link to the past.

ROGER: Oh yeah? Well that liquor's a prop, too, Floyd! You're mixing yourself a glass of water!

FLOYD: I know that, Roger. But notice how well I'm doing it . . . Now sit down, people. *(Roger and Julia uneasily resume their seats. Floyd continues to mix his elegant martini.)* Derivation of the word *prop:* short for *stage property,* people. Came into use in the eighteenth century. Think of it also as a support. It props you up. We academics are really actors, you know. We strut and fret our hour in front of the class, and we too need our props — a book, a piece of chalk, or in this case a drink — to lean on. They give us something to do. *(He finishes making his drink.)*

JULIA: You said earlier that this sort of play is dead.

FLOYD: I did. Yes, I did. Yes.

JULIA: If so, why are you bothering to stick around?

FLOYD: That's the first good question you've asked, Julia. And so I'll tell you. I am "sticking around" because there is one thing which intrigues me about this room.

ROGER: What thing?

FLOYD: This fourth wall.

ROGER: This fourth wall?

FLOYD: This, don't you see, redeems things. It's here, it dominates the room, and it implies a world beyond the world it is supposed to contain.

ROGER: And you think that's good?

FLOYD: I think it might be. Yes. You wonder if your wife is insane, Roger. My answer is possibly no. By insisting on this wall, she may be more in tune with the postmodern world than anyone else in this room — except myself. Simply through the configuration of this room, Roger, your wife may be subtly challenging western democratic capitalism at its very core.

ROGER: Like Melville's *Bartleby.*

FLOYD: Exactly, Roger! Very good! But she may be going farther. She may be saying that there is something more than material success and the quaint pleasures of hearth and home. At a time when communism has collapsed in ruins and the lowliest citizen of the poorest country secretly aspires to live in a room just like this, your wife may be saying: No, don't bother, it's not worth it, because there is a world elsewhere, a world beyond this wall, which is far more worth reaching for. It is a daring room, people, and therefore a dangerous one.

ROGER: Dangerous? You mean my wife is in danger?

JULIA: Nonsense. I noticed an excellent security system when I walked in the door.

FLOYD: It will take more than a suburban burglar alarm to keep out the reactionary forces of militant capitalism, Julia.

ROGER: Good lord.

FLOYD: Now look, I could be all wrong on this thing. This could simply be another domestic comedy, the kind of thing which the English have always done better, and we Americans have vulgarized into the sit-com on TV. It could be that, and if it is, I swear I'll dismiss you both as soon as I finish my drink.

ROGER: Or?

FLOYD: Or . . . it could be a deep and dangerous challenge to contemporary values, a major step into the twenty-first century, working within the rubrics of realistic drama yet systematically deconstructing them as it goes along.

ROGER: How will you be able to tell?

FLOYD: By talking to Peggy. Go get her immediately.

ROGER: *(Hesitantly.)* I will. But . . . *(Stops.)*

FLOYD: But what?

ROGER: I have to say, Floyd, I kind of hope this is just another conventional comedy. At least I hope it has a conventional happy ending. I mean, I really want my wife back.

FLOYD: Oh come on, Roger. Join the modern world. Allow for some dissonance around here. Embrace the random. Who knows? I might even end up with her myself.

JULIA: Yes, Roger. You heard him say how attractive she was.

FLOYD: They call that a plant in the theater. P-L-A-N-T. In the sense of a seed planted that will grow to fruition later on.

ROGER: Well I don't like that plant, thanks.

JULIA: Oh, Roger, grow up. Go with the flow. *(She takes his arm.)* Beside, you and I have our own little garden to cultivate, remember?

FLOYD: Your task is simply to send in Peggy. What happens offstage is no concern of mine.

JULIA: Hear that, Roger? Come. Let's go. It's time to make our garden grow. *(She drags Roger offstage. Floyd remains. He quickly thumbs through a magazine, then fusses with his hair. Then he moves to the piano. Slyly, he hits a key. Again the piano plays an introduction. He sings.)*

FLOYD: *(Singing.)*
 Why Shouldn't I
 Take a chance when romance passes by?
 Why shouldn't I know of love?
(He leans debonnairely on the piano.)
 Why wait around
 When each age has a sage who has found
 That upon this earth

Love is all that is really worth
Thinking of . . .
(He becomes more confident.)
It must be fun, lots of fun,
To be sure when day is done
That the hour is coming when
You'll be kissed and then you'll be kissed again.
(Peggy enters, now wearing a kitchen apron, wiping her hands.)

PEGGY: *(As the music continues under.)* You wanted to talk to me, Floyd?

FLOYD: I did, Peggy. But first I wonder if you'd help me finish this song.

PEGGY: Sure. Why not? *(Singing.)*
All debutantes say it's good,

FLOYD: *(Singing.)*
And ev'ry star out in far Hollywood
Seems to give it a try—

BOTH: *(In harmony.)*
So why shouldn't I?

FLOYD: Now sit down, Peggy.

PEGGY: All right. *(She sits.)*

FLOYD: If you don't mind, I'd like to switch from the lecture mode to the Socratic method and ask you a series of pointed questions.

PEGGY: Ask away.

FLOYD: I hope you'll answer them as clearly and thoroughly as you can.

PEGGY: I'll try.

FLOYD: First: What are we having for dinner?

PEGGY: Well I made this casserole. It's just chicken, and I threw in some cheese and some leftover broccoli. And then I added —

FLOYD: That's enough. It sounds good, and I think I'll stay.

PEGGY: I'm glad I made enough.

FLOYD: Now is it true, Peggy, that you think there are people beyond that wall?

PEGGY: *(Carefully.)* I think . . . there could be. I think . . . there should be.

FLOYD: Should be, Peggy?

PEGGY: I think it could be terrific if people could gather together somewhere, away from their CDs and TVs and VCRs, and see and hear live actors say serious things about what's going on in their city, in their country, and in their world.

FLOYD: What: you're saying is that any culture which cannot produce good theater, and a good, solid audience to respond to it, is no culture at all.

PEGGY: Maybe that's it.

FLOYD: What you're also saying — now don't let me put words in your mouth, but what you *might* be saying is that most great western nations — be it Greece in the age of Pericles or Elizabethan England — have produced great theater when they were at their peak.

PEGGY: Is that true?

FLOYD: It is indeed. And maybe you're saying that we ourselves have had a whiff of that greatness even in this country, in the period from Eugene O'Neill through Arthur Miller, when indeed our country was at the height of its power.

PEGGY: I . . . could be saying that. Yes.

FLOYD: And you're also saying that now that our theater has declined, you're concerned that our greatness as a nation is declining as well. And therefore, this wall, and your yearning to reach beyond it, is an attempt to revitalize theater in America and to keep our great country from sliding irrevocably into darkness and decay.

PEGGY: That could be it!

FLOYD: God, Peggy! You don't know how exciting this is! This afternoon, I was sitting alone in my office, hoping that one of my students in American Drama might stop by at least to chat. I knew this was unlikely, however, because this semester I am down to three students in that course: An ambitious young man who wants to write film scripts, a breathless young woman who once saw *Les Misérables,* and an exchange student from Bangladesh who signed up by mistake. Normally I would have used my spare time to prepare for next semester's course on World Drama, but I learned today that it's just been supplanted by a second section of a new course in Media Studies entitled "*The Brady Bunch* and Beyond."

PEGGY: You poor man.

FLOYD: No, no, not now! Because your husband called and invited me here. And suddenly I find myself not simply *discussing* but also actively *involved* in what could be a vital new American play! I mean, it's thrilling, Peggy! I feel we're on the brink of a major breakthrough! So I hope you'll forgive me if I ask a few more questions.

PEGGY: Shoot.

FLOYD: O.K. Here we go. Now. Let's suppose there are people there, Peggy, beyond that wall. You're here, and they're there, and suddenly here's your big moment: What would you do?

PEGGY: Um. Well. Hmmm. I think I'd make a speech.

FLOYD: All right, Peggy. And what would you say?

PEGGY: Can I talk about current issues?

FLOYD: You can do anything you want. This is your play, after all. You're the one who's hammering out a whole new form.

PEGGY: Then I'd say three things.

FLOYD: Just three?

PEGGY: Three, at the start.

FLOYD: O.K. Do it.

PEGGY: *(Gaining confidence.)* I'd start off easily. I'd use a simple example.

FLOYD: Example of what, Peggy?

PEGGY: Of how our country has gone off track. I'd talk about our obsession with Coca-Cola.

FLOYD: Coca-Cola?

PEGGY: And Pepsi, and all soft drinks, caffeinated or decaffeinated, carbonated or not. I'd say they're overpriced and nutritionally useless and terrible for your teeth. I'd say the amount of labor and money we spend producing, transporting, and consuming these useless beverages, and then dealing with their containers, is a total waste of time. I'd say we should all see to it that everyone in the world is able to drink and enjoy a free supply of cool, clear water.

FLOYD: That's quite a statement, Peggy. That hits at the heart of a consumer society.

PEGGY: But that's just the first thing I'd say.

FLOYD: Just the first?

PEGGY: The second would be to talk about Bill Clinton.

FLOYD: You'd name him directly?

PEGGY: Yes, I would.

FLOYD: So early in the game?

PEGGY: I absolutely would. I'd say here is a man who, at the end of the century — at the end of the millennium! — now holds the most powerful position in the world! Here is a man who has been given the chance to clean up the mess we've made over the last forty years.

FLOYD: Would you name names there as well?

PEGGY: Of course I would. I'd bring up all those people who took their eyes off the road and drove us into some ditch. I'd mention Johnson and Nixon and Reagan and Bush and —

FLOYD: What would you say about Bush, for example?

PEGGY: I'd say Bush had a special responsibility because he grew up in a room just like this. But did he make any attempt to reach beyond that fourth wall? He did not. Which is why he's not president today.

FLOYD: I'm not sure anyone in the theater has pointed a finger so directly at a political figure since Aristophanes attacked the demagogue Cleon in his comic masterpiece, *The Birds*.

PEGGY: Maybe, but I'd also say something about Cambodia.

FLOYD: Cambodia?

PEGGY: And Bosnia and the Sudan and anywhere else where people are in deep adversity. I'd say that the world is small enough now so that we can no longer ignore the suffering of our brothers and sisters in humanity, any more than we could ignore the suffering of our immediate family. I'd say we in this country have a human obligation to pull our selves together, not simply so we can improve our own lives here, but rather so we can help suffering people elsewhere live any life at all.

FLOYD: You'd say all that?

PEGGY: I would! But you know what, Floyd? Anyone can stand around a room and make speeches. The important thing is to have them connect . . . with other people. And I have to say that more and more I feel that connection.

FLOYD: Through that fourth wall.

PEGGY: Through that fourth wall. *(A pause. Then.)*

FLOYD: Wait here a minute.

PEGGY: Where are you going?

FLOYD: To get the others.

PEGGY: Why?

FLOYD: I want to tell them that we have a plot.

PEGGY: We do?

FLOYD: We most certainly do! In fact, we have the plot of one of the great plays of this, or any other century! *(He starts out again.)*

PEGGY: Would you mind telling me what it is?

FLOYD: *(Coming back in.)* Oh. Sorry. I thought you knew: It's the plot of *Saint Joan.*

PEGGY: *Saint Joan?*

FLOYD: *Saint Joan!* I'm thinking particularly of the version by George Bernard Shaw.

PEGGY: I've never seen it.

FLOYD: It's about a young French peasant girl who tries to change the world.

PEGGY: That's hardly me. I'm not so young and I'm not a peasant. In fact, my grandmother was in the Social Register.

FLOYD: But you have a peasant innocence, Peggy, and a taste for natural fibers in your clothes.

PEGGY: That's true, I do.

FLOYD: Furthermore, like Joan, you seem to hear special voices . . .

PEGGY: Beyond that fourth wall . . .

FLOYD: Beyond that fourth wall. And Joan acts on those voices. She goes to where the Dauphin is huddling with his cronies and persuades him to be the king he should be . . .

PEGGY: Just the way I'd go to Washington and get Bill Clinton to do the same . . .

FLOYD: That's it! Then Joan and the Dauphin win a series of battles against the English and try to kick them out of France.

PEGGY: Just the way Bill and I will kick the lobbyists and special interests and all the other dead wood out of Washington!

FLOYD: Precisely. And remember that Shaw's play is not just about a peculiar peasant girl and a few obscure battles during the Hundred Years War. What we are really seeing, Shaw tell us, is the rise of Protestantism and the birth of nationalism.

PEGGY: But how does that work with me?

FLOYD: With you, in your attack on a consumer society, we're seeing the rise of what we might call ecologism!

PEGGY: I see.

FLOYD: And in your concern to move beyond national boundaries, we have a new kind of *post*nationalism, or better yet, *trans*nationalism.

PEGGY: O.K.

FLOYD: But no matter what we name these things, you sense something outside yourself which is calling you to accomplish them — which means you're playing a new version of Joan of Arc.

PEGGY: I guess I am.

FLOYD: And that's what I have to go tell the others! *(He starts off.)*

PEGGY: Wait! One more question!

FLOYD: I have to say, Peggy, I'm becoming impatient with these delays. As a teacher, I'm eager to share my insights with others. As a lover of the theater, I'm concerned that we're slowing down the action.

PEGGY: I just want to know one more little thing.

FLOYD: *(Impatiently; at doorway.)* And what's that?

PEGGY: What about the ending?

FLOYD: What about it?

PEGGY: Well, I mean, Saint Joan dies, doesn't she?

FLOYD: Of course she dies. She gets captured by the English and burned at the stake.

PEGGY: But —

FLOYD: Stop quibbling, Peggy! We're talking big time now! I wouldn't be surprised if we ended up in New York! Now I've GOT to go tell the others. *(He goes off. Peggy staggers back into the piano. It sounds a dissonant chord, then plays.)*

PEGGY: *(Singing.)*

> Big Town, what's before me,
> Fair weather or stormy?
> Big Town, will I hit the heights
> And see my name in electric lights?
> Big Town, will I blunder,
> Fall down and go under
> Or will I rise and rise
> Till I scrape your skies?
> Big Town,
> Wise old town,
> What's the lowdown on me?

(The telephone rings. She answers it.)

PEGGY: *(On telephone.)* Hello? Yes, this is Peggy? What? *(She faces front in shock and horror.)* Who is this? *(Then defiantly.)* I don't care what you do! I plan to follow this through to the end! *(She slams down the receiver and starts to reprise the song proudly. Singing.)*

> Big Town, what's before me,
> Fair weather or stormy?
> Big Town, will I hit the heights
> And see my name in —

(Floyd comes back in.)

FLOYD: I have very bad news.

PEGGY: So do I. *(They look at each other. Curtain.)*

END OF ACT ONE

ACT TWO

Floyd and Peggy stand in exactly the same positions as at the end of Act One.

PEGGY: You said you had bad news.

FLOYD: I did. And you said the same.

PEGGY: Isn't it amazing how a sudden shock will affect our sense of time? I feel as if we'd been standing here, facing each other, for over fifteen minutes.

FLOYD: Ditto. Well. You tell me your news, then I'll tell you mine.

PEGGY: O.K. I just received a threatening phone call.

FLOYD: Hmmmm. I thought things might get dangerous. Was it a man or a woman?

PEGGY: Hard to tell. It was either a man who sings a decent tenor or a woman who smokes at least a pack a day. Either way, it was suggested in very sinister tones that I rearrange my furniture immediately.

FLOYD: They don't like the Fourth Wall.

PEGGY: They sure don't.

FLOYD: I can pretty well guess who it was.

PEGGY: You can?

FLOYD: Sure. It's obviously one of three possibilities, in view of those speeches you made.

PEGGY: Who, then?

FLOYD: First, it might have been a critic, warning you about your attempt to move beyond realism.

PEGGY: O.K. I can deal with that.

FLOYD: Or else it might have been a spokesperson for the soft drink industry, angry at what you said about Coke.

PEGGY: Well, I'm sorry. I'd say it again.

FLOYD: But frankly I think it's the third alternative.

PEGGY: Who?

FLOYD: Hillary Clinton.

PEGGY: You mean, because of what I said about Bill.

FLOYD: No. Because she wants to play Saint Joan herself.

PEGGY: But it was a hoarse voice. Does she smoke?

FLOYD: I imagine secretly. I imagine she has to.

PEGGY: Well I'm sorry, but no matter who threatens me, these things should be said.

FLOYD: Then keep saying them, Peggy!

PEGGY: O.K. Now for your bad news.

FLOYD: I — I've decided not to tell you.

PEGGY: Hey! No fair!

FLOYD: I can't, Peggy, and here's why. You may have noticed that tonight we are caught in a death struggle between two sorts of plays.

PEGGY: Two sorts of plays?

FLOYD: One represents a uniquely American yearning for the democratic experience. The other is a cheap throwback to the continental sex comedy.

PEGGY: I don't understand.

FLOYD: I'm glad you don't. *(He looks off.)* But my job, as I see it, is to prevent the bad play from destroying the good. Which is why I won't sully this stage by telling you my news.

PEGGY: But does it have to do with my husband?

FLOYD: I'm not saying any more. As the watchman says in the Agamemnon, "an ox stands on my tongue."

PEGGY: *(Starting off.)* Then I'll see for myself.

FLOYD: *(Quickly.)* No don't. *(Pause.)* There's another reason why I don't want to tell you, Peggy.

PEGGY: Another reason?

FLOYD: I'm nervous that you'll blame the messenger. I'm frightened you'll confuse the teller with the tale. I'm not sure why, but I don't think I could stand that, Peggy.

PEGGY: I won't do it then.

FLOYD: Promise?

PEGGY: I swear.

FLOYD: All right. Then here goes . . . You may remember I went off to tell Roger and Julia about the *Saint Joan* thing?

PEGGY: I remember very well. I thought you created a lot of suspense.

FLOYD: The suspense has evaporated, Peggy.

PEGGY: How come?

FLOYD: I couldn't tell them.

PEGGY: Why not?

FLOYD: They were unreceptive.

PEGGY: What do you mean?

FLOYD: They were in the bedroom. With the door locked.

PEGGY: What?

FLOYD: So I knocked. I even rattled the doorknob. Finally I put my ear to the door.

PEGGY: What did you hear?

FLOYD: Some of the most second-rate dialogue it has been my misfortune to listen to.

PEGGY: At least you heard dialogue.

FLOYD: I did. Then they opened the door.

PEGGY: Were their clothes in disarray?

FLOYD: Somewhat. And they behaved sheepishly.

PEGGY: Sheepishly?

FLOYD: They claimed they'd been watching television.

PEGGY: Do you believe that?

FLOYD: At least it explains the lousy dialogue. Television writing can be appalling.

PEGGY: Did you tell them about *Saint Joan?*

FLOYD: I tried. But they didn't listen.

PEGGY: Didn't listen?

FLOYD: They shushed me.

PEGGY: They SHUSHED you?

FLOYD: And waved me away.

PEGGY: Waved you AWAY?

FLOYD: And returned to the bed. Where they remained, sprawled on the bedspread, watching the tube.

PEGGY: No.

FLOYD: A sit-com, I might add.

PEGGY: No.

FLOYD: And a rerun at that.

PEGGY: Are you sure?

FLOYD: I am! — I mean the plot was vaguely familiar.

PEGGY: Oh God.

FLOYD: Exactly. "Oh God." Actually, the line from *Saint Joan* is: "Oh God that madest this beautiful earth, when will it be ready to receive Thy saints?"

PEGGY: Not by watching TV, I can tell you that.

FLOYD: Of course not.

PEGGY: This is horrible.

FLOYD: You can see why I was a reluctant messenger.

PEGGY: I should have known Julia would try to seduce Roger! It's been on her mind ever since she saw his underpants in third grade.

FLOYD: And in their attempt to recapture these juvenile feelings, they've regressed to television.

PEGGY: Which they're probably not even watching now. Which is probably just blabbing away in the background.

FLOYD: I wouldn't be surprised.

PEGGY: Oh, Floyd.

FLOYD: I'm sorry, Peggy. I really am.

PEGGY: I wonder what Saint Joan would do about this.

FLOYD: She'd ignore it. She'd have more on her mind than the backstage gropings of a couple of stock characters.

PEGGY: That's true . . .

FLOYD: So don't let this throw a vulgar light on all we've accomplished so far.

PEGGY: I'll try not to. *(A pause; they look off.)*

FLOYD: *(Exploding.)* Television! I should have known! A major threat to the contemporary theater! We could compete with the movies, but television!

PEGGY: In our bedroom! With another woman!

FLOYD: Oh hell. Maybe our country deserves to decline. Rome had its bread and circuses. We have TV.

PEGGY: *(Starting off)* Not necessarily! I'm going to break up the party!

FLOYD: *(Grabbing her arm.)* Wait!

PEGGY: No! This time I'm off! They want sit-com, they'll get sit-com!

FLOYD: *(Still holding her.)* Please, Peggy, stay just a little longer. I have one more thing to say.

PEGGY: But it's time for me to act!

FLOYD: Half of acting is listening, Peggy. I listened to your speeches. Now you listen to mine.

PEGGY: O.K. But if I lose concentration, I'm sure you'll know why. *(She sits reluctantly.)*

FLOYD: *(Speaking with difficulty.)* Peggy, I want you to know that I have never, in all my years of teaching, made any kind of sexual advance toward any of my female students, no matter how attractive they may be.

PEGGY: Good for you, Floyd.

FLOYD: This is because I've always considered myself gay.

PEGGY: You're sweet to tell me. Now can I go?

FLOYD: No, listen. Please. There's something about this room which has reoriented me. As we've played our scenes together, Peggy, I've begun to have second thoughts about my sexuality. Even as I've announced the infidelity of your husband, I've had the strange yearning to take his place at your side.

PEGGY: Floyd . . .

FLOYD: No, really. In fact, I think I love you, Peggy. I want to be with you wherever you go. All right, I may be gay but why should that stop me? Gays on stage make spectacular lovers. English actors have been proving this for years. Well, they have the technique, but we have the feelings, Peggy. At least I have. For you. Tonight.

PEGGY: Aren't you slipping into the continental sex comedy, Floyd?

FLOYD: Maybe I am, but what the hell. Oh look, I don't have to sleep with you, though Lord knows I'd love to take a crack at it. I won't even play the frustrated lover, mooning at your side! May I simply hang out with you occasionally, screening your phone calls, opening your hate mail, maybe even sharing a pizza with you in lonely hotel rooms when you take this play on the road?

PEGGY: But what about your teaching career? Don't you want tenure?

FLOYD: *(Kneeling before her.)* How can I teach *Saint Joan* when I've met the real thing?

(Roger and Julia enter.)

ROGER: Are we interrupting something?

PEGGY: *(Keeping Floyd on his knees.)* You certainly are.

ROGER: We were watching TV.

PEGGY: So I have heard.

ROGER: No, darling, really. We were.

PEGGY: With the door locked?

ROGER: That was automatic, darling. A hangover from the days when the children used to barge in.

PEGGY: Don't drag the children into this!

ROGER: All right, darling. Here's the thing. Julia and I may have entered the bedroom with other intentions, but during the preliminaries I happened to roll onto the remote. The TV went on and naturally we watched it.

JULIA: It just shows how television dominates our lives.

ROGER: It turned out to be crummy. I was bored with it almost immediately.

PEGGY: Oh yes? Then why did you continue to watch it?

ROGER: I hoped it would get better.

FLOYD: "Hoped it would get better, hoped it would get better." That's what they said about postwar Russian drama! *(The others look at each other, confused.)*

PEGGY: And did it get better, Roger? After Floyd came and went?

FLOYD: And left you to your own devices?

ROGER: No it didn't, darling. It got worse.

JULIA: I disagree completely. I thought it was getting quite good.

PEGGY: Now I'm confused. Are we talking about sex or television?

FLOYD: Only in America could such a question arise.

JULIA: Well the answer is that he grabbed the remote and switched to the sports channel.

PEGGY: This suddenly has the ring of truth. Men are always doing that. They remotely control almost every aspect of our lives, and we women have to accommodate ourselves passively to every channel they switch to.

ROGER: Now hold on here! Just hold on! Who has accommodated himself to whom around here? Who's been putting up with this frigging fourth wall? Oh Peggy, I've loved you for a hell of a long time, but sometimes you're a royal pain in the ass! Now I'm telling you that nothing happened between Julia and me, and that's a hard thing to say because Julia is an extremely exciting woman!

JULIA: Thank you, Roger.

ROGER: And what if something *had*, Peggy? What if a guy happens to put his wee-wee into the wong woman — I mean, wrong woman? So the hell what? Maybe a man gets tired of the approved diet occasionally and wants to bite into a good, unhealthy, sizzling steak?

JULIA: Thank you, Roger.

ROGER: I mean the French do it all the time. We're disappointed when they don't. Hindu Gods do it on temples. Hollywood stars do it on screen.

JULIA: Folks in Siam do it. Look at Siamese twins.

ROGER: And your buddy Bill Clinton did it!

PEGGY: He did not!

ROGER: I say he did! And Hillary welcomed him back, and the country elected him president!

JULIA: That's why I voted for him.

FLOYD: This scene will stand as the most insidious defense of adultery in all of western drama.

PEGGY: *(Taking Floyd's arm.)* All right, Roger. Then may I do it, too?

ROGER: No.

PEGGY: Why not?

ROGER: Because it would be completely out of character.

PEGGY: My character has changed!

JULIA: There. You see? As with most arguments between husbands and wives, you've both gotten absolutely nowhere.

PEGGY: *(To Roger.)* Why don't you just go watch the Playboy Channel? That might solve everything.

ROGER: I don't want to watch TV any more, Peggy. Ever. Except for the Buffalo Bills.

FLOYD: Then welcome back to the living stage.

PEGGY: No, Floyd. Wait. Not so fast, please. *(To Roger and Julia.)* First I have one final question to ask of Roger and Julia.

ROGER: Shoot. I'm ready for it.

JULIA: I have nothing to be ashamed of, at least this far in the plot.

PEGGY: *(Carefully.)* Roger and Julia: When you were demonstrating your limited attention span in the bedroom, and Floyd and I were working through a very difficult scene here in the living room, did either of you give a thought to what might be happening in the kitchen?

ROGER: The kitchen?

PEGGY: Did either of you, for example, bother to look at what might be happening in the oven, or think about what we might do for a green vegetable, or check the freezer for any ideas on dessert? *(Roger and Julia look at each other guiltily.)*

ROGER: I didn't.

JULIA: Nor, I'm afraid, did I.

PEGGY: I didn't think so. *(She starts off.)* Excuse me, Floyd. Apparently Saint Joan is still responsible for a meal.

ROGER: Let me help you, sweetheart.

PEGGY: No thanks. You'll just try to butter me up.

ROGER: Let me at least wash the lettuce.

PEGGY: All right. But no goosing or nuzzling or fooling around. I'm still very mad at you, Roger. You can't switch my channels so easily. *(She goes. He follows. Pause.)*

JULIA: I'm hopeless in the kitchen. Being a New Yorker, I either order in, or eat out. *(No answer from Floyd.)* Even breakfast poses a problem. I don't understand stoves. I always burn my buns. *(Her little joke. Floyd opens a book, reads.)* Are you a good cook?

FLOYD: *(Vaguely.)* Hmmm?

JULIA: *(Shouting.)* I said are you a good cook?

FLOYD: Umm-hmmm.

JULIA: Really? Do you have any specialties?

FLOYD: *(Vaguely; as he reads.)* Noisettes de veaux Angleterre . . . gnocci e porcini di Firenze . . . Trout Tel Aviv with Dead Sea dumplings . . .

JULIA: Yummy. Sounds delicious . . . Maybe you'd cook for me sometime.

FLOYD: No thanks. *(He closes his book, gets another, reads that.)*

JULIA: Mind if I smoke?

FLOYD: Yes.

JULIA: You do? You really do?

FLOYD: I really do.

JULIA: Don't tell me you're one of those Health Nazis.

FLOYD: I'm glad to say I am.

JULIA: Then suppose I joined the Resistance and did it anyway?

FLOYD: I wouldn't.

JULIA: But I want to.

FLOYD: There are no ashtrays here.

JULIA: I'll use this little plate of Staffordshire china.

FLOYD: I don't believe the good craftsmen in Staffordshire designed that plate as a receptacle for lipstick-stained butts.

JULIA: Nonetheless, I think I'll employ it for such. *(She opens her purse, takes out a lovely cigarette case, a holder, and an expensive lighter.)*

FLOYD: You might want to know that no one smokes on stage any more.

JULIA: Oh really?

FLOYD: It's a piece of stage business that's totally obsolete.

JULIA: Then the theater has lost another fine, old custom. If it's done well, it both looks seductive and reveals character. *(She takes a cigarette out of the case, taps it, puts it in the holder, and is about to light it.)* For example, watch how attractively I do this. You'll be reminded of the Lunts.

FLOYD: If you light that butt, lady, I'll take it with all your other smoking paraphernalia and shove it attractively up your twat.

(Long pause. Julia removes the cigarette from the holder, puts it back in the box, puts everything back in her purse, snapping each container closed with grim precision.)

JULIA: *(Finally.)* You're not very polite. You know that, I suppose.

FLOYD: Yes. I know that.

JULIA: I mean, all I'm trying to do is have a short scene with you, and you're making it virtually impossible.

FLOYD: We don't belong in the same *play*, lady, much less the same scene.

JULIA: And why, pray tell, do you say that?

FLOYD: Because we've made a major breakthrough here today. We've opened the whole thing up. We've been talking about big issues here, and you're bringing it all back down to some second-rate, middle-class comedy of manners.

JULIA: Oh really. And what "big issues" have you been talking about?

FLOYD: Reforming this country, changing the world, all that.

JULIA: Oh now come on.

FLOYD: In fact, we've found certain strong parallels to Saint Joan.

JULIA: *Saint Joan? (A tinkling laugh.)* Joan of Lorraine? The Arc family's little girl Joan? That Joan?

FLOYD: That Joan.

JULIA: *(More laughter.)* You must be kidding. *Saint Joan* as a subject in today's world? Why even the movie was a failure forty years ago! Grow up, Professor Loesser! Join the twentieth century!

FLOYD: Yeah well, you might be interested to know that it's an eternal story. It stretches back to Antigone and forward to *Thelma and Louise.*

JULIA: Oh yes?

FLOYD: Oh yes! And in all its many manifestations, there's no place in the cast for a type like you. So please find a reason to get off this stage, or I'll find one for you.

JULIA: *(After a pause.)* Floyd . . . May I call you Floyd?

FLOYD: I don't give a shit.

JULIA: Floyd, I have a friend . . .

FLOYD: I doubt that, Julia.

JULIA: No, I do, Floyd. I have a friend who is a professional actress. She told me once that whenever she got into trouble in a scene, she tried to remember her original objective. Now what is *my* original objective? My original objective was simply to give an opinion of this wall.

FLOYD: And? So?

JULIA: But then, as things progressed, I revised that objective, Floyd. My objective became to seduce someone.

FLOYD: You mean Roger.

JULIA: I mean Roger. But recently, as you may have observed, Roger "passed," as they say in the theater. Therefore, being a woman, I am capable of lowering my sights.

FLOYD: Don't get any ideas, lady.

JULIA: *(More tinkling laughter.)* What? You mean, you? With me? Oh heavens, no. What I meant was that I am modifying my objective once again. My objective is now simply and solely to engage you in casual conversation. All I want to do is keep the ball in the air and the air in the ball. That's my only objective at this point.

FLOYD: My objective remains what it has always been — to keep good theater alive in this country in order to create and maintain a healthy and self-critical society.

JULIA: But we'll *keep* theater alive, dear heart, just by talking to each other.

FLOYD: Conversation is not dramatic dialogue.

JULIA: Oh come on. We've got to do *some*thing. I mean, here we are, in front of this stupid fourth wall. At least, tell me where you're from.

FLOYD: I'm not saying.

JULIA: Oh please. Just as an improvisation. Just to jump start us.

FLOYD: *(With a sigh.)* I happen to come from a very underestimated town.

JULIA: Name it, and we'll see.

FLOYD: I happen to come from right here.

JULIA: What? Buffalo? Beau Fleuve? Which is cruelly called The Mistake on the Lake?

FLOYD: This is my hometown.

JULIA: But I'm from Buffalo, too!

FLOYD: Come off it.

JULIA: I am. You would have known that if you had been here for the exposition.

FLOYD: I'm amazed.

JULIA: You see? You see where casual conversation can take us? Already we've struck a common chord. Shall we pursue the thread?

FLOYD: Oh hell, why not?

JULIA: Tell me about your family, for example.

FLOYD: You wouldn't know them.

JULIA: Oh please. I might.

FLOYD: I come from a very different world.

JULIA: But maybe your mother cleaned for us.

FLOYD: Actually, I have no family, Julia.

JULIA: Don't be silly. There must be more Loessers.

FLOYD: The name Loesser was given to me by my drama teacher in high school, who admired the composer of *Guys and Dolls*.

JULIA: But what was your surname before that?

FLOYD: I didn't have one. I was an orphan.

JULIA: An orphan?

FLOYD: When I was barely a few hours old, I was deposited on the steps of the Niagara Home for Little Wanderers by an unwed mother.

JULIA: No!

FLOYD: Yes. And I was raised there by a group of kindly social workers. No one ever adopted me because I had a slight bed-wetting problem, which now, goddammit, is virtually cured. *(Pause.)*

JULIA: You're not going to believe this, Floyd.

FLOYD: What?

JULIA: Well, here's the thing: I, yours truly, little old me, once had an illegitimate child.

FLOYD: You're kidding.

JULIA: No really. I did. I never thought I could talk about it unless I was asked onto the *Oprah Winfrey Show.*

FLOYD: You? A mother?

JULIA: When I was very young. Before I became involved with Planned Parenthood . . . And guess what I did with my illegitimate child.

FLOYD: I'd hate to think.

JULIA: I deposited it on the steps of the same institution which you referred to in your own narrative.

FLOYD: The Niagara Home for Little Wanderers?

JULIA: The same.

FLOYD: Fantastic.

JULIA: I know it.

FLOYD: Talk about coincidence.

JULIA: Talk about plot.

FLOYD: Small world, huh?

JULIA: Old Home week.

FLOYD: Niagara Home week.

JULIA: Exactly! *(Both laugh.)* Now you see? You see what fun it can be when people just loosen up and converse?

FLOYD: *(Putting aside his book.)* I do. I'm beginning to see that.

JULIA: All right, now let's just keep going, shall we? Just to see where things lead?

FLOYD: Oh hell. Sure. Why not?

JULIA: All right. Now tell me, Floyd: How old are you, more or less? Just give me a ballpark figure.

FLOYD: I'll tell you this: Today's my birthday.

JULIA: Well happy same!

FLOYD: Thanks, Julia.

JULIA: I should have a present or something. *(She looks around, then offers him a knickknack from a nearby table.)*

FLOYD: Oh no, no, no.

JULIA: Now wouldn't it be amusing if my lost child were approximately the same age?

FLOYD: That would be a good one, wouldn't it!

JULIA: Well now, you wait. We can actually check.

FLOYD: You can check?

JULIA: Absolutely. I just happen to be wearing . . . *(She takes a locket from around her neck.)* This locket, containing the date of birth and a scrap of the little nightgown the infant wore when I presented it to the orphanage. I wear this everywhere. Except on the subway, of course. *(She gets it out.)* There. See? The birth date? Read it, would you please? I don't have my glasses.

FLOYD: *(Reading.)* It's today's date!

JULIA: No!

FLOYD: I swear!

JULIA: I just can't believe this! We're beginning to sound like Dickens! It must be this silly fourth wall!

FLOYD: *(Getting out his wallet.)* Actually, I always carry with me a scrap of the nightshirt I was found in.

JULIA: Wouldn't it be fun if they compared favorably?

FLOYD: That would be too much. *(Comparing the two pieces of cloth.)* Julia . . .

JULIA: Now don't tell me.

FLOYD: No seriously. They compare! Look! They're virtually identical! And see? Only when you put them together, can you read the following message: "Tumble dry under moderate heat."

JULIA: I can't believe this!

FLOYD: I mean, Jesus, we were just talking, and out all this stuff comes. You were right, Julia, about the natural flow of conversation. It makes me think I've been much too structured, both in the classroom and outside.

JULIA: I'm very tempted to tell the others.

FLOYD: Think we should?

JULIA: They might get a kick out of it.

FLOYD: Maybe we ought to make a call first.

JULIA: A call?

FLOYD: To the Niagara Home for Little Wanderers. Just to make sure.

JULIA: You think so?

FLOYD: I've learned in academia never to leap to conclusions.

JULIA: I suppose you're right.

FLOYD: I mean, take the little nightshirts, for example. Lots of babies might have worn them.

JULIA: I suppose. The Fifties were conformist times.

FLOYD: *(Picking up the phone.)* May I have directory assistance, please?

JULIA: Wait, Floyd, I noticed a telephone in the den. Maybe we should call from there. I mean this is a rather private issue.

FLOYD: *(Hanging up.)* You're right.

JULIA: *(Taking his arm.)* Let's go, then! I wonder if these orphanages give out information over the phone?

FLOYD: They have to these days. It's the law. All you need is a valid credit card. *(They start out.)*

JULIA: *(Stopping.)* Floyd. . .

FLOYD: What?

JULIA: In view of how far we've come, I wonder if now you might let me celebrate by smoking one little ciggy-poo?

FLOYD: Only if you let me bum one.

JULIA: Oh you! You are a piece of work, Floyd! You really are! *(They go off laughing. After a moment, Roger comes in, looks at the piano, moodily hits a key. It plays.)*

ROGER: *(Singing.)*
>After you, who
>Could supply my sky of blue?
>After you, who
>Could I love?
>After you, why
>Should I take the time to try
>For who else could qualify
>After you, who?
>Hold my hand and swear
>You'll never cease to care
>For without you there,
>What could I do?
>I could search years
>But who else could change my tears
>Into laughter after you.

(The piano continues to play, as Roger looks off longingly. He reprises the last part of the song downstage. As he finishes the song, Peggy comes in carrying two plates of food, which she sets down on the coffee table in front of the couch.)

PEGGY: Come eat.

ROGER: Where are the others?

PEGGY: Telephoning in the den. They said to go ahead.

ROGER: I'll see how long they'll be.

PEGGY: Roger . . .

ROGER: What?

PEGGY: I think we should have a scene together. By ourselves.

ROGER: Couldn't we have it in the kitchen?

PEGGY: It belongs here. In front of that wall.

ROGER: But I love eating in the kitchen. Remember when the kids were still around? Eating in the kitchen and watching *Jeopardy?* I loved all that.

PEGGY: See? There you are. Always falling back on the television. Now please. Sit down. *(He does.)*

ROGER: Suddenly I feel very nervous.

PEGGY: So do I. Maybe we're both subconsciously reminded of the final scene in *The Doll's House,* by Henrik Ibsen.

ROGER: Uh-oh. We read that my freshman year in college.

PEGGY: So did we. In those days, everyone seemed to read the same thing.

ROGER: Would you refresh my memory on that final scene? I got a C in English because I spent too much time playing freshman lacrosse.

PEGGY: I only got a B minus, but I think what happens is the wife sits her husband down and explains to him why she's leaving him.

ROGER: Leaving?

PEGGY: Walking out.

ROGER: Forever?

PEGGY: You have that feeling.

ROGER: Why?

PEGGY: Because he never took her seriously.

ROGER: I've taken you seriously.

PEGGY: As a wife, yes. As a mother, oh yes. But as me, as a person in my own right, never. When it comes to things that have nothing to do with our cozy little family, you've never really listened to what I had to say.

ROGER: Peggy . . .

PEGGY: No, I mean this now. If you and I had just sat down and had this scene at the beginning, we probably wouldn't be having it at all.

ROGER: Your logic eludes me, darling.

PEGGY: No it doesn't. You know exactly what I mean. You just don't want to deal with it.

ROGER: Sweetheart . . .

PEGGY: You never do. We've been very lucky, you and I, Roger. With the kids, with your work, with everything. And that's made us smug and safe and selfish. I had to shake things up.

ROGER: Consider me shook.

PEGGY: I wonder. I try to open up our life, and what do you do? You bring in Julia to trivialize the problem, and then you bring in Floyd to categorize it academically.

ROGER: Sweetheart. . .

PEGGY: And you think if everyone sings Cole Porter, it will solve every-thing . . .

ROGER: I love Cole Porter.

PEGGY: I know you do, darling, and so do I. But he's no solution for what ails us.

ROGER: He's a serious guy, Peggy. There's an oh-such-a hungry-yearning burn-ing inside of him.

PEGGY: I'm not going to argue about the score, Roger. There's a certain inevitability in plays. And a certain progression in the history of modern drama. I also learned that in freshman English. After Ibsen comes Shaw. Which means that after we do *The Doll's House*, I've got to go off and play *Saint Joan.*

ROGER: Are you going to put on armor, or can you play it in pantyhose?

PEGGY: Goddammit Roger, I've just discovered a fifth wall there tonight.

ROGER: Oh no! Not a fifth! Please! I can't even handle the fourth.

PEGGY: Well when you do, there's still a fifth to get through. And that's the wall between men and women . . . which may be the toughest of all to crack. Now good-bye . . . I'm on my way to Washington.

ROGER: Washington? Floyd mentioned New York.

PEGGY: I've decided Washington.

ROGER: That's a dangerous town, love.

PEGGY: I'll change that. I plan to put a fourth wall in the White House.

ROGER: That may not be feasible, Peggy. It's an oval office.

PEGGY: Still I'll do it. Then I'll put one in every house in America.

ROGER: Lots of people don't have one wall these days, darling, much less four.

PEGGY: All the more reason to get going.

ROGER: Why you, darling?

PEGGY: Because I want to. Because I said I would. Because people are count-ing on me.

ROGER: What people?

PEGGY: Those people! Beyond the wall! Oh Roger, where the hell have you been?

ROGER: I've been here, love. All evening. And I have to tell you, in all hon-esty, I don't think there's anyone there.

PEGGY: You don't?

ROGER: I don't. That wall just holds up our house. Period.

PEGGY: That's all?

ROGER: And that's enough. And even supposing there were people beyond it, Peg, I don't think they'd expect you to change the world. Maybe they'd be amused. Maybe even interested. But in the end, they wouldn't take this Saint Joan thing terribly seriously.

PEGGY: You don't think so?

ROGER: I really don't, sweetheart. Plays never change the world, Peg. And the ones that try are the ones that never last.

PEGGY: *(Sitting down.)* Oh boy.

ROGER: *(Sitting beside her; putting his arm around her.)* Oh sweetheart, look. We've had a good time here tonight. We've had a laugh or two. You've said some things that ought to be said. But now don't you think it's time we put the furniture back the way it was?

PEGGY: The way it was?

ROGER: I promise I'll turn off the TV and talk eyeball to eyeball with you any time you want!

PEGGY: You mean you want to just sit around and grow old?

ROGER: *(Putting his arm around her.)* And enjoy each other. And our friends. And our kids. And maybe grandchildren some day. Leave politics to the politicians. Let's hunker down at home.

PEGGY: So what you're saying is I've run up against a blank wall.

ROGER: That's what I'm saying, darling.

PEGGY: Like Melville's *Bartleby?*

ROGER: Like Melville's *Bartleby.*

(Julia and Floyd come in.)

JULIA: *(Seeing them together on the couch.)* You look so gloomy. Has somebody died?

PEGGY: Only a dream.

JULIA: Well I want to thank you for the use of your telephone.

ROGER: I hope it served its purpose.

FLOYD: It did and it didn't.

ROGER: Meaning?

FLOYD: We thought we'd have a surprise for both of you.

JULIA: We thought we'd discovered we were related.

FLOYD: In fact, I secretly hoped we'd be able to dramatize the connectedness of all human beings.

PEGGY: Oh that would have been wonderful!

FLOYD: But this was not to be.

JULIA: It turns out that the illegitimate child I deposited at an orphanage years ago was female, rather than male. It simply slipped my mind.

FLOYD: The child was obviously not me, and I'd be glad to prove it.

JULIA: *(To Floyd.)* That won't be necessary, dear. *(To others.)* In my eagerness to carry on a conversation, I assumed too much.

FLOYD: And in my eagerness for a recognition scene I went along with it. Art is not life, people. And what happens on stage tends to be modified once we're in the wings.

JULIA: *(Taking Floyd's arm.)* On the other hand, we've been on a meaningful journey together, and have formed a friendship with no sexual component whatsoever. This is new to me, of course. You might say I have broken through my own personal fourth wall.

FLOYD: And as for me, I feel that life has at last penetrated the academic shell I've built around myself. Next semester, I plan to take a sabbatical from teaching and concentrate simply and solely on my bedwetting problem.

JULIA: I'll help you, dear.

FLOYD: I'd appreciate that.

ROGER: Then here's what we do. *(He goes to the piano, hits a note. The piano plays an introduction.)*

PEGGY: Knew it. He's trying to end this thing with Cole Porter.

ROGER: *(Singing.)*
    What say? Let's be buddies,
    What say? Let's be pals . . .
    (Julia joins him.)

JULIA: *(Singing.)*
    What say? Let's be buddies,
    And keep up each other's morales.
    (Floyd joins them.)

FLOYD: *(Singing.)*
    I may never shout it,
    But many's the time I'm blue . . .

ROGER: Come on, Peg . . .
    (Peggy joins them reluctantly.)

ALL: *(In good harmony.)*
    What say? How's about it?
    Can't I be a buddy with you?

ROGER: O.K. Once again, now. From the top . . .

ALL: *(Singing.)*
    What say, let's be buddies . . .

JULIA: *(Improvising.)*
    Bosom buddies . . .

ALL: *(Singing.)*

> What say, let's be pals . . .

ROGER: *(Improvising.)*

> Like Hope and Crosby . . .

ALL: *(Singing.)*

> What say, let's be buddies . . .

FLOYD: *(Improvising.)*

> Like Beaumont and Fletcher!

ALL: *(Singing.)*

> And keep up each other's morales . . .

ROGER: *(Spoken.)* Take it, Peg!

PEGGY: *(Singing.)*

> I may never shout it . . .
>
> *(Suddenly breaking away from the group.)* I can't do this. *(The piano dies out.)*

ROGER: Why not? You were doing fine.

PEGGY: That's just it. It reminds me how great it is when people get together and sing.

JULIA: Only in small groups, darling. When they're old friends. And know the words.

PEGGY: But I want other people to get it on it. I want everyone in the world to be singing different parts to some basic underlying melody.

JULIA: *(To Floyd.)* Is she talking about opera?

FLOYD: No, she's talking about the social contract, as proposed by Jean-Jacques Rousseau in the eighteenth century.

PEGGY: Whatever it is, I've got to get people to do it. *(She starts out.)*

ROGER: Not everyone can carry a tune, Peg.

PEGGY: Then they can beat the drum. Come on, Floyd. Time to march into battle.

FLOYD: March? I'm just learning how to walk, Peggy.

PEGGY: O.K. Then I'll go alone.

ROGER: No, wait. What about the exam? Early in the evening, Floyd mentioned an exam.

JULIA: Yes. That was a plant, Peggy. You just can't leave it hanging there.

ROGER: Right. You've got to take the exam, Peg.

FLOYD: She's already passed summa cum laude.

PEGGY: Thank you, Floyd. *(She kisses him on the cheek.)* And thanks for my plot . . . Good-bye, Julia. *(Kisses Julia, remembers both cheeks; turns to Roger, gives him a warm kiss.)* Good-bye, darling. I'll miss you. Now there are lots of leftovers in the freezer. They'll last till you learn how to cook.

ROGER: I won't bother! I'll eat Chinese! I'll have an affair!

JULIA: *(Taking Floyd's arm.)* Not with me, please. I'm over all that.

ROGER: *(Blocking the doorway.)* I won't let you go, Peggy! I'll keep you here by force!

PEGGY: *(Touching his lips.)* Don't be silly, darling. Good-bye. *(She exits blithely through the fourth wall, is hit by a lovely light. She sees the audience.)* I KNEW it! I knew you'd be there! Oh I wish we could all get together, but first I've got to go to Washington and change the world! . . . *(She greets people as she goes up the aisle.)* Good-bye . . . Good-bye . . . Anything you want me to tell Bill? . . . Wish me luck . . . Good-bye! *(She exits through the audience. Pause.)*

FLOYD: Wow! Did you see that? She broke the proscenium!

JULIA: She must have done it with mirrors.

ROGER: Quickly, Floyd. Was Saint Joan married?

FLOYD: Of course not.

ROGER: She must have had lovers.

FLOYD: Only in Schiller and Verdi.

ROGER: Shit! I can't speak German or Italian!

FLOYD: In Shaw, there's a loyal soldier who follows her around. I wanted to play it once upon a time.

ROGER: I could do that.

FLOYD: It's kind of a minor role.

ROGER: Maybe I've played the lead too long. *(He hesitates, then closes his eyes, and steps through the wall; again a new light hits him. He sees the audience.)* Well, what d'you know? She was right! *(Calls after Peggy.)* Wait, darling! Wait! I'm coming, too!

(He greets people as he hurries up the aisle.) Hello . . . Hello . . . Peg! I've got the credit cards! *(He exits through the audience. Pause.)*

JULIA: *(Looking out blankly.)* Hmmm. *(Pause; then shrugging it off.)* Oh well. That's the end of a rather pleasant little evening.

FLOYD: *(Looking at the wall.)* As Shaw says at the end of *Saint Joan*, I wonder . . . *(The piano sounds a note. They look at each other.)*

JULIA: *(Singing.)*
  Can't I be a buddy?

FLOYD: *(Singing.)*
  Can't I be a buddy?

BOTH: *(Singing.)*
  Can't I be a buddy to you?
  (They embrace. Curtain.)

THE END

LATER LIFE

Later Life was produced at Playwrights Horizons (Don Scardino, Artistic Director) in New York City on May 23, 1993. It was directed by Don Scardino; the scene design was by Ben Edwards; the costume design was by Jennifer Von Mayrhauser; the lighting design was by Brian MacDevitt; the sound design was by Guy Sherman/Aural Fixation; the wig and hair design was by Daniel Platten; and the production stage manager was Dianne Trulock. The cast was as follows:

AUSTIN . . . . Charles Kimbrough
RUTH . . . . Maureen Anderson
OTHER WOMEN . . . . Carole Shelly
OTHER MEN . . . . Anthony Heald

The Playwrights Horizons production of *Later Life* was produced by Steven Baruch, Richard Frankel, and Thomas Viertel in association with the Shubert Organization and Capital Cities/ABC Inc., at the Westside Theatre in New York City on September 12, 1993. In this production, the part of Austin was played by Josef Somer.

AUTHOR'S NOTE
A while back, I used to teach literature in the Department of Humanities at MIT. One of the most intriguing stories we studied in a course on American Literature was "The Beast in the Jungle" by Henry James. I like to think my students responded to it as strongly as I did. It's a study of a man who is so convinced that something terrible will happen to him in life that he guards himself continually against the possibility. As a result, nothing ever does happen, until, in a final twist, he realizes that the terrible thing is exactly that: the recognition that he has never really lived. When I started writing *Later Life*, I had no intention of adapting James, but as the plot began to take shape, I realized that I was at least touching on the work that we had talked about so many times in class. My ending, particularly, echoes that of the James's story, though I admit it doesn't go quite as far.

There are many elements in my play, however, that are obviously different from James. All the characters, with the possible exception of Austin, are my own invention, and the idea that the play takes place in continuous time, during one evening, at a Labor Day party overlooking the Boston harbor, is all mine. When the play was first presented, I gave credit to James, but I purposely didn't name the specific story because I didn't want people, particularly the critics, rushing to make specific comparisons. I was sure to lose in any contest with the Master. *Later Life*, being a play, also has thematic elements that are different from "The Beast in the Jungle." It is about the possible romance between Austin and Ruth, who are both locked into playing pretty much the same roles all their lives, in contrast to the various characters who visit them on the terrace. The very fact that the hostess and all her guests are played by the same two actors throughout underscores the possibility of the many roles available to us, even in middle age. On the other hand, the fact that Austin and Ruth are played by the same actors throughout makes their choices seem all the more achingly inhibited. James's story has a tragic dimension, a kind of crushing inevitability punctuated with two significant deaths. My play has a more comic tone and throbs with the idea of "if only. . . ."

We all had a good time working on this play, the first time out. The actors were all first rate, and Don Scardino, the director, and I got along very well. The play was too short when we began rehearsals, but it grew organically as we worked on it, and many of its best scenes emerged out of the rehearsal process. The original set by Ben Edwards was gorgeously romantic, with a lovely sense of the Boston harbor glistening under a vast canopy of stars. If Austin and Ruth were to fall in love, this was the place to do it. We opened at Playwrights Horizons, transferred to the Westside Theatre for an extended run, and then were picked up by many regional and summer theaters. The play has received generally good reviews and audiences seem to like it. With its single set and small cast, it has continued to be performed over the years. Amateur and community groups tend to cast the second roles with a number of different actors, a device which allows more people to be on stage but which somewhat diminishes the theme of the play. *Later Life* also has had some success abroad, particularly in Germany. The French couldn't possibly understand Austin's problem, and the English wouldn't want to.

The play is not easy to do, however. The only real suspense comes from whether Austin and Ruth will finally get together, along with the issue of what "terrible thing" is obsessing Austin, so the two lead actors have to drive the play with real urgency for it to work. Pregnant pauses don't help much. Similarly, the other two actors have to play their parts with as much reality as they can, otherwise they'll look like cartoons as they take their short turns on stage. Because they have such quick changes, they usually need some efficient help in the wings.

CHARACTERS

AUSTIN

RUTH

All the other parts to be played by one additional actor and actress.

SETTING

The terrace off an apartment in a high-rise building overlooking Boston Harbor. Good outdoor furniture, including a chaise. Occasional greenery. Several chrysanthemum plants to suggest the fall. A romantic, starry sky behind.

The play is to be performed without an intermission.

The author is indebted to Henry James.

LATER LIFE

Before Rise: Elegant music such as Scarlotti or Vivaldi.
At Rise: Evening light, early September. The music is now heard coming from
within, along with sounds of a lively party. The stage is empty. We hear occa-
sional harbor sounds—a buoy bell, a foghorn. Then Sally comes on, busily.
She wears whatever a hostess would wear.

SALLY: *(Beckoning toward within.)* Come out here, Austin! *(She adjusts a cou-*
ple of chairs so that they face more toward each other. She speaks more to her-
self.) I'm setting the stage here. That's all I can do. Just set the stage . . .
(Again toward within.) I said, come on out. *(Austin comes out, somewhat*
hesitatingly. He is a distinguished, good-looking, middle-aged man, who wears
a gray suit, a blue shirt, and a conservative tie. He carries a glass.) Now wait
here.

AUSTIN: Why should I wait here?

SALLY: So you can talk.

AUSTIN: To you?

SALLY: No, not to me, Austin. I'm much too busy to talk. *(She lights the out-*
door candle.) I want you to talk to *her.*

AUSTIN: Who's "her?"

SALLY: You'll see.

AUSTIN: Oh Sally . . .

SALLY: No Austin, it's time you took a chance. I'll go get her. *(She starts back*
in.) Now, please. Just wait.

AUSTIN: *(Calling after her.)* What do I do while I wait?

SALLY: *(Adjusting his tie.)* You think. You admire the view of the Boston Harbor.
You examine your immortal soul. I don't care, as long as you wait. *(She*
hurries off. Austin waits, uneasily. Jim comes out. He might wear a beard or
a mustache and is rather scruffily dressed.)

JIM: I believe this is where people may still smoke.

AUSTIN: I should think so. Yes.

JIM: *(Going to the ashtray on the table.)* That looks very much like an ashtray.

AUSTIN: I guess it is.

JIM: *(Examining it.)* It is indeed. It is definitely an ashtray. *(Holding it up.)*
Appealing object, isn't it? Notice the shape.

AUSTIN: Yes.

JIM: Do you suppose there are still people in the world who design ashtrays?

AUSTIN: I imagine there are . . . in Europe.

JIM: *(Producing an unopened pack of Marlboros.)* Speaking of design, this pack itself also has a subtle appeal. Notice the brightness of the red, the crispness of the lettering, the abstract white mountain peak behind, luring us on.

AUSTIN: Oh yes. I see.

JIM: Do you realize that at least eighty percent of the price we pay for cigarettes goes for packaging and taxes.

AUSTIN: I didn't know that.

JIM: And with Clinton in, the tax will be substantially higher.

AUSTIN: Yes, well, Clinton . . .

JIM: *(Opening the pack carefully.* On the other hand, the packaging is important. There is nothing sweeter than the smell of fresh tobacco. *(Holds it out to Austin.)* Smell.

AUSTIN: Oh well . . .

JIM: No, I'm serious. Smell. *(Austin takes the pack and sniffs.)* You see?

AUSTIN: *(Handing it back.)* It's quite pleasant.

JIM: Pleasant? That is the aroma of rural America. There is a hint of the Virginia planter in that, and the stolid yeomen farmers of the North Carolina plains, coupled with the personal cologne of Senator Jesse Helms.

AUSTIN: Ha ha.

JIM: *(Beginning to tap out a cigarette.)* This is also a pleasant process. Tapping the first one out. Gently coaxing him away from his companions. All the time knowing that there are nineteen others, waiting patiently for their turn . . . . Oh. Excuse me. Want one? *(Offers him one.)*

AUSTIN: No, thanks.

JIM: Sure?

AUSTIN: Positive.

JIM: You don't smoke?

AUSTIN: No.

JIM: Never did?

AUSTIN: No.

JIM: Not even when everyone else did?

AUSTIN: No.

JIM: Never even tried it?

AUSTIN: Oh well, I suppose behind the barn . . .

JIM: *(Taking a cigarette for himself.)* That's too bad. You've missed something in life. Smoking is one of the great pleasures of the phenomenal world. It's the closest we come to heaven on earth—particularly now it's forbidden fruit. *(Takes out a lighter.)* It adds depth and dimension to whatever we say or do. Oh, I know, I know: it corrupts children, it exploits the Third World, it is gross, addictive, and unnecessary. It is an image of capitalism in its last, most self-destructive stages. But . . . *(Puts the cigarette in his mouth, lights the lighter, holds it almost to his cigarette.)* it is also a gesture of freedom in an absurd universe. *(Suddenly snaps lighter shut.)* And I'm giving it up.

AUSTIN: Are you serious?

JIM: I am. I have made the decision. That's why I'm behaving like such an ass-hole.

AUSTIN: Oh I wouldn't say that.

JIM: No really. I've given it up before, of course, but tonight is the big night. I bought this fresh pack, and came out here because this time I'm trying to confront temptation. I am shaking hands with the Devil. I am deliberately immersing myself in the dangerous element.

AUSTIN: Do you teach around here?

JIM: That's not important. What I do—or rather, what I did, was smoke. I was an existential smoker. I smoked, therefore I was.

AUSTIN: I'm sure you teach.

JIM: No, I smoked. I am what they call a recovering nicoholic. Or what *I* call, tobacco-challenged. My days were comforted by this pleasant haze. My nights were highlighted by this glowing ash. Cigarettes provided the only significant punctuation in the sprawling, ungrammatical sentences which composed my life. And therefore, even though I was an outcast, a pariah, a scapegoat, I wore my badge of shame with honor. I flaunted it. Hey, it was my Scarlet Letter. *(Returns the cigarette to the pack.)*

AUSTIN: *(Laughing.)* Come on. Where do you teach? Harvard? BU? MIT? Where?

JIM: All right. I confess. I have taught. Philosophy. At Brandeis. They made me take early retirement last year. They claimed I slept with too many students.

AUSTIN: Oh now . . .

JIM: But I think the real reason was I smoked.

AUSTIN: All right now. Enough's enough.

JIM: I agree. You must forgive me. *(Caressing the pack of cigarettes.)* But you see, I'm saying good-bye to a lifelong companion. Nothing becomes it like the leaving thereof. *(He sniffs it longingly.)* Yet it's an agonizing decision! All decisions are, at our age. For us, there's no turning back. Younger people can change their minds, change their lives, that's fine, they have a lifetime ahead of them to change again. But for us who have had a whiff of the grave—it all boils down to our last chance. *(Sally comes back out, with Ruth in tow. Ruth is a lovely woman who wears a simple, slightly artsy dress. She carries a glass of white wine.)*

SALLY: Here we are! . . . Now go away, Jimmy. *(To Austin.)* Has he been boring you about smoking?

JIM: I've given it up, Sal.

SALLY: So you said last week.

JIM: This time I am.

SALLY: Then go away and *do* it, Jimmy. I want these two people to talk,

JIM: *(To Austin, as he leaves.)* Next time you see me, I'll be a shadow of my former self. I'll be a negative entity, defined not by what I am but by what I am not. You will perceive and know me simply as a nonsmoker.

SALLY: Just go, Jimmy. Please.

JIM: All right. But I hope you'll remember me for when I came. And saw. And conquered the habit. *(Jim goes. The party sounds continue within.)*

SALLY: He's a nice man, but he smokes.

AUSTIN: Give him a chance, Sally.

SALLY: I'm giving *you* a chance, Austin . . . this is Ruth . . . and Ruth, this is Austin . . .

AUSTIN: *(Extending his hand.)* How do you do.

RUTH: Hello. *(They shake hands.)*

SALLY: Ruth's from out of town.

AUSTIN: Then welcome to Boston.

SALLY: *(Looking from one to the other.)* And?

RUTH: He doesn't remember.

SALLY: *(To Austin.)* You don't remember Ruth?

AUSTIN: Should I?

SALLY: She remembers you.

RUTH: I do. I definitely do.

SALLY: She said she noticed you the minute you walked into the room.

RUTH: Oh not the *minute* . . .

SALLY: *(To Austin.)* Did you notice *her?*

AUSTIN: *(With a polite bow.)* I certainly do now.

RUTH: I told you he wouldn't remember.

SALLY: Well then *get* him to.

RUTH: I'll try.

SALLY: And let me break the ice here: Austin, I told Ruth you were divorced, and I'm hereby telling you that Ruth is.

RUTH: Not divorced. Separated.

SALLY: *(Coming down to Ruth.)* Judith said you were divorced.

114 A. R. GURNEY

RUTH: Judith thinks I should be.

SALLY: *(Recovering her equanimity.)* Well, the point is, here you are. Now make the most of it. *(She goes. Pause.)*

AUSTIN: We've met?

RUTH: We have.

AUSTIN: When?

RUTH: Think back.

AUSTIN: To when?

RUTH: Just think.

AUSTIN: I'm thinking . . . *(He looks at her carefully.)* Ruth, eh?

RUTH: Ruth.

AUSTIN: What's your last name?

RUTH: That won't help.

AUSTIN: What was your last name when we met?

RUTH: You never knew my last name.

AUSTIN: I just knew Ruth.

RUTH: That's all you knew. *(Pause.)*

AUSTIN: Were you married?

RUTH: When?

AUSTIN: When we met.

RUTH: Oh no.

AUSTIN: Was I?

RUTH: No.

AUSTIN: Ah. Then we're talking about way back.

RUTH: Way, way back.

AUSTIN: Were we in college?

RUTH: No.

AUSTIN: School, then.

RUTH: I doubt if we would have met either at school or at college.

AUSTIN: Why not?

RUTH: Not everybody in the world went to Groton and Harvard.

AUSTIN: So I have learned in the course of my life. *(She laughs.)* I feel like a fool.

RUTH: Why?

AUSTIN: An attractive woman came into my life. And I don't remember.

RUTH: My hair was different then.

AUSTIN: Still. This is embarrassing.

RUTH: You want a hint?

AUSTIN: No, I should get it on my own . . . *(Looks at her carefully.)* There's something . . . . Goddammit, I pride myself on my memory. I can remember when I was two and a half years old.

RUTH: You can not.

AUSTIN: I can. I can remember still being in my crib.

RUTH: I doubt that.

AUSTIN: No really. I can remember . . .

RUTH: What?

AUSTIN: It's a little racy.

RUTH: Tell me.

AUSTIN: I don't know you well enough.

RUTH: Oh come on. We're both adults.

AUSTIN: I can remember being wakened in my crib by a strange sound. A kind of soft, rustling sound. And . . . *(He stops.)* Never mind.

RUTH: Go on. You can't stop now.

AUSTIN: It was my nurse—we had this young nurse. I specifically remember seeing her through the bars of my crib. Standing by the window. In the moonlight. Naked. Stroking her body. And I lay there watching her.

RUTH: Through the bars of your crib.

AUSTIN: Through the bars of my crib. *(Pause.)*

RUTH: Austin.

AUSTIN: What?

RUTH: *(Melodramatically.)* I am that nurse.

AUSTIN: No.

RUTH: No. Just kidding. *(Both laugh.)* No, we met after college.

AUSTIN: After college, but before I was married.

RUTH: And before I was.

AUSTIN: You are presenting a rather narrow window of opportunity, madam.

RUTH: I know it.

AUSTIN: I got married soon after college.

RUTH: As I did, sir. As did I.

AUSTIN: So we are talking about a moment in our lives when we were both . . . what? Relative free and clear.

RUTH: That's what we were. Relatively. Free and clear.

AUSTIN: Those moments are rare.

RUTH: They certainly are. *(Sounds of the party within. Marion comes out, gray-haired and maternal.)*

MARION: *(Looking out and around.)* Oh! . . . . Ah! . . . . Oh! . . . . Now that is what I call a beautiful view! *(She calls toward offstage.)* Roy, just come out here and look at this view! You can see all of Boston harbor! *(Roy comes out hesitatingly. He is grim and cold.)* See, sweetheart? There's the USS Constitution right over there, with the lights on the rigging! *(To Ruth.)* Old Ironsides! *(Looking out.)* And behind it is Revere Beach! And that must be Salem to the north. And those little lights way off to the right might even be Cape Cod. *(To Austin.)* Excuse me, sir. You look like one of those people who know everything.

AUSTIN: Oh I'd hardly say that.

MARION: Do you at least know Boston?

AUSTIN: I've lived here all my life.

MARION: Well then could you tell me: are those little lights Cape Cod?

AUSTIN: They are indeed. They're the lights of Provincetown.

MARION: And I imagine on the other side of the building you can see the Old North Church, and the Charles River, and the spires of Harvard.

AUSTIN: I imagine you can.

MARION: *(Taking his arm.)* Oh, isn't that spectacular! Look, Roy! Just look! It's all here, sweetie! *(Roy moves up reluctantly; Marion turns to Austin.)* And he wants to leave it.

ROY: I have to leave it.

MARION: You don't have to at all.

ROY: *(To Ruth.)* I have to move south.

MARION: *(To Austin.)* He doesn't have to at all.

ROY: *(To Ruth.)* The weather is getting me down.

MARION: Now you'll hear about his arthritis.

ROY: I've got terrible arthritis.

MARION: It's all in his mind.

ROY: Notice how cold it is. Early September and you can already feel the chill.

MARION: *(To Ruth.)* Are you cold?

ROY: Of course she's cold.

MARION: *I'm* not cold at all.

ROY: Let the lady talk. *(To Ruth.)* Are you cold?

RUTH: *(With a glance at Austin.)* Actually since we've been out here, we've been getting warmer.

MARION: *(To Roy.)* You see? It's all in your mind.

ROY: *(To Ruth.)* Last night it got down to fifty-eight.

MARION: *(To Austin.)* He talks about temperatures all day long. He wanders around the house tapping thermometers.

ROY: *(To Ruth.)* I've got arthritis in my knees and hips.

MARION: *(To Austin.)* Will he take a pill? Will he submit to medication? He will not.

ROY: I was once a runner.

MARION: He's never gotten over it.

ROY: I ran the Marathon six times.

MARION: I had to line up the whole family on Commonwealth Avenue every Patriot's Day and cheer him on towards the Prudential Center.

RUTH: What's Patriot's Day?

AUSTIN: *(To Ruth.)* Ah. It's our own special holiday. It commemorates Paul Revere's ride to Lexington and Concord. " 'Twas the Eighteenth of April, in '75 . . ."

MARION: *(Taking over.)* ". . . and hardly a man who is now alive
Who remembers that famous day and year . . ."

AUSTIN: Good for you. *(To Ruth.)* These days we celebrate it by running a marathon.

RUTH: Sounds very Boston.

AUSTIN: What do you mean?

RUTH: Everyone running madly towards an insurance building.

AUSTIN: *(Laughing.)* Ah well I look at it in another way. We celebrate a Greek Marathon because we're the Athens of America.

MARION: Exactly! *(To Roy.)* Listen to this man, Roy. He knows. He's chosen to live here all his life. *(To Austin.)* I wish you'd tell my husband why.

RUTH: Yes. I'd be interested in that, too.

AUSTIN: Chosen to live here? Oh I don't think I ever *chose*. I was born here, I've lived here, I've been here, and now I don't think I could be anywhere else.

MARION: That because it's the most civilized city in America.

RUTH: *(To Austin.)* Do you agree?

AUSTIN: *(Bowing to Marion.)* I'd never disagree with such a passionate advocate.

MARION: Thank you, sir.

ROY: *(To Ruth.)* I did the Marathon of seventy-eight under four hours.

MARION: She doesn't *care*, Roy.

ROY: I came in six hundred and seventy-nine out of over fifteen thousand registered contenders.

MARION: Roy . . .

ROY: Now I'm paying for it. Now it's bone against bone. You should see the X-rays.

MARION: *(To Austin.)* He's found this retirement community in Florida.

ROY: *(To Ruth.)* It has its own golf course.

MARION: It looks like a concentration camp.

ROY: Oh for Chrissake!

MARION: It has gates! It has guards!

ROY: At least I can stagger around a golf course.

MARION: *(To Austin.)* It's an armed camp. He's moving me from Athens to Sparta.

ROY: At least I'll get exercise. At least I'll be out of doors.

MARION: We'd be leaving our friends, leaving our children . . .

ROY: A man's got to do something. A man can't just sit and grow old.

MARION: Leaving our grandchildren . . .

ROY: Brace yourselves. Here it comes. I sense it coming.

MARION: We have two grandchildren living almost around the corner. *(She opens her purse.)*

ROY: Here come the pictures.

MARION: I just want them to see.

ROY: *(Walking away.)* Watch it. Sometimes she flashes her pornography collection.

MARION: *(Sitting down; getting out the pictures.)* That's not even funny, Roy! *(Shows Ruth a picture.)* There. See? Could you walk away from that? *(Austin stops walking away.)* I mean, don't you just want to take a bite out them?

ROY: *(Now warming his hands at the outdoor candle.)* They're not interested, Marion.

MARION: You mean *you're* not interested, Roy. *(To others.)* He doesn't like his grandchildren.

ROY: *(Coming down.)* I like it when they come, I like it when they go.

MARION: He won't help, he won't pitch in.

ROY: You have the instinct. I don't.

MARION: Everyone has the instinct.

ROY: *(With increasing passion.)* I have the instinct to migrate south! I have the instinct to land on a golf course!

MARION: See what I'm up against?

ROY: And now I have the instinct to go inside and get warm!

MARION: *(With equal passion.)* All I want to do is enjoy my own grandchildren!

ROY: You can enjoy them after I'm dead! *(He goes in. An embarrassing pause.)*

MARION: *(To Austin and Ruth.)* Why have I followed that man around all my life? Answer me that. Do I have to follow him to Florida, just so *he* can follow a golf ball around? *(Slaps her knees.)* My knees are fine! There's nothing wrong with *my* knees. *(Gets up, starts out.)* One of these days he might look over his shoulder and find *me* running my *own* marathon! Right back here. To this wonderful city. And that perfectly marvelous view! *(She looks at the view one more time, glances at Austin and Ruth, and then hurries in after Roy.)* Roy! . . . Roy! *(And she is off. Pause.)*

AUSTIN: *(To Ruth.)* That view may change.

RUTH: Oh yes?

AUSTIN: There is a group—a consortium—which has approaches our bank with a serious proposal to turn Boston harbor into—what is the expression?— a "theme park." Can you imagine? One of the great natural harbors of the New World! These old wharves have already given way to condominia, such as this one. And soon, if the developers get their way, that lovely string of islands, which once guided the great sailing vessels into port, will be transformed into fake Indian encampments and phony Pilgrim villages. We'll be invaded by tourists from all over multicultural America, lining up to see daily reenactments of the Boston Tea Party and the landing at Plymouth Rock.

RUTH: And are you fighting it, tooth and nail?

AUSTIN: No.

RUTH: No?

AUSTIN: How can you fight history?

RUTH: I suppose by making it.

AUSTIN: Yes, well, apparently you and I made our own private chronicle sometime ago, didn't we? Where were we?

RUTH: BM.

AUSTIN: I beg your pardon.

RUTH: Before Marriage.

AUSTIN: Ah.

RUTH: But after college.

AUSTIN: Was I working then?

RUTH: No.

AUSTIN: No?

RUTH: You claimed you were working. But you were really playing.

AUSTIN: You mean, I was taking time out from my obligations at home to serve my country abroad.

RUTH: I mean, you were a very handsome young Naval officer steaming around the Mediterranean.

AUSTIN: You mean, I was defending western democracy against the constant threat of Soviet domination.

RUTH: I mean, you were living it up while you had the chance.

AUSTIN: Hmmm.

RUTH: Yes. Hmmm. *(Pause. Ruth hums a tune, "The Isle of Capri.")*

AUSTIN: Is that a hint?

RUTH: Of course. *(She hums a few more bars.)*

AUSTIN: Sing the words.

RUTH: You sing them. *(She hums again.)*

AUSTIN: *(Singing.)* "Twas on the Isle of Tra-Lee . . ."

RUTH: Wrong.

AUSTIN: " 'Twas on the Isle of Capri that I met her . . ."

RUTH: Right.

AUSTIN: The Isle of Capri?

RUTH: Right.

AUSTIN: Let's see . . . . Capri . . . . Our ship came into Naples . . . . And a bunch of us had liberty . . . so we took a boat out to the Isle of Capri.

RUTH: And?

AUSTIN: And . . . . God, let's see . . . . We saw the Blue Grotto, and we took a cable car or something . . .

RUTH: *(Singing.)* "Funiculi, funicula . . ."

AUSTIN: We took a funicular up some hill. And there was a restaurant on top. And we had some beers . . . *(It begins to come back.)* . . . And at the next table was a bunch of American girls who were touring Italy . . .

RUTH: Marsh Tours. See Italy in ten days. Summer Special for the sisters of Sigma Nu from the University of Southern Illinois.

AUSTIN: I struck up a conversation with a girl named . . . Ruth!

RUTH: *(Italian accent.)* Bravo!

AUSTIN: Hello, Ruth!

RUTH: Hello, Austin. *(They shake hands again.)*

AUSTIN: What a memory!

RUTH: For that at least.

AUSTIN: We got along, didn't we?

RUTH: We did. Immediately.

AUSTIN: I remember cutting you off from the herd . . .

RUTH: Oh no. I cut *you* off. From *your* herd.

AUSTIN: Anyway we ended up out on some terrace . . .

RUTH: Overlooking the bay of Naples . . .

AUSTIN: Which is one of the great natural harbors of the *old* world.

RUTH: Sorento to the south . . .

AUSTIN: Ischia to the north . . .

RUTH: Vesuvius smoking in the distance . . .

AUSTIN: Actually, I think Vesuvius had given up smoking.

RUTH: I suppose it had to. There must have been pressure from the people of Pompeii.

AUSTIN: I should think so. *(Both laugh. The party within is getting livelier, with livelier music. Duane sticks his head out. He wears a short-sleeved shirt and high-waisted pants.)*

DUANE: Hi there. I'm Duane.

AUSTIN: Hello, Duane . . .

RUTH: Hello, Duane . . .

AUSTIN: Austin and Ruth.

DUANE: Seem to have lost the wife.

AUSTIN: I don't believe she's here, Duane.

DUANE: Small woman? Maybe a little . . . overemotional? *(He peers over the upstage railing.)* She's been upset lately.

AUSTIN: Oh.

DUANE: Reason is, I don't think she wants me to upgrade.

AUSTIN: Upgrade?

DUANE: I've been shopping around for a new IBM compatible with an Intel 486 processor.

AUSTIN: Ah.

DUANE: I think she'd prefer I stay with my old machine.

AUSTIN: I see.

DUANE: So tonight we meet this VP from Data-Tech out on 128, and the guy's just *bought* one! With a new scanner that would knock your socks off! He starts telling us about it, and my wife just turns tail and walks away. *(Ruth walks away.)*

AUSTIN: Oh dear.

DUANE: I keep saying I'll upgrade her, too, if she wants. I'd be glad to upgrade her. I mean, she's still using DOS 2.0, if you can believe it.

AUSTIN: Oh.

DUANE: I tell her she's backspacing herself into the dark ages.

AUSTIN: Ah.

DUANE: Well, she's in the files somewhere. I'll just have to search and locate, that's all. I've checked the bar, now I'll check the bathroom. I mean, she may not appreciate a premium machine, but she sure appreciates premium vodka.

AUSTIN: We'll keep an eye out for her, Duane.

DUANE: Thanks guys. *(Starts off; then stops.)* Say. You folks look like Power-book users.

AUSTIN: What?

DUANE: Just point and click, am I right?

RUTH: That's one way of putting it.

DUANE: Well, you're way ahead of my wife. She's still hung up on Wordstar 2000. Won't install Word Perfect. Refuses even to touch the mouse. *(Duane goes off.)*

AUSTIN: *(To Ruth.)* Touch the mouse?

RUTH: Skip it.

AUSTIN: Maybe we'd better . . . Let's sail back to the bay of Naples.

RUTH: Yes. Quickly. Let's.

AUSTIN: Suddenly I want to know . . . . Did I . . .

RUTH: Did you what?

AUSTIN: Did I kiss you on Capri?

RUTH: Yes you did.

AUSTIN: I did?

RUTH: Oh yes. Almost immediately.

AUSTIN: I was a horny bastard.

RUTH: You seemed so. Yes.

AUSTIN: What else did I do?

RUTH: You talked.

AUSTIN: I talked?

RUTH: You said things.

AUSTIN: Did you say things?

RUTH: No. Not really.

AUSTIN: What did you do?

RUTH: I listened.

AUSTIN: I talked, you listened.

RUTH: Primarily. *(They are sitting down by now.)*

AUSTIN: Was I drunk?

RUTH: A little.

AUSTIN: I used to get smashed whenever I went ashore.

RUTH: Smashed or not, you seemed dead serious.

AUSTIN: About you?

RUTH: About yourself.

AUSTIN: Good God.

RUTH: I don't think I've ever heard anyone else say the things you said. Before or since. That's really why I remembered you. *(More party sounds; moody jazz music. Nancy comes out, carrying a plate of food and a bottle of beer. She wears slacks and might have a Louise Brooks–style hairdo. She might speak with a Long Island lockjaw accent.)*

NANCY: They have food in there. Don't let me interrupt, but they have food. *(Shows them her plate.)* See? Food. *(Looks at it.)* I think it's food. *(Tastes it.)* Yes. It's definitely food. *(She noisily drags the chaise downstage.)* Don't think I'm antisocial, but someone else is joining me, so I'll sit over here. *(Gets settled.)* Continue your conversation. Don't mind me.

AUSTIN: *(To Ruth.)* Are you hungry?

RUTH: Not really. Are you?

AUSTIN: Not yet.

RUTH: Why rush for food?

AUSTIN: I agree. *(Pause.)*

NANCY: *(Looking at her food.)* I don't know what this is exactly. It looks like chicken. Shall I taste it? I'd better taste it. *(She tastes it.)* Yes. This is definitely chicken. In a kind of cream of curry sauce. *(Takes another bite.)* And there's dill in this. Just a tad of dill. It's quite good, actually. I recommend it. *(She begins to eat.)* But please: go on with what you were saying. You both look terribly intense.

AUSTIN: *(To Ruth.)* How about another drink?

RUTH: No thanks. I'm fine.

AUSTIN: Sure?

RUTH: Absolutely.

AUSTIN: People drink less these days. *(Nancy is chugalugging her bottle of beer.)*

RUTH: Some people. *(Pause.)*

NANCY: I don't know where my companion is. We were having a perfectly pleasant conversation, and she said, "Oh there comes the food. Let's get food," so we got into line, and I thought out here we might be able to least to sit *down*. So here I am. *(Looks off.)* But where is *she*?

AUSTIN: I imagine it's quite crowded in there.

NANCY: It is. It's a mob scene.

RUTH: Maybe your friend got lost in the shuffle.

NANCY: Maybe she wanted to get lost . . . . Or maybe she wanted *me* to get lost.

AUSTIN: Oh I doubt that.

NANCY: You never know. People can be very peculiar. It's too bad, though. I thought I was getting on this one. I thought we clicked. *(Austin looks at her, is a little taken aback, then turns to Ruth.)*

AUSTIN: Are you cold?

RUTH: Oh no.

AUSTIN: It's not summer any more. That's why people are staying indoors.

RUTH: I think it's fine.

AUSTIN: Tell me if you're cold. We'll go in.

RUTH: Do you want to go in?

AUSTIN: No I don't. Do you?

RUTH: No I really don't.

AUSTIN: If we went in, we might get lost in the shuffle, too.

RUTH: Exactly. *(Pause.)*

NANCY: *(Eating something else.)* Now *this* is a vegetable casserole. That's all this is. Zucchini, of course. *(Sticks her tongue out.)* And tomatoes. And a bean or two. It's all right. It'll pass. C minus, I'd say. If that. *(She takes a bite of bread.)* But the bread is good. Very chewy. It would be better with butter. No one serves butter in Boston any more. But still, it's fine. *(She continues to eat.)*

AUSTIN: *(To Ruth.)* So. You were saying . . .

RUTH: *(Softly.)* Wait.

AUSTIN: We were talking about . . .

RUTH: *(Putting a hand on his arm.)* Just wait.

AUSTIN: I'm always waiting.

RUTH: I know.

AUSTIN: You *know?*

RUTH: That's one of the things you told me on Capri.

AUSTIN: I told you that?

RUTH: Sshh. *(Nancy is now looking at them. Pause.)*

NANCY: *(Crumpling up her napkin.)* Well that's that. *(Puts her plate aside, gets up.)* That is definitely that. That was very pleasant. Of course, it might have been slightly *more* pleasant if I hadn't had to eat alone. I mean, she was right behind me in the line. And then she just disappears. It was really very rude. *(She opens her compact, puts on lipstick.)* Are you two married?

AUSTIN: Oh no. God, no. No.

NANCY: I thought you might be married and were having a fight.

AUSTIN: No, no.

NANCY: Are you lovers, then?

RUTH: No.

NANCY: Be frank.

RUTH: No, we're not.

NANCY: *(Hovering over them.)* Then you're arranging an affair, aren't you? You're arranging an assignation.

AUSTIN: No, we're not doing that either. I don't think we're doing that. *(To Ruth.)* Are we doing that?

RUTH: I don't know. Are we?

AUSTIN: I think we're just talking

RUTH: That's right. That's all. Just talking.

AUSTIN: Just two old friends, catching up.

NANCY: *(Looking them up and down; then focusing particularly on Ruth.)* I see. Well. Life has taught me this: even if the main course is somewhat disappointing, there's always dessert. *(She goes out. Pause.)*

AUSTIN: A rather disconcerting woman.

RUTH: I'll say.

AUSTIN: We might have been a little rude to her.

RUTH: Rude?

AUSTIN: We didn't . . . bring her in.

RUTH: I didn't want to bring her in.

AUSTIN: We should have.

RUTH: Why?

AUSTIN: It was the polite thing to do.

RUTH: Oh hell.

AUSTIN: I worry about these things.

RUTH: That's because you went to prep school.

AUSTIN: No, not just because of that. I believe in civility.

RUTH: Being from Boston . . .

AUSTIN: Well, I do. The more the world falls apart, the more I believe in it. Some guy elbows ahead of me in a line, I like to bow and say, "Go ahead, sir, if it's that important to you." Treat people with civility and maybe they'll learn to behave that way.

RUTH: It's been my experience that they'll feel guilty and behave worse.

AUSTIN: Well *I* feel guilty now. Because I wasn't polite.

RUTH: I feel fine.

AUSTIN: You do?

RUTH: Yes I do. Because we were doing something very rare in this world that is falling apart. We were making a connection. That's something that happens only once in a while, and less and less as we get older, so we shouldn't let anything get in its way.

AUSTIN: O.K., Ruth. I'll buy that. O.K. *(Sounds of party laughter from within. Duane sticks his head again.)*

DUANE: Hi there again.

AUSTIN: Hello . . . ah . . .

DUANE: Duane.

AUSTIN: Duane.

RUTH: Duane.

DUANE: Thought you folks should know: I found the wife.

AUSTIN: In the bathroom?

DUANE: In the kitchen. The caterer was feeding her coffee.

AUSTIN: Uh-oh.

DUANE: No, no. Everything's batched and patched. *(Glances off.)* She's right there in the hall, having a quiet conversation with an old friend from Wellesley. *(Waves to her.)*

AUSTIN: I'm glad, Duane. .

DUANE: You see, what we did was sit right down at the kitchen table and talked things over.

AUSTIN: Sounds very cozy.

DUANE: Sure was. We put our cards on the table. And I suddenly retrieved the fact that today's her birthday!

AUSTIN: Really!

DUANE: No wonder she was upset. There I was, yakking away about the 486, and she just wanted personal recognition.

AUSTIN: Why don't you buy her a present, Duane?

DUANE: Right. Hey, how about a gift certificate to Radio Shack? . . . Just kidding . . . . No, I'm a romantic guy if you push the right buttons. In fact, I already have a present for her.

AUSTIN: Already?

DUANE: What I did was telephone the kids immediately and tell them to modem into the new twenty-four hour nationwide home shopping free delivery channel. Tonight, when we get home, my wife is going to find one dozen long-stem red roses waiting in the bedroom, personal note attached.

AUSTIN: That might do it.

DUANE: It sure should. Maybe I'm learning something in my old age. *(Calling off.)* Right, honey? Maybe I'm finally learning that women like to be put in their own special subdirectory! . . . Honey? *(To Austin and Ruth.)* Pardon, folks. Once again the wife seems to have scooted off the screen. *(Duane goes off.)*

AUSTIN: I have the terrible feeling that our future grandchildren will be able to respond to Duane more than to anyone else at this party.

RUTH: Austin . . .

AUSTIN: Hmmm?

RUTH: Tell me. Did it ever happen?

AUSTIN: Did what ever happen?

RUTH: What you told me about. On Capri.

AUSTIN: What did I tell you about, on Capri.

RUTH: I guess it never happened.

AUSTIN: You've lost me, Ruth.

RUTH: When we had our long talk, you told me you had this problem.

AUSTIN: I did?

RUTH: You did. You said you have a major problem. That's what I remember most about the whole evening. That's really why I wanted to talk to you again. I had to know how it came out.

AUSTIN: What was my problem?

RUTH: Want me to say it?

AUSTIN: Sure.

RUTH: You won't be embarrassed?

AUSTIN: I hope not.

RUTH: You said—and I can quote you almost exactly . . .

AUSTIN: After all these years?

RUTH: After all these years . . . . You said that you were sure something terrible was going to happen to you in the course of your life.

AUSTIN: Did I say that?

RUTH: You did.

AUSTIN: Something terrible?

RUTH: That's what you said. You said you were waiting for it to happen. You said you'd already spent most of your life waiting.

AUSTIN: What? All of twenty-two years? Just waiting?

RUTH: You said it again a few minutes ago.

AUSTIN: Oh well . . .

RUTH: No, but that's what you said. You said that you were sure that sooner or later something awful was going to descend on you and ruin your life forever.

AUSTIN: God. How melodramatic.

RUTH: It didn't seem so, then.

AUSTIN: You took me seriously?

RUTH: Absolutely.

AUSTIN: I must have been bombed out of my mind.

RUTH: I'm not so sure . . .

AUSTIN: And I must have been trying to snow you.

RUTH: Maybe . . .

AUSTIN: I mean, there we were on the Isle of Capri, overlooking the Bay of Naples . . . me, ashore on liberty after ten days at sea . . . you, an attractive young girl . . .

RUTH: Thank you.

AUSTIN: I must have been trying to snow the pants off you.

RUTH: Well if you were, you succeeded.

AUSTIN: I did?

RUTH: You most certainly did. In fact, after we got back to the mainland, I invited you up to my room.

AUSTIN: Come on! Surely I'd remember that.

RUTH: The reason you don't remember it is, you said no.

AUSTIN: I said no?

RUTH: Or rather, no thank you.

AUSTIN: And did I give a reason for saying no thank you?

RUTH: Oh yes. You said you couldn't get involved, because of your problem.

AUSTIN: What?

RUTH: You said you liked me much too much to drag me into it.

AUSTIN: I said that?

RUTH: I swear. You said you liked me very much, you liked me more than anyone you'd ever met, and therefore you had to say goodnight. *(Pause.)*

AUSTIN: I must have been drunk as a skunk.

RUTH: By then you were sober as a judge.

AUSTIN: Hmmm.

RUTH: So. You gave me a big kiss goodnight and went back to your ship.

AUSTIN: And what did you do?

RUTH: Well, if you remember, everybody else was hanging around the hotel bar, drinking beer . . .

AUSTIN: Did you do that? *(Pause.)*

RUTH: No.

AUSTIN: No?

RUTH: I went out on the town with a friend of yours.

AUSTIN: A friend?

RUTH: Another officer.

AUSTIN: Who?

RUTH: Oh Lord, I don't remember. I think he had an Irish name.

AUSTIN: *(Immediately.)* Denny Doyle? Assistant Gunnery Officer on the forward turret?

RUTH: That could have been the one.

AUSTIN: Denny Doyle? That son of a bitch! He's from Boston, too, you know. He came back and ran for the State Legislature!

RUTH: I'll be he won.

AUSTIN: He sure did. He had every cop in South Boston in his hip pocket . . . .
Oh Christ! You did *Naples* with Denny *Doyle?*

RUTH: I didn't feel like rejoining the "herd."

AUSTIN: That guy was a mover from the word go!

RUTH: He was full of life, I'll say that.

AUSTIN: He was full of bull!

RUTH: Well, he was fun.

AUSTIN: I don't think he ever told me he took you out.

RUTH: I'm glad he didn't.

AUSTIN: He must have thought you were my girl.

RUTH: For a moment there, I thought I was.

AUSTIN: *(Bowing to her.)* I apologize, madam. For turning such a lovely lady down. And leaving her to the lascivious advances of Denny Doyle.

RUTH: Well you have your reasons.

AUSTIN: Apparently I did.

RUTH: I'll never forget it, though. What you told me. I've met lots of men with lots of lines before and since—but no one ever told me anything like that.

AUSTIN: Some line. What a dumb thing to tell anyone.

RUTH: Oh no. It worked, in the long run.

AUSTIN: It worked?

RUTH: It's made me think about you ever since.

AUSTIN: Really? More than Denny Doyle?

RUTH: Much more. Particularly when . . .

AUSTIN: When what?

RUTH: When terrible things happened to me. *(Pause.)*

AUSTIN: *Now* would you like a drink?

RUTH: No thanks.

AUSTIN: Actually, I would.

RUTH: I'll bet you would.

AUSTIN: Shall we go in while I get a drink?

RUTH: You go in, if you want.

AUSTIN: I'm not going to leave you out here alone.

RUTH: Why not?

AUSTIN: It's rude.

RUTH: Oh nuts to that.

AUSTIN: You're not cold?

RUTH: Not at all.

AUSTIN: Then I'll be back. *(He starts in.)*

RUTH: Austin . . . *(He stops.)* How do I know you're not retreating back to your ship?

AUSTIN: Because I'm older now.

RUTH: Which means?

AUSTIN: Which means I learn from my mistakes.

RUTH: That's good to hear. *(He starts in again, then stops.)*

AUSTIN: Will you be here when I get back.

RUTH: Sure. Unless Denny Doyle shows up again.

AUSTIN: He just might. He's now head of the Port Authority and wild as a Kennedy.

RUTH: Then you better hurry.

AUSTIN: I will. And I'll get us both drinks. *(He goes. Pause. Ruth settles onto the chaise, looks out. We hear the party within, with more sentimental music now in the background. Ted and Esther come out. They wear bright colors and have southern accents.)*

TED: *(To Ruth.)* Hi there. We're the McAlisters.

RUTH: Hello, McAlisters.

ESTHER: Ted and Esther.

RUTH: I'm Ruth.

TED: *(As they look at the views.)* We just moved north six months ago.

ESTHER: Can't you tell from how we talk?

TED: We're trying to make the most of Boston.

ESTHER: It's a fascinating experience.

TED: We thought it would be a stuffy old town.

ESTHER: You know: stuffy New England . . .

TED: But it's not at all.

ESTHER: It's different, it's exciting. No wonder they call it the New Boston. *(They come down to Ruth on the chaise.)*

TED: We're making a point of meeting everyone at this party.

ESTHER: And everyone has a story.

TED: If you can just find out what it is. For example, we met man, a perfectly ordinary looking man, who turns out to be a real Indian . . .

ESTHER: Native-American, honey . . .

TED: That's right. A Tuscarora, actually.

ESTHER: He teaches history at Tufts.

TED: Think of that. A Tuscarora chief. Teaching history at Tufts. And there he was, drinking a dry martini.

ESTHER: Teddy said, be careful of the old firewater.

TED: And he laughed.

ESTHER: He did. He laughed.

TED: Oh yes. And we met a couple who travels to Asia Minor every year.

ESTHER: To do archeology.

TED: So I said, maybe we should all talk Turkey.

ESTHER: They didn't laugh.

TED: He did. She didn't.

ESTHER: Oh well. She's from Cambridge.

TED: And we met several Jewish people.

ESTHER: They're all so *frank*.

TED: That's because they've suffered throughout history. You'd be frank, too, if you'd suffered throughout history.

ESTHER: Oh, and there's an African-American woman in there. Who writes poetry.

TED: And we met this Hispanic gentleman . . .

ESTHER: Latino, honey. He prefers Latino. And he wants to . . . . Shall I say this, Ted?

TED: Sure, say it, we're among friends.

ESTHER: He says he wants to become a woman.

TED: Said he was seriously thinking about it.

ESTHER: Can you imagine? Of course, they say Boston doctors are the finest in the world.

TED: He may have been pulling our leg.

ESTHER: I know. But still . . . I mean, ouch.

TED: And we met a woman from Cambodia, and a man from Peru . . .

ESTHER: He looked like an Aztec prince.

TED: Half-Aztec, anyway. *(Both laugh.)*

ESTHER: Anyway he had a story. Everyone has a story.

TED: What's your story, Ruth?

RUTH: Mine? Oh gosh. That would take years. Are you prepared to sit down and listen to all three volumes. *(Ted and Esther pull up chairs.)*

ESTHER: Are you a Bostonian, at least?

TED: At least tell us that.

RUTH: Oh no. That's the last thing I am. I'm just visiting my friend Judith. She's the Bostonian. She moved specially from New York to play in the Symphony.

ESTHER: We *met* her! She plays the viola?

RUTH: That's the one.

TED: We met her! She's a little . . . nervous, isn't she?

RUTH: Oh, she just gets upset when things get out of tune.

TED: She thinks things are out of tune?

RUTH: She sure thinks I am.

ESTHER: Where are you from, Ruth?

RUTH: Originally? Oh well, I was born in the Midwest, but I've kind of kicked around over the years.

TED: And now?

RUTH: And now you might say I'm circling over Logan Airport. Wondering whether to land.

TED: Do it. Come on in.

ESTHER: It's a real nice place to live.

RUTH: That's what Judith says. She thinks I could use a little stability.

ESTHER: Why?

RUTH: Oh, she thinks I court disaster.

TED: That must mean you're married. *(Everyone laughs.)*

ESTHER: Are you?

RUTH: Four times.

TED: Hey, we're talking to a veteran here.

RUTH: Twice to the same man.

ESTHER: Oh my.

RUTH: He was very . . . persuasive. *(Pause.)* Still is.

TED: We're talking to a real veteran here.

RUTH: I was married to my first husband for only seven days.

ESTHER: Mercy! What happened?

RUTH: Bad luck. He was killed in Asia.

TED: A real veteran here. A veteran of foreign wars.

RUTH: Korea. Long after the war. A land mine exploded. And he just happened to be there.

ESTHER: Oh dear.

RUTH: It was just bad luck, that's all. Just very bad luck.

ESTHER: That's a sad story. But at least it's a story. You see? Everyone has a story.

TED: Any children, Ruth?

RUTH: *(After a pause.)* One daughter. *(Pause.)* Not by him. *(Pause.)* By my second husband. *(Pause.)* You don't want to hear this.

ESTHER: No, we do, we do.

TED: If you want to tell us. *(Pause.)*

RUTH: We lost her. *(Pause.)* To leukemia. *(Pause.)* When she was eleven years old.

TED: It must be terrible to lose a child.

ESTHER: It must be the worst thing in the world.

RUTH: It is. It's . . . hell. *(Pause.)* We brought her home. She died at home. That . . . helped.

ESTHER: You and your husband pulled together . . .

RUTH: Yes, we did. We pulled together. But when she was gone, we had nothing left to . . . pull. So we pulled apart.

ESTHER: Oh dear.

RUTH: But. Life goes on.

TED: It does, Ruth. It definitely does.

RUTH: So I married a Man of the West.

ESTHER: Number three?

RUTH: And four.

ESTHER: Oh my.

TED: He's a cowboy?

RUTH: He thinks he is . . . . He'd like to be . . . . He drives a Ford Bronco.

TED: At least he buys an American vehicle.

RUTH: Oh yes. He's very—American.

ESTHER: Do you like the West, Ruth?

RUTH: The answer to that is yes and no. *(Pause.)* I'm a little at sea about that. *(Looks out.)* Maybe I'll find my moorings in Boston Harbor.

ESTHER: We're all wanderers, aren't we?

TED: Ships that pass in the night.

RUTH: Some are. *(Glances off where Austin has gone.)* Some aren't. *(Pause.)* Lord knows I am.

TED: I didn't think we would be. But we are now.

ESTHER: We got sent here from Atlanta by his company.

TED: Out of the blue. Just pick up stakes and go, they said.

ESTHER: We didn't want to do at all.

TED: We thought we'd freeze to death, to begin with.

ESTHER: But finally we just said what the hell.

TED: We held our noses and jumped, and here we are.

ESTHER: We got an apartment on Marlborough Street . . .

TED: Surrounded by students . . .

ESTHER: And we've taken the Freedom Trail.

TED: And we walk to the Gardiner Museum . . .

ESTHER: And Symphony Hall . . .

TED: And we even got mugged once . . .

ESTHER: All he took was our Red Sox tickets . . .

TED: And we're taking a course on Italian at the Harvard Extension . . .

ESTHER: "Nel mezzo di mia vita . . ."

TED: *(Quietly; seriously.)* That's Dante. "In the middle of my life."

ESTHER: *(Looking at him tenderly.)* Which is the way we feel. In the middle of our lives. *(They nuzzle each other.)*

TED: I think everyone over fifty should change their life, Ruth.

RUTH: Oh well, I've done that, all right. That I have definitely done. Trouble is, I keep doing it.

TED: We were in a rut before, I'll tell you that.

ESTHER: We were. Maybe we didn't remarry, but we sure remade our bed.

TED: Now it's more fun sleeping in it.

ESTHER: Oh now Ted . . .

TED: The sex has perked way up.

ESTHER: Ted, please . . .

TED: *(Shyly.)* The South shall rise again!

ESTHER: Teddy!

TED: So welcome to Boston, Ruth. It's a great town.

RUTH: I hope you're right. *(Austin comes back carrying two drinks in one hand and two plates of food in the other.)*

AUSTIN: I'm back.

RUTH: These are the McAlisters.

TED: Ted and Esther.

AUSTIN: *(Bowing.)* Austin here.

ESTHER: *(Checking her watch.)* Actually, we've got to go.

TED: Right you are. *(To Austin and Ruth.)* We made reservations.

ESTHER: There's a place on Route One where you dance.

TED: The old kind of dancing. And not too Laurence Welky, either. *(They begin to demonstrate.)*

ESTHER: And the new. We do the new, too.

TED: *(Demonstrating.)* We do disco.

ESTHER: *(Demonstrating.)* We've learned some new moves.

TED: Some students taught us.

RUTH: Sounds like fun.

TED: Say, want to join us? *(Ruth looks at Austin.)*

AUSTIN: Oh I don't think so. Not tonight, thanks.

RUTH: *(To Ted and Esther.)* We haven't seen each other in years and we're trying to catch up.

AUSTIN: Thank you very much for asking us, though. Thank you.

ESTHER: Next time I want to find our *your* story, Austin.

AUSTIN: I don't have a story.

RUTH: Oh yes you do.

ESTHER: Of course you do.

TED: Everyone has a story.

RUTH: Austin has a special story.

ESTHER: Well then get him to tell it.

RUTH: I'm working on that.

TED: Good-bye, you two.

RUTH: Good-bye, McAlisters.

ESTHER: Ciao.

AUSTIN: Good-bye all. *(The McAlisters go off.)* That must be what they call the New South.

RUTH: *(Getting up, crossing to table.)* They sure fit into the New Boston.

AUSTIN: I suppose every place is getting pretty much the same these days. Like airports.

RUTH: No. Boston seems different.

AUSTIN: In what way?

RUTH: Well. For one thing, it has you.

AUSTIN: *(Laughing.)* I suppose I am peculiar to these parts. Like baked beans. Though I hope I don't produce the same results. *(Hands her a drink.)* I brought you a vodka and tonic.

RUTH: Thank you.

AUSTIN: Is that what you were drinking?

RUTH: It is now.

AUSTIN: I thought, one last echo of summer.

RUTH: Yes.

AUSTIN: And food. In case you were hungry.

RUTH: Looks delicious.

AUSTIN: There's more sumptuous fare within. But I tried to select what Julia Child tells us is a balanced diet. *(They sit.)*

RUTH: It all looks fine. *(He takes silverware and a couple of paper napkins out of his pocket.)*

AUSTIN: Silverware . . . and napkins . . .

RUTH: You're a thoughtful man, Austin.

AUSTIN: Try to be, try to be. *(Pause. Sounds of the party within; quieter talking and more lush, romantic music.)*

RUTH: So.

AUSTIN: So.

RUTH: So it never happened.

AUSTIN: What?

RUTH: The terrible thing.

AUSTIN: Oh that.

RUTH: It never happened?

AUSTIN: Oh no. God no. No.

RUTH: You never made some terrible mistake?

A? Not that I know of. No.

RUTH: You were never hit by some awful doom? Things always worked out?

AUSTIN: Absolutely. I mean, I think so. I mean, sure. After the Navy, I came back. Went to the Business School. Got a good job with the Bank of Boston. Married, married the boss's daughter, actually. Two kids. Both educated. Both launched. Both doing well. Can't complain at all.

RUTH: Sally said you were divorced.

AUSTIN: Oh well that . . . *(Pause.)* That doesn't . . . she wasn't . . . we weren't . . . *(Pause.)* She fell in love . . . *claimed* she had fallen in love . . . . With this . . . this *creep*. I mean, the guy's half her age! . . . So she got her face lifted. Dyed her hair. Does aerobics on demand . . . I mean, it's pathetic.

RUTH: So that's not the terrible thing?

AUSTIN: Her leaving? Christ no. That was a good thing. That was the best thing to happen in a long, long time.

RUTH: And nothing else even remotely terrible happened in your life?

AUSTIN: I don't think so. *(Looks for some wood to knock on.)* At least, not yet.

RUTH: You still think something might? *(He looks off into space.)* Austin? Hello? *(He looks at her.)* Do you? *(Pause.)*

AUSTIN: I think it all the time.

RUTH: Really?

AUSTIN: All. The. Time. *(Pause.)* I've been very lucky, you know. Too lucky. From the beginning. It's not fair. Something's bound to . . . *(Pause.)* Want to know something?

RUTH: What?

AUSTIN: I'm on Prozac right now.

RUTH: You are?

AUSTIN: It's a drug. It calms you down.

RUTH: Oh I know Prozac. I know what it does. And doesn't do.

AUSTIN: I don't tell people I'm on it. But I am.

RUTH: Does it help?

AUSTIN: Yes . . . . No . . . . A little.

RUTH: You shouldn't drink with it.

AUSTIN: I don't. Normally. That was a Perrier I was drinking before.

RUTH: But not now?

AUSTIN: This is a white wine spritzer. Tonight I'm becoming very reckless.

RUTH: Be careful. You might make some terrible mistake.

AUSTIN: Sometimes I wish I would. At least the shoe would drop. *(Sally comes out, carrying a cardigan sweater. She goes to a light switch. Austin gets to his feet.)*

SALLY: Let's have some light on the subject . . . *(The outside light comes on.)* You two seem to be having a perfectly marvelous time.

AUSTIN: *(Getting to his feet.)* We are indeed, Sally.

SALLY: *(To Ruth, holding out the sweater.)* Judith thinks you should wear your sweater.

RUTH: Oh I'm not cold.

SALLY: Well Judith thinks you will be.

RUTH: Judith is very solicitous. *(She takes the sweater.)* But I'm perfectly fine. *(She doesn't put it on.)*

SALLY: Did you two ever figure out where you met?

AUSTIN: We did. It was very romantic.

SALLY: Oh good. But it doesn't have to be. *(She starts gathering up plates.)* I met my sweet, dear Ben, after class, in Room 120 of Eliot Hall, when I was auditing his course on Renaissance Architecture. He was a superb teacher, he knew everything in the world, but I remember thinking, all during his lectures, "I can teach *him* a thing or two." So I married him, and did.

AUSTIN: I took Ben's course.

SALLY: Everyone took Ben's course. Those were the days when we all tried to learn the same things. *(Starts out, then stops.)* Oh. Which reminds me. There's a little man in there from the Berkeley School of Music who has been sniffing around Ben's old Steinway. So when things settle down, we're going to dust it off and try singing some of the old songs. It's probably hopelessly out of tune—*we're* probably hopelessly out of tune—but that's just a risk we'll have to take. *(She goes out. Pause.)*

RUTH: I like it here. *(She moves upstage; tosses her sweater somewhere.)*

AUSTIN: Boston?

RUTH: My friend Judith says it's very livable. The universities, the music . . .

AUSTIN: My family has had the same two seats at Symphony Hall for four generations.

RUTH: I'm sure.

AUSTIN: Maybe you'd join me some Wednesday evening. If you stay.

RUTH: I'd like that. If I stay. *(Pause.)* One thing scares me, though. About Boston.

AUSTIN: What's that?

RUTH: Is it a little . . . well, Puritan.

AUSTIN: Whatever that means.

RUTH: Shouldn't do this, have to do that.

AUSTIN: Ah. Yes. Well, some people say there's that.

RUTH: Are they right?

AUSTIN: Puritan? Oh well. I'm a little . . . close to it. You're probably a better judge.

RUTH: I sense it a little.

AUSTIN: With me?

RUTH: A lot. *(Pause.)*

AUSTIN: You sound like my shrink.

RUTH: What? You go to a psychiatrist?

AUSTIN: She's the one who prescribed the Prozac.

RUTH: I can't see you with a psychiatrist.

AUSTIN: Neither can I. My kids conned me into it. After the divorce, I happened to be feeling a little . . . well, glum . . . so they gave me two sessions as a Christmas present.

RUTH: Good for them.

AUSTIN: I went so I wouldn't hurt their feelings.

RUTH: And you've stayed so you wouldn't hurt the psychiatrist's feelings.

AUSTIN: Right.

RUTH: God, Austin! You're so polite! When you die, you'll probably say excuse me.

AUSTIN: *(Laughing.)* Maybe so. *(Pause.)* Anyway, it doesn't work. Psychiatry. At least for me. It may work for them—the younger generation. They're so much at home with all that lingo. And they're all so aware of their own feelings. I mean, they strum on their own psyches like guitars. So it probably works for them. I hope it does. After all, their life is ahead of them. But me? Even if I . . . could say . . . even if I found some way of . . . I mean, it's a little late, isn't it?

RUTH: Don't say that. You should never say that.

AUSTIN: Anyway she hasn't a clue. My psychiatrist. Not a clue. I sit there in this hot room on Copley Square, overlooking Trinity Church, trying to explain. But she hasn't the foggiest. It was all so different. The world I came from. It was a totally different culture. All those . . . surrogates. That's what she calls them. Surrogates breathing down your neck. Nurses. Cooks. Maids. Gardeners. Aunts and uncles. Parents, too, of course. And Godparents. Grandparents. *Great*-grandparents, for Christ sake. All this pressure. Vertical and horizontal. You were like a fly caught in this very intricate, very complicated spider web, and if you struggled, if you made

a move, if you even tweaked one strand of the web, why the spider might
. . . *(Pause.)* Anyway, what does she know about a world like that? My
shrink. She grew up in a cozy little nuclear family in some kitchen in the
Bronx.

RUTH: Nuclear families can be explosive.

AUSTIN: I'd take a good explosion over Death by Spider. Caught in that web,
being systematically wrapped in silk, carefully preserved, until you can't
. . . breathe.

RUTH: Oh now . . .

AUSTIN: Anyway. Puritan. She says I have a Puritan sense of damnation.

RUTH: Oh yes?

AUSTIN: She says I've inherited a basically Calvinistic perspective from my fore-
fathers in Salem and points north.

RUTH: She says that, does she?

AUSTIN: *(Settling back on the chaise.)* Let's see. How does it go? I've been brought
up all my life to think of myself as one of the Elect.

RUTH: I see.

AUSTIN: But it's hard to feel Elect in a diverse and open-ended democracy.
Particularly after George Bush lost the election.

RUTH: So?

AUSTIN: So therefore I'm terrified that I may actually be one of the Damned,
exiled forever from the community of righteous men and women.

RUTH: Isn't that what they used to call predestination?

AUSTIN: Oh yes. But she says I'm constantly struggling against it. That's why
I'm so polite. I'm trying to propitiate an angry god before he lowers the
boom.

RUTH: She's got all the answers, hasn't she? This shrink.

AUSTIN: Oh well. She went to Radcliffe.

RUTH: And this is what I get if I move to Boston?

AUSTIN: We like patterns here. We like categorizing things. Even our subway
system is carefully color-coded. The good guys ride the Red Line.

RUTH: I'm someone who likes to ride anywhere I want.

AUSTIN: Right! And I'm full of bullshit.

RUTH: Austin! Watch your language. They'll sentence you to the ducking stool.

AUSTIN: *(Laughing.)* Hey, this has been good. I feel good now. You've got me
talking about these things. I've never done that before.

RUTH: Except with your shrink.

AUSTIN: It's different with you.

RUTH: You never talked about it with your wife?

140 A. R. GURNEY

AUSTIN: Oh God no. Not with her. Never.

RUTH: Maybe that's why she left.

AUSTIN: Maybe. And maybe that's why you've stayed.

RUTH: Maybe.

AUSTIN: See? I've been snowing you again, just as I did on the Isle of Capri.

RUTH: Oh, is that what you've been doing?

AUSTIN: Has it worked?

RUTH: Oh yes. It's worked all over again.

AUSTIN: I'm glad. *(He leans over and kisses her. Behind them the sky is a deep, starry blue as it was in Naples. Then Walt comes out, a little drunk. He wears a Navy blazer with a crest on it, and gray flannels.)*

WALT: Austin! Sally tells me you've found a . . . *(Sees the kiss.)* Wooops. Sorry to interrupt. *(He goes off.)*

RUTH: Who was that?

AUSTIN: That was my friend Walt. *(Walt comes back on again.)*

WALT: I heard that. "My friend Walt." I like that. "My friend Walt" . . . *(To Ruth.)* I happen to be his best friend in the entire free world.

AUSTIN: That's true. He is.

WALT: Damn right it's true. *(To Ruth.)* We roomed together at Groton. We had a suite together in Dunster House. I was his Best Man, when he married the lovely Cynthia Drinkwater, of Marblehead, Mass. *(He starts to leave.)* Anything you want to know about this guy, just ask me.

RUTH: *(More to Austin.)* Is he saved or damned?

WALT: *(Coming back.)* Say again?

RUTH: Is he as good a man as I think he is?

WALT: Better. Austin is—and I now quote from the Groton School Yearbook— a prince among men.

AUSTIN: Thanks and good-bye, Walt.

WALT: No, and I'll tell you why, uh . . .

RUTH: Ruth.

WALT: Ruth . . . . He hails from one of the finest families in the greater Boston area. As a banker, he has unimpeachable credentials. As a father, he is fair to a fault. As a husband, he is . . . was . . . gentle, thoughtful, and ultimately forgiving. As a friend, he—

AUSTIN: Cut it out, Walt.

WALT: No, Ruth should know these things. You have been occupying Ruth's time, you have been preventing the rest of us from enjoying the pleasure of Ruth's company, you have obviously been attempting to lure Ruth into your bed—has he been doing that, Ruth?

RUTH: No, he hasn't.

AUSTIN: Yes, I have.

RUTH: News to me.

AUSTIN: The Lord moves in strange and devious ways.

WALT: Then Ruth should know what she's in for. So I'll tell you this, Ruth. You are about to go to bed with a great squash player. He'd be nationally ranked in the over-fifties bracket, except he won't play outside of Boston. But put this guy in a squash court, and you'll see his true colors.

AUSTIN: Ruth doesn't care about squash.

WALT: I'll bet Ruth does. Because Ruth knows, in her deep heart's core, that good at squash means good in bed.

AUSTIN: Oh Jesus, Walt. *(He walks upstage.)*

WALT: Would you like me to describe Austin's squash game, Ruth?

AUSTIN: I wish you wouldn't.

RUTH: I wish you would.

WALT: The ayes have it. So. Now the secret to squash—we're talking about squash racquets here—is that you're obliged to be both brutally aggressive and ultimately courteous at the same time. At this, my friend Austin is a master. He will hit a cannon ball of a shot right down the rail and then bow elegantly out of your way so you can hit it back.

RUTH: And what if you don't?

WALT: Then he'll ask if you'd like to play the point over.

AUSTIN: God, Walt.

RUTH: He sounds very special.

WALT: He is, Ruth. Now as you may know, Boston is a great sports town. We produce champions around here: Ted Williams, Bobby Orr, Larry Byrd. And we've also produced Austin.

AUSTIN: This is pitiful . . . pitiful . . .

WALT: No, now listen to me, Ruth. Squash is a very old game. And very British. Henry the Eighth played a version of it at Hampton Court. The British Raj played it in India. We Americans picked it up in our Anglophilic days and naturally made some improvements. But lately the game has come to be considered somewhat obsolete. It is deemed obscure, elitist, and somewhat dangerous. So in an attempt to adjust to the modern world— to accommodate women, to make it more telegenic—they've softened the ball, widened the court, and modified the rules. It is only played the old way in a few old cities: New York, Philadelphia, and of course Boston. And here Austin is still unbeatable. Put him in a clean white box, with thin red lines and the old rules, and by his squash, thou shalt know him.

RUTH: And what happens when he steps out of that clean, white box?

WALT: Ah well. Then he likes to take a cold shower.

AUSTIN: *(Coming down.)* Knock it off, Walt! This is embarrassing.

WALT: O.K. Sorry.

RUTH: You like him a lot, don't you, Walt?

WALT: Like him? I love the guy. *(Kissing Austin on the cheek.)* I love him a lot.

AUSTIN: *(Backing away.)* Dammit, Walt.

WALT: Hey, it's 1993, man. We can do that now and not even get called on it. *(Party sounds. Judith creeps out self-consciously, beckoning to Ruth. She looks like someone who plays in an orchestra. She wears a plain, dark, velvet dress and has rather wild, unruly hair. She speaks with a New York accent.)*

JUDITH: *(Portentously.)* Ruth, there's a telephone call for you.

RUTH: For me?

JUDITH: He's tracked you down.

RUTH: Oh. *(To Austin and Walt.)* Excuse me. *(Starts in.)*

JUDITH: Ruth . . . I could easily say you're not here.

RUTH: Um. Well. No.

JUDITH: Oh Ruth: now listen. I could simply say you don't want to talk to him. Period. I could say that point blank.

RUTH: No. I'll—talk to him. *(Starts in again.)* Where's the phone?

JUDITH: I don't want to tell you.

RUTH: Where is it, Judith?

JUDITH: In Sally's bedroom.

RUTH: I can at least talk to him.

AUSTIN: Will you be back?

RUTH: Of course I'll be back.

JUDITH: Of course she'll be back. *(To Ruth.)* Come back, Ruth. Rejoin the human race.

RUTH: Yes. That's right . . . *(Ruth starts out again, then stops, returns, puts her arm around Judith. To Austin and Walt.)* Oh. This is *my* friend. Judith. *(She goes.)*

JUDITH: *(Shrugging.)* Some friend. I shouldn't even have brought the message. I should have walked right into Sally's bedroom and slammed down the phone.

AUSTIN: I'm afraid you have the advantage on this particular subject.

JUDITH: What? Oh. Sorry. That was him.

AUSTIN: Who?

JUDITH: Her husband. He's a deeply flawed person.

AUSTIN: How? How is he flawed?

JUDITH: *(Looking from one to the other.)* Am I among friends here?

WALT: You sure are.

JUDITH: *(After a moment.)* He hit her. That's for openers.

AUSTIN: No.

JUDITH: He *hit* her! She had to hit him back!

AUSTIN: Oh boy.

JUDITH: She told the whole group!

AUSTIN: What group?

JUDITH: I'm sorry. I'm so keyed up I forgot to play the overture. *(She does some breathing exercises.)* We met in this women's group two summers ago at the Aspen Music Festival. My husband and I played Mozart in the morning, and I signed up for Assertiveness Training thing in the afternoon. There was Ruth, dealing with her divorce. I though we were all making great strides, but in the end she went back to her husband.

AUSTIN: So the group didn't help.

JUDITH: It helped me. I decided to leave mine.

AUSTIN: Oh dear.

JUDITH: I decided he was a weak man.

WALT: Weak—uh—physically?

JUDITH: Weak musically. Weak on Mozart, weak on Mahler, weak even on *Moon River.*

AUSTIN: And this—group had a say in all that?

WALT: These women's groups work, man. *(To Judith.)* My wife Ginny went to one. It improved her net game enormously.

JUDITH: *(To Walt.)* There you are. They open new horizons. I learned there's more to life than the string section. I'm now seriously involved with a French horn.

AUSTIN: May we talk about Ruth, please.

JUDITH: Ruth? Ruth was unable to release. I mean, the man is a disaster. Once she almost called the police.

WALT: Oh Christ. One of those.

JUDITH: You got it. One of those. Still, back she goes.

AUSTIN: To where?

JUDITH: Are you ready? Las Vegas.

AUSTIN: I'm unfamiliar with Las Vegas.

JUDITH: So am I, and pray to God I remain so. But that's where they live. Furthermore, he's gone through every nickel she's got. She starts this very lucrative little art gallery—creates an oasis of civilization out there—and what does he do but bankrupt her.

AUSTIN: Why is she even talking to him, then?

JUDITH: *(With an elaborate, complicated, hopeless shrug.)* You tell me.

WALT: The guy must have some hold.

JUDITH: Some hammer lock, I call it.

AUSTIN: What does he do in life?

JUDITH: Do? Do? The man gambles. Period. End of sentence.

AUSTIN: Uh oh.

JUDITH: And to support his habit, he manages a car rental business.

AUSTIN: Oh boy. I can tell you, as a banker, that is a very erratic business.

JUDITH: She says he likes all that. He likes being out on a limb.

AUSTIN: Have you met him?

JUDITH: No, thank God. But she showed me his picture. That's another problem. He looks like the Marlboro Man.

WALT: Uh oh. Better load up your six-shooter, Austin.

JUDITH: Please. No macho stuff. Please. It's her choice. She's got to learn to kick the habit.

AUSTIN: Maybe she will.

JUDITH: From your mouth! I mean, the man's a barbarian! Once he grabbed her television and threw it out the window!

AUSTIN: Good Lord.

JUDITH: While she was watching *Jewel in the Crown.*

WALT: *(To Austin.)* There's the bell, buddy.

AUSTIN: What?

WALT: Your serve, man! Time to make your move.

JUDITH: It's time for everyone to make a move. It's time for a concerted effort.

WALT: Damsel in distress, pal.

JUDITH: Which is why I brought her here tonight. I wanted to show her what civilized life was all about.

WALT: You wanted to show her Austin.

JUDITH: Austin? Austin was just luck. But when she said she *knew* you, Austin, and when Sally said you were *free*, I thought, YES! At least there's *hope!*

AUSTIN: Hey, gang. Don't paint me into a corner here.

JUDITH: All I now is she's a sweet person, and she's had a rough life, and she deserves a better break than she's had so far . . . . Let me see if I can pry her loose from that goddam telephone! *(She goes off quickly.)*

WALT: You like her?

AUSTIN: Ruth?

WALT: Of course Ruth.

AUSTIN: I hardly know her.

WALT: She seems like a good gal.

AUSTIN: She's very . . . simpatico.

WALT: You need someone, buddy.

AUSTIN: I've got somebody, buddy.

WALT: Who? Your little friend up in Nashua?

AUSTIN: She's there when I need her.

WALT: I'm talking about more than a dirty weekend in New Hampshire, Austin.

AUSTIN: Oh are you, Walt?

WALT: Give this one a change.

AUSTIN: I'm not sure what you mean.

WALT: I mean Ginny and I have tried to fix you up several times. But you gave those ladies short shift, or shrift, or whatever the fuck the expression is.

AUSTIN: Of course I'll give her a chance. I like to think I give everyone a chance. Why wouldn't I give her a chance?

WALT: Because you're acting like a jerk, that's why.

AUSTIN: What is it with you people in this town? Who do you think I am? Some new boy back at boarding school, being set up for the spring dance? I am a divorced man, Walt! I am a father of two grown children! I'll be a *grand*father any day! At our age, we don't just . . . *date* people, Walt. We don't just idly fool around. Every move is a big move. Every decision is a major decision. You ask a woman out, you take her to dinner, that's a statement, Walt. That says something important. Because there's no second chance this time, Walt. This is our last time at bat!

WALT: All the more reason not to be alone.

AUSTIN: And did you ever think, Walt, did you and Ginny ever think that maybe I like being alone? Ever think of that? Maybe I've discovered the pleasures of listening to opera while I'm shaving. And *walking* to work through the Commons—rather than riding that damn train. And having a late lunch with a good book at the Union Oyster House! And reading it in bed at night! Maybe I like all that! Maybe I like feeling free to fart! *(Ruth comes in, carrying dessert and two demitasses.)* Excuse me, Ruth.

RUTH: No problem.

AUSTIN: I was just letting off a little—steam.

RUTH: Good for you.

WALT: I'll get back to the party.

RUTH: Good-bye, Walt.

WALT: So long, Ruth. I hope we'll meet again.

RUTH: I hope so, too. *(Walt goes; Ruth sets her plates down.)* I brought dessert.

AUSTIN: *(Settling at the table.)* Very thoughtful.

RUTH: And coffee.

AUSTIN: Decaf, I hope.

RUTH: *(Sliding him his cup.)* What else. *(They eat brownies or something.)* Mmmm.

AUSTIN: A little rich, isn't it?

RUTH: Well, we deserve it. We were so healthy with the main course.

AUSTIN: Right. In Boston, they'd say we're getting our just desserts. *(Ruth gives him a weak smile. Pause.)* Everything all right, by the way?

RUTH: With the telephone call?

AUSTIN: Judith told us who it was. *(Pause.)*

RUTH: He's at the . . . what is it? The Skyway Lounge, out at the airport.

AUSTIN: What? He's there?

RUTH: He's there.

AUSTIN: And?

RUTH: He wants me to join him.

AUSTIN: When?

RUTH: Now. Right now.

AUSTIN: But you're here.

RUTH: That's right. I'm here. Which is what I said. I said I'm having a very good time right here.

AUSTIN: What did he say to that?

RUTH: He said he could give me a better one, right there.

AUSTIN: Could he?

RUTH: He can . . . fun.

AUSTIN: Did you tell him about me?

RUTH: No.

AUSTIN: Why not?

RUTH: He might have shown up with a baseball bat.

AUSTIN: I could have dealt with that.

RUTH: Oh yes? With your squash racquet.

AUSTIN: I would have done something.

RUTH: *(Touching him.)* I know you would have, Austin. *(She gets up.)* I just don't want you to, that's all. *(She looks out.)* He's got two tickets on tonight's red-eye back west. First class. And he wants to order a bottle of champagne to drink while we wait.

AUSTIN: Champagne? At an airport bar?

RUTH: He knows I like it. *(Pause.)* First class, too. He knows I'm a sucker for that. *(Pause.)* And he'll charge everything to *my* credit card.

AUSTIN: Sounds like a nice guy.

RUTH: Oh he . . . has his problems.

AUSTIN: Sure sounds like it.

RUTH: Of course we all do, don't we?

AUSTIN: Ouch.

RUTH: No, but I mean we do. Lord knows I do, too.

AUSTIN: Name one.

RUTH: Him.

AUSTIN: O.K.

RUTH: He's not good for me.

AUSTIN: That's an understatement.

RUTH: But he was some redeeming social virtues.

AUSTIN: Such as?

RUTH: Well . . . for one thing, he loves me.

AUSTIN: Oh sure.

RUTH: He does . . . . He's never traded me in for some young bimbo. He's never taken me for granted. He loves me . . . I walk out, I leave him, I say this is it, and what does he do? He telephones all over the country till he finds out where I am. Then he grabs a flight to Boston. Calls me here. Offers me champagne. And begs me to come back . . . . He loves me.

AUSTIN: How can he love you if he hits you?

RUTH: He doesn't hit me.

AUSTIN: I hear he does.

RUTH: *(More to herself.)* Judith? . . . *(To Austin.)* Once, maybe.

AUSTIN: Once is enough.

RUTH: By mistake.

AUSTIN: Oh Ruth.

RUTH: It was by *mistake*, Austin!

AUSTIN: Some mistake. That's a big mistake.

RUTH: Sometimes he gets . . . carried away.

AUSTIN: Yes well, that's not love in my book.

RUTH: Oh really?

AUSTIN: That has nothing to do with love. Rape, violence, things of that kind, I'm sorry, they elude me. They totally elude me. If that's love, then I'm afraid I know nothing about it. *(She looks at him as if for the first time. Pause. Sounds of people singing around a piano come from within. They sing a lively song.)* Well. How about a song at twilight?

RUTH: Maybe it's better if I just . . . *(She makes a move to go.)*

AUSTIN: *(Getting in her way.)* Ruth. *(She stops.)* Tell you what. We'll go to the Ritz Bar, you and I. It's a very pleasant, very quiet place. And *I'll* buy you champagne. And I promise you it will be a better brand than what your Marlboro Man comes up with, out at the airport. And I'll pay for it my*self.*

RUTH: Austin . . .

AUSTIN: No, and I'll tell you something else. After we've had champagne, we'll go to my place. If you'd like.

RUTH: Oh Austin . . .

AUSTIN: No, now I don't want you to feel obligated in any way. But I have a very nice apartment on Beacon Street, and we can walk there, right down Arlington Street from the Ritz. And I have a guest room, Ruth. It's a nice room. With its own bath. I keep it for the kids. You can sleep there if you prefer. I'll even lend you a pair of decent pajamas.

RUTH: Decent pajamas . . .

AUSTIN: No, now wait. If, where we're there, you'd like to . . . to join me in my room, if you'd care to slip into my bed, naturally I'd like that very much. Very much indeed. But you wouldn't have to. Either way, you'd be most welcome. And if things worked out, why we might . . . we might make things more permanent . . . I mean, it's a thought, at least. And if they don't, well hell, you should always feel free to leave any time you want.

RUTH: Oh well . . .

AUSTIN: I mean, we obviously get along. That's obvious. We did on Capri and we do now. Hey, come to think of it, this is a second chance, isn't it? We're back where we were, but this time we're getting a second chance. *(Pause.)* So. What do you say?

RUTH: *(Kissing him.)* Oh Austin. Austin from Boston. You're such a good man. *(She starts out. Singing continues within.)*

AUSTIN: Where are you going?

RUTH: I don't want to tell you.

AUSTIN: To him?

RUTH: I think so. Yes.

AUSTIN: Why?

RUTH: Why?

AUSTIN: Why him and not me?

RUTH: Oh dear.

AUSTIN: How can you love that guy?

RUTH: If you don't know, I can't tell you.

AUSTIN: *(Turning away from her.)* You don't think I'm attractive?

RUTH: I think you're one of the most attractive men I've ever met.

AUSTIN: Then it must be my problem.

RUTH: Yes.

AUSTIN: You think it's a crock of shit!

RUTH: No! Not at all. No! I take it very seriously. I take it more seriously than you do.

AUSTIN: You think something terrible is going to happen to me?

RUTH: I think it already has.

AUSTIN: When?

RUTH: I don't know.

AUSTIN: Where?

RUTH: I don't know that either.

AUSTIN: But you think I'm damned into outer darkness?

RUTH: I do. I really do.

AUSTIN: But you won't tell me why.

RUTH: I can't.

AUSTIN: Why not?

RUTH: It's too painful, Austin.

AUSTIN: Do you think I'll ever find out?

RUTH: Oh I hope not.

AUSTIN: Why?

RUTH: Because you'll go through absolute hell.

AUSTIN: You mean I'll weep and wail and gnash my teeth?

RUTH: I don't think so, Austin. No. I think you'll clear your throat, and square your shoulders, and straighten your tie—and stand there quietly and take it. That's the hellish part. *(She looks at him feelingly.)* I've got to dash. *(Sally enters.)* Oh Sally . . . Good-bye! *(Ruth goes quickly. Singing offstage:)*

> The bells are ringing
> For me and my gal,
> The birds are singing,
> For me and my gal . . .

SALLY: *(Looking after Ruth.)* That was a little abrupt.

AUSTIN: She was in a hurry.

SALLY: She certainly was.

AUSTIN: She asked me to thank you for her. She said she had a wonderful time.

SALLY: You're lying, Austin. *(Kisses him on the cheek.)* But you're also very thoughtful and polite. Now if I were you I'd call her up at Judith's, first thing in the morning.

AUSTIN: She's going back to her husband. Tonight.

SALLY: Oh no.

AUSTIN: Flying back to Las Vegas.

SALLY: No.

AUSTIN: That's what she's choosing to do.

SALLY: I hear he's bad news.

AUSTIN: How could she go back to a guy like that?

SALLY: Maybe she thinks he'll change.

AUSTIN: People don't change, Sally.

SALLY: Maybe they do in Las Vegas.

AUSTIN: Not at our age. We are who we are, only more so.

SALLY: No, Austin. No. I can't agree with that. No. If that were true, I'd still be rattling around Ben's house on Brattle Street, having tea with his colleagues, talking about his books. But I sold the house, Austin, soon after he died. And I gave his books to the Widener. And I moved down here to the harbor so I could live a different life, with different people, who talk about different things.

AUSTIN: Different they are, Sally. I'll say that.

SALLY: And they keep me *alive!* . . . Oh Austin, give it a try. Why not go after her?

AUSTIN: Sally . . .

SALLY: I mean it. She can't have gone that far! *(She sees the sweater.)* Look! She even left her sweater! You see? You're in luck! She's even given you a good excuse! Take it to her! Right now! Please!

AUSTIN: Sally, I'm not going to scamper off to some airport bar to deliver some sweater . . . . She can come back any time she wants.

SALLY: Maybe she *wants* to be swept off her feet!

AUSTIN: I'm a little old to be sweeping people off their feet, Sally. Just a little too old for that.

SALLY: Austin, you're hopeless. *(She begins to clean up the dessert plates.)* Well. Come join the party. We found the Fireside Songbook stuck away in the piano bench, and after we get through that, there's talk of rolling back the rug and doing some serious dancing! *(Within, they are now singing:)*

>   In a cavern, in a canyon,
>   Excavating for a mine . . .

(Jim comes out, lighting his cigarette.)

JIM: I'm sorry. I'm afraid I have to smoke again.

SALLY: At least you tried, Jimmy.

JIM: *(His hand shaking as he lights up.)* I went almost the whole evening smoke-free, but now look at me, puffing like a chimney.

SALLY: Well, try again tomorrow.

JIM: Right. *(Sitting down, inhaling deeply.)* Meanwhile, gather tumors while ye may . . . *(The singing continues:)*

> Oh my darlin', oh my darlin',
> Oh my darlin' Clementine . . .

I was fine till we started in on that fucking song. It made me think of a cat I had. *(To Sally.)* Remember my cat, Sal? Clementine?

SALLY: *(Standing behind him.)* Of course I remember Clementine.

JIM: *(To Austin.)* But it isn't really the cat at all. It's the association with my friend Dalton. *(To Sally.)* Remember Dalton, Sal?

SALLY: I remember him well. I liked Dalton.

JIM: *(To Austin.)* I had a friend named Dalton, and we'd put our cat in the car and sing to her, driving down to Provincetown. Have you ever sung to a cat?

AUSTIN: Can't say that I have.

SALLY: *(Stroking Jim's hair.)* My poor dear Ben loved music.

JIM: *(Putting out his cigarette.)* I'd take the melody, he's would take the harmony. We were fantastic! . . .

SALLY: Ben played all the old songs on the piano. Sigmund Romber, Rogers and Hart . . .

JIM: *(Starting to cry.)* Oh boy. Now look at me. Now I'm starting to cry . . .

SALLY: *(Holding him.)* Now, Jimmy. Now, now.

JIM: Shit. I'm going to pieces here. I'm totally falling apart. *(He breaks down, cries unabashedly. Austin stares at him, almost hypnotized.)* Why are you staring? I'm just a sentimental old fag who smokes.

SALLY: Let's go in, Jimmy. It's cold out here.

JIM: *(Pulling himself together.)* You're right. I'm embarrassing you, Sal, in front of your guest. *(He blows his nose, gets up.)*

SALLY: *(Pulling the chaise back to where it was.)* Austin understands, don't you, Austin? *(She hands him Ruth's sweater.)*

AUSTIN: *(Taking the sweater.)* Oh yes.

SALLY: Everyone in the world loves *some*thing. Am I right, Austin?

AUSTIN: Oh yes . . . . Yes . . . .

JIM: *(Taking off the dessert plates and coffee cups.)* Still, it's terrible to let go that way . . . *(He goes.)*

SALLY: *(To Jim, as he goes.)* Think how much more terrible it would be if you couldn't! *(She blows out the candle; starts out.)* Coming, Austin?

AUSTIN: In a minute. *(Sally goes, turning off the terrace light. Austin stands, clutching Ruth's sweater, lit only by the shaft of light coming from indoors. He takes a deep breath, clears his throat, squares his shoulders, straightens his tie, and looks longingly toward the life within, as the lights fade and the singing ends.)*

　　Thou art lost and gone forever,
　　O my darlin' Clementine . . .
(Slow fade.)

THE END

A CHEEVER EVENING

A New Play Based on the Stories of John Cheever

for Mary Cheever

ORIGINAL PRODUCTION

A Cheever Evening was produced by Playwrights Horizons (Don Scardino, Artistic Director; Leslie Marcus, Managing Director) in New York City, in October, 1994. It was directed by Don Scardino; the set design was by John Lee Beatty; the costume design was by Jennifer Von Mayrhauser; the lighting design was by Kenneth Posner; the sound design was by Aural Fixation; the production manager was Jack O'Connor and the production stage manager was Lloyd Davis, Jr. The ensemble cast included John Cunningham, Jack Gilpin, Julie Hagerty, Mary Beth Peil, Robert Stanton, and Jennifer Van Dyck.

NOTE

Over the years, I have adapted several John Cheever short stories for the stage or television. Here I have tried to shape a more complicated tapestry by interweaving elements from a sizable number of his works. Wherever possible, I have used Cheever's language and events, but I also have made changes to accommodate the special demands of the stage. What I hope to do is pay homage to a major American author and a major influence on my own writing.

AUTHOR'S NOTE

I've always had a special fondness for the work of John Cheever. I used to read with almost religious fervor his stories in *The New Yorker*, and I especially admired his keen ear for the rhythms and repetitions in the dialogue of his anxious Easterners. My first assignment at the Yale School of Drama was to write an adaptation of some sort, so I chose a story by Cheever, and my second full-length play, *Children*, was suggested by another of his works. In the late 70's, I adapted his short story "O Youth and Beauty!" into an hour long television play for P.B.S. I also taught his stories, and sometimes his Wapshot novels in a course on American Literature at M.I.T. Cheever and I had a short, but, for me, very rewarding correspondence during this period.

In the early nineties, I found myself rereading his anthology of stories, and once again falling in love with his loopy dialogue and quirky turns of event. I began to wonder if I could fashion a play which might celebrate this distinguished American writer without reducing or altering his special qualities by confining them within an alien medium. I'd written episodic plays before, with *Scenes From American Life* and *The Dining Room*, so I set about making a collage of those Cheever stories which I felt might work best on the stage. I combined some stories, reworked others, and little by little the evening began to take shape. I tried to organize the evening so that the earlier city and suburban stories would occupy Act One, whereas Act Two would deal primarily with those set during the summer. Through both acts, I also attempted to track the idea of the family as it builds, blooms, and disperses over the years.

Don Scardino, who then was Artistic Director at Playwrights Horizons, read a draft of my *Cheever Evening* and responded to it enough to try a simple reading for some of his subscribers. I asked Mary Cheever, the author's widow, if she'd come take a look before we went any further, and after she did, she allowed us to take the piece a step further. The following year Playwrights Horizons presented a full production. We had a first-rate scenic concept by John Lee Beatty, which included a turntable that only occasionally broke down. The cast also was exceptionally good. The result was that we were pretty much a success, well reviewed and well attended, and we extended the run a couple of times.

Despite the simple requirements for production and number of excellent parts, *A Cheever Evening* hasn't subsequently been performed elsewhere as much as I had hoped. I don't know whether the problem is that people aren't as interested in John Cheever as they should be, or that they don't like what I did to him. Obviously, the stage can never do justice to some of his complicated tonalities, but one would hope that his aching sense of the limitations of "the

American dream" would have a general appeal, and his weird comic perspectives would also have some resonance beyond New York City and its commuting suburbs. I can say that this is the kind of play that brings a cast together in an excitingly interdependent way, and we all had a great time working on it at Playwrights Horizons.

PRODUCTION NOTES

CAST
A minimum of six: three men, three women. The distribution of roles is indicated in the script. Parts have been assigned to reflect equality, fluidity and versatility.

COSTUMES
Simple, basic suits or dresses with minor accessories added as needed. There might be some attention to changing styles as the play moves from the late forties through the fifties and sixties into the early seventies.

PROPS AND ACCESSORIES
Only what is essential.

SET
A number of pieces of good, simple, Early American furniture, set against backgrounds which invoke, first, a Manhattan skyline, then a Westchester backyard, and finally a seascape. The furniture should look inherited, the kind that might belong in any of these locales. For example, a couch, a school bench, a table and several Windsor chairs. A dry sink may be used as a bar and as a source and repository for props and accessories.

LIGHTING
Interiors and exteriors. Light is essential in Cheever. We should move from the yellow, slanting light of New York to the lush green foliage of the suburbs on to the gray-blue sky of the seashore.

SOUND
Music from the Fifties and Sixties. Other sounds as indicated.

NOTE: This play may also be presented simply as a reading with actors using stools and music stands.

A CHEEVER EVENING

ACT ONE

At Rise: A party is in progress. Lush fifties music in the background, say, the Harry James recording of "You'll Never Know." Everyone is onstage. First Actor is making First Actress a drink. Second Actor and Second Actress are conversing and smoking. Third Actor and Third Actress are dancing an easy fox-trot. All are talking animatedly. The music modulates to a Benny Goodman quartet as the Actors come downstage to address the audience.

FIRST ACTOR: *(As if bringing us into the party.)* We are talking of a time when the city of New York was filled with a river light . . .

FIRST ACTRESS: And when you heard the Benny Goodman quartets from a radio in the corner stationery store . . .

SECOND ACTOR: And almost everybody wore a hat . . .

SECOND ACTRESS: *(Putting out her cigarette.)* We are the last of that generation of chain smokers who woke the world in the morning with their coughing . . .

THIRD ACTOR: Who sailed for Europe on ships . . .

THIRD ACTRESS: Who were truly nostalgic for love and happiness . . .

SECOND ACTRESS: And whose gods were as ancient as yours, whoever you are.

FIRST ACTOR: It was long ago . . .

FIRST ACTRESS: So long ago that the foliage of elm trees was part of the summer night . . .

THIRD ACTOR: So long ago that when you wanted to make a left turn, you cranked down the car window and pointed in that direction . . .

THIRD ACTRESS: Otherwise you were not allowed to point.

SECOND ACTOR: "Don't point," you were told.

SECOND ACTRESS: I can't imagine why.

FIRST ACTOR: *(Affectionately.)* Maybe the gesture was thought to be erotic.

FIRST ACTRESS: *(Taking his arm.)* And maybe it was . . .
(First Actor and Actress withdraw upstage with the Third Actor and Third Actress. The Second Actor and Second Actress remain downstage. They become Jim and Irene.)

JIM: *(To audience; arm around Irene.)* Jim and Irene Westcott were the kind of people who seem to strike that satisfactory average of income, endeavor, and respectability that is reached by the statistical reports in college alumni bulletins.

IRENE: *(To audience.)* They were the parents of two young children, had been married nine years, and lived on the twelfth floor of an apartment near Sutton Place.

JIM: They went to the theater on an average of 10.3 times a year . . .

IRENE: That much?

JIM: According to the statistics.

IRENE: And they hoped someday to live up in Westchester County . . .

JIM: *(Settling into a chair.)* They differed from their neighbors only in an interest they shared in serious music . . .

IRENE: *(Turning on a "radio," which might be suggested by a patch of light downstage.)* They had a new Magnavox console radio, and they spent a good deal of time listening to music on it.

(She settles down with her needlepoint. Music such as a Chopin prelude is heard. They listen. Then.)

FIRST ACTOR: *(Behind them, slamming his hand on the "keyboard.")* For Chrissake, Kathy, do you always have to play the piano when I get home?

FIRST ACTRESS: *(Behind them.)* It's the only chance I have. I'm at the office all day.

FIRST ACTOR: So am I! Which makes it hell to come home to that shitty piano!

(Sound of a door slamming. The Chopin resumes. Pause.)

IRENE: *(To Jim.)* Did you hear that?

JIM: I did.

IRENE: On the radio?

JIM: I heard.

IRENE: The man said something dirty.

JIM: It's probably a play.

IRENE: It didn't sound like a play . . . . Try another station.

(Jim gets up and turns a "dial.")

THIRD ACTOR: *(Behind them.)* Have you seen my garters?

THIRD ACTRESS: *(Behind them.)* Button me up.

THIRD ACTOR: I said, have you seen my garters?

THIRD ACTRESS: Just button me up and I'll find your garters.

THIRD ACTOR: I wish you wouldn't leave apple cores in the ashtrays. I hate the smell.

(Another pause.)

JIM: Strange, isn't it?

IRENE: Isn't it.

(Jim turns the "dial" again.)

FIRST ACTRESS: *(Singing in an English accent; rocking a "baby.")*
"Trot, trot, trot to Boston,
Trot, trot, trot to Lynn!"
IRENE: My God! That's the Sweeney's nurse, in 17-B!
FIRST ACTRESS:
"Trot, trot, trot to Salem,
And then come home again . . ."
IRENE: Turn that thing off!
JIM: Why?
IRENE: Maybe they can hear us! *(Jim turns it off.)* We must be getting other
people's apartments.
JIM: Impossible.
IRENE: But that was the Sweeney's nurse! She sings that song in the elevator!
JIM: Let me try it again.
(Jim turns on "radio" again.)
FIRST ACTRESS: *(Singing.)* "Ride a cock horse to Banbury cross . . ."
IRENE: There she is again!
JIM: *(Into "radio.")* Hello? . . . Hello? . . . *(To Irene.)* They can't hear us.
IRENE: Then try something else.
(Jim turns the "dial." The others sing a song like "The Whiffenpoof Song.")
THIRD ACTRESS: Eat some more sandwiches!
(Others sing exuberantly underneath.)
IRENE: *(Joining Jim by the "radio.")* That's the Fullers in 11-E.
JIM: No.
IRENE: That's the Fullers. She was in the liquor store this afternoon, planning
a party tonight.
JIM: Why weren't we invited?
IRENE: Because we don't know them, Jim.
JIM: Maybe we will now.
IRENE: See if you can get those peculiar people in 18-C.
JIM: *(To audience, as he fiddles with the "dial.")* And so that night we heard a
monologue on salmon fishing in Canada, and a bridge game, and later
on . . .
FIRST ACTOR: What's the matter, honey?
FIRST ACTRESS: I can't sleep.
FIRST ACTOR: Do you feel all right?
FIRST ACTRESS: I don't really feel like myself. There are only fifteen or twenty
minutes in the week when I feel like myself.
FIRST ACTOR: We'll try another doctor tomorrow.

FIRST ACTRESS: Oh these doctors. These bills . . .

(They go off. Jim and Irene look at each other.)

JIM: *(Turning off the "radio.")* Maybe we should go to bed.

IRENE: Maybe we should.

JIM: *(To audience.)* But the next evening, when I came home . . .

IRENE: Quickly! Go up to 16-C, Jim! Mr. Osborne's beating his wife! They've been quarreling since four o'clock!

JIM: I can't just —

IRENE: *(Turning on the "radio.")* But he's hurting her! Listen! *(They listen. Sounds of bedsprings and love-making. They look at each other.)* Well now it's stopped.

JIM: *(Turning it off.)* Have you been listening all *day?*

IRENE: Of course not! *(Pause.)* Just occasionally. *(Pause.)* It's been horrible. Mrs. Melville's mother died, and some woman is having an affair with the handyman, and that girl who walks the poodle is a whore.

JIM: Irene . . .

IRENE: What?

JIM: I spent a great deal of money on that radio. I bought it to give you some pleasure.

IRENE: You bought it for yourself too, Jim.

JIM: I bought it mainly for you. I'm not here all day.

IRENE: You seem to be blaming me for something.

JIM: Not blaming. Just pointing out a simple fact.

IRENE: Don't, don't, DON'T quarrel with me, Jimmy, please. Everybody in the world has been quarreling, all day long.

JIM: Then don't listen.

IRENE: I won't. I'm trying not to. *(They look at the "radio.")* We've never been like that, have we, darling? I mean we've always been good and decent and loving to one another. We've got two sweet children, and we're happy, aren't we?

JIM: Of course we're happy. I'll have that damned radio fixed first thing. *(To audience.)* So I called the store. *(The piano now plays music such as Debussy's La Mer. Jim turns to Irene.)* Better?

IRENE: *(Somewhat disappointedly.)* Oh yes. The man came, and it's been fine ever since.

JIM: I saw the repair bill on the hall table. Four hundred dollars.

IRENE: Apparently it required some major adjustment.

JIM: That's our last extravagance this year.

IRENE: Let's hope . . . *(They listen to the music.)*

JIM: I also noticed, on the hall table, a bill from Saks.

IRENE: Oh. Yes.

JIM: You haven't paid the Saks bill yet?

IRENE: I'll pay it next month.

JIM: Why did you tell me you'd already paid it?

IRENE: I didn't want you to worry.

JIM: You lied to me.

IRENE: I didn't *lie*, Jim.

JIM: I'm not at all sure of the future, and frankly I don't like to see all my labors wasted in fur coats and slipcovers and expensive radios!

IRENE: *(Turning off the "radio." The piano stops.)* Please, Jim. They'll hear us.

JIM: Who'll hear us?

IRENE: The radio.

JIM: The radio can't hear us. Nobody can hear us. *(Shouting.)* Nobody in the goddamn world can hear us!

IRENE: Oh Jim. Please!

JIM: And what if they can? Who gives a shit?

IRENE: Stop it. You know I hate that word.

JIM: Why are you so Christly all of a sudden. What's turned you overnight into a convent girl? You stole your mother's jewelry before they probated her will. You never gave your sister a cent — not even when she needed it. And where was all your piety when you went to that abortionist? I'll never forget how cool you were. You packed your bag and went off to have that child murdered as if you were going to Nassau! Oh hell, I'm getting a drink.

(He goes to the "bar.")

IRENE: *(Kneeling by the "radio." To audience.)* She thought of the radio and hoped it might once again speak to her kindly.

JIM: *(Crossing behind her.)* I've worked my ass off for you and the kids! I've broken my back for you guys!

(He goes out.)

IRENE: *(To audience.)* Maybe she'd hear some Chopin, or at least the soothing song of the Sweeney's nurse . . . *(Turns on the "radio.")*

FIRST ACTOR'S VOICE: An early morning railroad disaster in Tokyo killed twenty-nine people and injured at least . . .

FIRST ACTRESS'S VOICE: *(Overlapping.)* A fire in a Catholic hospital near Buffalo was extinguished early this morning, after causing several deaths and thousands of dollars worth of . . .

FIRST ACTOR'S VOICE: *(Overlapping.)* The temperature is forty-seven . . .

FIRST ACTRESS'S VOICE: The humidity is eighty-nine . . .

IRENE: But that's all she heard, so she turned it off.

> *(She turns off the "radio," as we hear party sounds. Laura comes on, played by Third Actress.)*

LAURA: Is this where we powder our noses?

IRENE: *(Vaguely.)* What? . . . Oh yes . . . . Feel free . . .

> *(She goes off. Laura pulls up a chair as if to a dressing table and powders her nose as if in a mirror. Alice comes on, played by First Actress.)*

ALICE: Hi.

LAURA: Oh hi.

ALICE: Say, could I borrow a splash of perfume? I seem to have left mine at home.

LAURA: Certainly. Certainly you can, Alice. *(Hands her a perfume spray.)*

ALICE: *(Looking at it.)* Hmmm. Taboo . . . How fancy. *(She sprays herself, hands it back.)*

LAURA: Ralph gave it to me for Christmas.

ALICE: *(Now combing her hair.)* I hear you're moving to California.

LAURA: We hope so. We'll know tomorrow.

ALICE: It is a good job?

LAURA: Ralph thinks so.

ALICE: You're lucky.

LAURA: I suppose we are.

ALICE: California . . .

LAURA: It's kind of scary, actually. To pick up stakes.

ALICE: Scary, hell. You're very, very lucky. You don't know how lucky you are. *(Brushing her hair angrily.)* I have this cake of soap. I mean, I *had* this cake of soap. Somebody gave it to me when I was married. Some maid, some music teacher. It was good English soap, the kind I like, and I decided to save it for when Larry made a killing and could take me to Bermuda. First I thought I could use it when he got the job in Hartford. Then when we went to Boston. And then, when he got work here, I thought maybe this time, maybe now I get to take the kids out of public schools and pay the bills and move out of those second-rate rentals we've been living in. Well, last week, I was looking through my bureau drawers, and there it was, this cake of soap. It was all cracked, so I threw it out. I threw it out because I knew I never was going to have a chance to use it. I'm never going to Bermuda. I'm never even going to get to Florida. I'll never get out of hock, ever, ever, *ever.* For the rest of my life, for the rest of my *life,* I'll be wearing ragged slips and torn nightgowns and shoes that hurt. And every taxi driver and doorman and headwaiter in this town is going to know in a minute that I haven't got five bucks in this black imitation-suede purse that I've been brushing and brushing and brushing for the past ten years. *(She sits down next to Laura.)* How do you rate it, Laura? What's so wonderful about you that you get a break like this? *(She runs her fingers down Laura's arm.)* Can I rub it off you? Will that make me lucky? I swear to Jesus I would murder somebody if I thought it would bring us any money. I'd wring somebody's neck — yours, anybody's — I swear to Jesus I would — ! *(She stops herself.)* Well anyway. Thanks for the Taboo. *(She hurries off. Laura becomes Betsy as she ties on an apron and sets two silver candlesticks on the table. Bob comes on, wearing a hat, carrying a briefcase. He is played by the Third Actor. He scuffs his feet.)*

BOB: *(To audience, tossing off his hat.)* Betsy and I both come from that enormous stratum of the middle class that is distinguished by its ability to recall better times. Lost money is so much a part of our lives that I am sometimes reminded of a group of expatriates who have adapted themselves energetically to some alien soil, but who are reminded, now and then, of the escarpments of their native coast. *(Betsy has gone to a "window" downstage, and stands staring out.)* I'm home! *(He kisses her on the cheek; she continues to stare out.)* Sometimes my wife stands in the middle of the room, as if she had lost or forgotten something, and this moment of reflection is so deep that she will not hear me if I speak to her, or the children if they call. *(He puts down his briefcase.)* Is it O.K. if the kids listen to *The Lone Ranger?* *(No response.)* Do I smell corned beef hash on the stove? Mmmmm. Yummy. *(No response.)* Want me to light the candles? *(Still no response; he takes some bills from his briefcase, goes to the table, starts to work.)*

BETSY: *(Finally.)* Do you remember the Trenchers?

BOB: The Trenchers?

BETSY: We met them last month at the Newsome's. He's a doctor. She's older. Talk constantly about her dog.

BOB: Oh right.

BETSY: He's there.

BOB: Where?

BETSY: *(Indicating.)* Down there. On the street.

BOB: Trencher?

BETSY: Come here and see.

(Bob comes to the window.)

BOB: *(Looking out.)* Ah. Walking the dog.

BETSY: He wasn't walking the dog when I first looked out. He was just stand-ing there, staring up at this building.

BOB: This building?

BETSY: That's what he says he does. He says he comes over here and stares up at our lighted windows.

BOB: When did he say this?

BETSY: At the playground.

BOB: At the playground?

BETSY: He stands outside the gate and stares at me. Yesterday he walked me home. That's when he made his declaration.

BOB: What declaration?

BETSY: He said he loves me. He can't live without me. He'd walk through fire to hear the notes of my voice. *(She laughs.)* That's what he said.

BOB: You'd better go to another playground.

BETSY: I did. But he followed me there . . . Oh I know he's crazy, darling, but I feel so sorry for him. He says that he's never compromised in his life and he's not going to compromise about this.

BOB: What does that mean?

BETSY: I'm not sure . . . Well, I'll get dinner. *(She goes off.)*

BOB: *(To audience as he returns to working on his bills.)* I was tired that night and worried about taxes and bills, and I could think of Trencher's "dec-laration" only as a comical mistake. I felt that he, like every other man I knew, was a captive of financial and sentimental commitments. He was no more free to fall in love with a strange woman he met at some party than he was to take a walking trip through French Guyana . . . *(The tele-phone rings; Bob answers.)* Yes? . . . Hello? . . . Who is this? *(He slams down the phone.)* Then I wondered if it might be more serious. In his help-lessness, Trencher might have touched that wayward passion my wife shares with some women — that inability to refuse any cry for help. It is not a reasonable passion, and I would almost rather have had her desire him than pity him. *(The telephone rings again; he answers.)* Hello? . . . Lookit, I know it's you, Trencher! . . . It's late, we are trying to have din-ner, so get off the line, you creep, or I'll call the cops! *(Slams down the phone. To audience.)* And that seemed to work. But then the kids got sick. *(Betsy crosses the stage with a tray; her shoes are off.)*

BETSY: *(To audience.)* I had to deal with them all day . . . *(She goes off.)*

BOB: *(To audience.)* We took turns getting up at night. And I often fell asleep at my desk . . .

BETSY: *(Coming back on, carrying a vase of roses.)* As did I, in my chair, after dinner . . . *(She puts the flowers on a table, fusses with them.)*

BOB: What are those?

BETSY: What do they look like?

BOB: Don't get wise, Betsy. I'm too tired.

BETSY: They arrived this afternoon. I just haven't had time to deal with them.

BOB: From your mother?

BETSY: From Trencher.

BOB: Oh, Christ.

BETSY: He said they were to cheer me up.

BOB: He *said?*

BETSY: He brought them to the door.

BOB: Oh Jesus, Betsy.

BETSY: I didn't let him in, Bob.

BOB: *(Taking the vase.)* Out they go, down the incinerator.

BETSY: Don't you dare!

BOB: Now! *(He starts off.)*

BETSY: Bob! *(He stops.)* Do you realize I haven't been out of this apartment in two weeks?

BOB: It hasn't been quite two weeks.

BETSY: It's been *over* two weeks.

BOB: Well let's figure it out. The children got sick on a Saturday, which was the fourth —

BETSY: Stop it, Bob! Just *stop* it! I know how long it's been. I haven't had my shoes on in two weeks.

BOB: It could be worse.

BETSY: My mother's cooks had a better life.

BOB: I doubt that.

BETSY: *(Taking off her apron; throwing it onto a chair.)* My mother's cooks had a better *life!* They had pleasant rooms. No one could come into the kitchen without their permission. They had days *off!*

BOB: How long was he were this afternoon?

BETSY: A minute. I told you.

BOB: He got *in?* He *stayed?*

BETSY: No. I did not let him in! And you know why? Because I looked so terrible. I didn't want to discourage him.

BOB: Oh God!

BETSY: He makes me feel marvelous. The things he tells me make me feel marvelous!

BOB: I don't believe this! *(A tapping sound from above.)* What's that?

BETSY: That? I'll tell you what that is. That is the people upstairs, tapping on the radiator! That is our fellow prisoners in our common penitentiary, signaling through the plumbing! That's what that is!

BOB: Do you want to go?

BETSY: Go?

BOB: Leave.

BETSY: Where would I go? Dobbs Ferry? Mount Kisco?

BOB: I mean with Trencher.

BETSY: I don't know, Bob. I don't *know.* What harm would it do if I did? Is divorce so dreadful? Is marriage the most wonderful thing in the world? When I was at school in France, I wrote a long paper on Flaubert in French. A professor from the University of Chicago wrote me a letter. Today I couldn't read a French *news*paper without a dictionary. I don't read any newspaper. I am ashamed of my incompetence. I am ashamed of how I look. Do you know what I mean? Have you the slightest idea of what I mean? *(A buzzer from off.)*

BOB: Now what? *(Buzzer again.)* That's him, isn't it? Down in the lobby.

BETSY: Maybe it is.

BOB: I'm going to tell the guy to come up.

BETSY: No, Bob.

BOB: I'm going to tell the guy to come *up!* And when he does, when he makes his so-called declaration, I'm going to knock him DOWN!

BETSY: Bobby, no.

BOB: I am! And then I'm going to tell him to get the hell out of our lives! *(He goes off, carrying the flowers.)*

BETSY: *(Calling after him.)* Bobby! Don't! Please! *(To audience.)* He didn't hit him, thank God. Trencher never got close enough for that. But the poor man stood in the vestibule, hat in hand, while Bob yelled and swore at him, and then, when Trencher turned to go, Bob threw the vase of flowers at him, which hit him right in the small of his back. *(Bob comes back on.)*

BOB: He's gone.

BETSY: I know he's gone.

BOB: Are you crying?

BETSY: Yes.

BOB: Why?

BETSY: Why? Why am I crying? I am crying because my father died when I was twelve and my mother married a man I detested. I am crying because I had to wear an ugly dress to dancing school, and didn't have a good time. I'm crying because I'm tired and can't sleep. *(She goes upstage; looks off.)*

BOB: *(To audience.)* Now, when I come home in the evenings, Betsy and I go right to the children's room. Sometimes they have built something preposterous, and their sweetness, their compulsion to build, and the brightness of the light are reflected perfectly in Betsy's face. We feed them, we bathe them, we get them to bed. Afterwards she stands for a moment in the middle of the room, trying to make some connection between the evening and the day. Then I light the candles in the candlesticks she inherited from her grandmother . . . *(He does.)* . . . and we sit down to our supper.

(Jane and Bill come on, making their way down a "row" as if for a meeting. Jane is played by the Second Actress, Bill by the Second Actor. We might hear an Episcopal hymn. Simultaneously the lights dim on Betsy and Bob as they carry off the lighted candles.)

JANE: Excuse me . . . Excuse me . . . I'm sorry . . . Excuse me.

BILL: Sorry . . . Are those your toes? . . . Sorry . . . Excuse us, please.

(They settle into their seats. Charlie, played by First Actor, comes on and stands somewhat behind them. The Rector of St James' School comes on to address a parents meeting. He is played by the Third Actor.)

RECTOR: . . . and we believe very strongly here at St. James that all our children should be grounded in at least one year of Latin before they go off to boarding school, and be able to play at least two team sports. Furthermore, all students are pledged to abide by the honor system. Courage, good sportsmanship, and honor — these are the coin of our realm. *(Jane and Bill are now whispering animatedly between themselves.)* I might conclude by pointing out that this year there are sixteen children enrolled in St. James whose parents *and* grandparents also went there. I doubt if any other day school in the city could equal that.

JANE: *(Raising her hand.)* Doctor Frisbee . . .

BILL: *(Whispering to Jane.)* Don't.

JANE: Doctor Frisbee . . .

BILL: I warned you . . . DON'T!

JANE: *(Whispering to Bill.)* I want to.

BILL: Goodnight, then. *(He gets up; to "others" in the row.)* Excuse me . . . Sorry about those toes . . . Excuse me . . . Goodnight . . . *(He edges his way out.)*

JANE: *(Defiantly.)* Dr. Frisbee . . .

RECTOR: Yes, Mrs. Sheridan.

JANE: *(Standing up.)* I wonder if you have ever thought of enrolling Negro children in Saint James?

RECTOR: *(Pause.)* That question came up three years ago. A report was submitted to the board of trustees. There have been very few requests for it. *(She waits.)* But if you'd like a copy, I will have one sent to you.

JANE: Yes. I would like to read it.

(The Rector goes off. A piano now plays dancing school music, such as "Alice Blue Gown."*Mrs. Bailey, the Dancing School Mistress, played by the First Actress, addresses the audience.)

MRS. BAILEY: We will now attempt the waltz, children . . . One two three, one two three . . .

(She fades off as Jane comes downstage as if to watch the class. Charlie approaches her.)

CHARLIE: Hello.

JANE: Hello.

CHARLIE: I was interested in the question you asked at the Saint James parents meeting the other night.

JANE: I'm glad someone was interested. The Rector wasn't. My husband certainly wasn't.

CHARLIE: That's what was interesting. *(She looks at him.)* I mean, the Rector's reply.

JANE: Yes . . . It just seems so dumb not to respond to the changing times.

CHARLIE: I agree. *(They look out.)*

JANE: This is dumb, too. When you think about it. Dancing school.

CHARLIE: I went. Didn't you?

JANE: Oh yes. Yes.

CHARLIE: At least it taught us to be courteous and polite.

JANE: Yes . . . *(They watch the dancing.)*

CHARLIE: Haven't we seen each other waiting for the school bus? At 68th and Park?

JANE: Oh yes.

CHARLIE: You have your daughter, and I have my son.

JANE: *(Carefully.)* Somebody said your wife had died.

CHARLIE: Yes. I've remarried.

JANE: Yes.

CHARLIE: *(Looking out.)* She's very cute, your little girl.

JANE: Not cute enough, I'm afraid. She seems to have been delegated to the sidelines.

CHARLIE: Oh well.

JANE: That velvet dress was supposed to do the trick. It was a present from my mother.

CHARLIE: I notice my boy is misbehaving again.

JANE: Mine won't even smile.

CHARLIE: I'll tell mine to dance with her next week.

JANE: If she'll come. She's becoming totally uncooperative. She's hopeless on the piano, and I drag her kicking and screaming to her riding lessons . . . *(The music ends; they applaud.)*

CHARLIE: Would you have lunch with me some time?

JANE: *(Immediately.)* Yes.

CHARLIE: Next Tuesday? One o'clock? Rocco's, at 31st and 1st?

JANE: Sounds interesting.

CHARLIE: It's — out of the way.

JANE: That's what sounds interesting.

CHARLIE: We can talk about Saint James' School.

JANE: Yes. Oh yes.

CHARLIE: *(Calling out, as he crosses the stage.)* Billy! Behave! *(They are now on either side of the stage.)*

JANE: *(To audience.)* The menu at Rocco's was soiled, and so was the waiter's tuxedo, but we met again — for dinner, when my husband was away.

CHARLIE: *(To audience.)* She was excited at finding someone who was interested in her opinions. Which I was. And we kissed in the taxi when I took her home. *(They move closer to each other.)*

JANE: *(To audience.)* And then we met in the rotunda at the Metropolitan Museum, and again for lunch at a restaurant in an uptown apartment house.

CHARLIE: The reason I asked you to come here is that my firm has an apartment upstairs.

JANE: Yes. All right.

CHARLIE: Do you want to walk up? The elevator men in these buildings . . .

JANE: I don't care about the elevator men in these buildings.

CHARLIE: *(To audience.)* And so we went up. *(They step into the "elevator"; their hands touch.)*

JANE: *(To audience.)* For lovers, touch is metamorphosis. All the parts of their bodies seem to change into something different and better.

CHARLIE: That part of their experience, the totality of years before they met, is changed, and redirected toward this moment.

JANE: They feel they have reached an ecstasy of rightness that they command in every part . . .

CHARLIE: And any recollection that occurs to them takes on this final clarity. . .

JANE: Whether it be a Chicago railroad station on Christmas Eve . . .

CHARLIE: Or running a ski trail at that hour when, although the sun is still in the sky, the north face of every mountain lies in the dark. *(They are about to kiss when Charlie's Wife storms on behind them. She is played by the Third Actress in raincoat and hat.)*

WIFE: *(Pounding on the "door.")* Let me in there! Charles, I know you're in there! I can hear you! I can hear you whispering!

JANE: *(Whispering.)* How did she . . .

CHARLIE: *(Whispering.)* Mrs. Woodruff in the rotunda . . . She must have told her.

WIFE: *(More pounding.)* All right then, Charles! I intend to call her husband immediately! *(She storms off. Pause.)*

CHARLIE: I'd better go put out the fire.

JANE: Yes. *(He goes off. Jane turns to the audience.)* And then it struck her that they were all too confused to abide by the forms that guarantee the permanence of a society, as their fathers and mothers had done. *(Dancing school music again; she gets up.)* Instead, they put the burden of order onto their children and filled their days with specious rites and ceremonies . . . *(Mrs. Bailey come up to her. Charlie comes on in time to hear.)*

MRS. BAILEY: Oh I'm so glad to see you, Mrs. Sheridan. We were afraid you were sick. Right after class began, Mr. Sheridan came and took your girl.

JANE: Took her? Where?

MRS. BAILEY: He mentioned something about Europe. He seemed very upset.

JANE: Thank you, Mrs. Bailey. *(Mrs. Bailey moves off. Charlie comes up to her.)* What do we do?

CHARLIE: *(Whispering.)* It will be all right, my darling. It will be all right.

JANE: I'm not sure it will be, at all!

(She hurries off. He starts to follow her off.)

MRS. BAILEY: *(To "class.")* Dance, children! . . . Straight backs! . . . One two three, one two three . . . *(She goes off.)*

CHARLIE: *(Turning to audience.)* I am perceived as a somewhat retiring man. Here's why . . . *(The piano waltz modulates to skating music, as if played on a Wurlitzer organ.)* You may have seen my mother, waltzing on ice skates in Rockefeller Center. *(Behind him, First Actress "skates" with Third Actor.)* She's seventy-eight years old, but very wiry, and she wears a red velvet costume with a short shirt. Her tights are flesh colored, and she has spectacles and a red ribbon in her hair, and she waltzes with one of the rink attendants. *(We see this.)* I suppose I should be grateful for the fact that she amuses herself and is not a burden to me, but I sincerely wish she had hit on some less conspicuous recreation. Whenever I see gracious old ladies arranging chrysanthemums and pouring tea, I think of my own mother, dressed like a hat-check girl, pushing some paid rink attendant around the ice, in the middle of the third-biggest city in the world . . . *(Harding, his father, comes out and sits in a chair at a table. Harding is played by the Second Actor.)*

HARDING: *(Calling off.)* Kellner! Garçon! Cameriere! You! Could we have a little service here!

CHARLIE: *(To audience.)* And this was my father. My mother divorced him long ago. *(He pulls up a chair and joins Harding.)* Hi, Dad.

HARDING: *(Still calling off.)* Chop! Chop! *(To Charlie.)* You hungry?

CHARLIE: Sure.

HARDING: We'll stoke you up before you have to go back to that lousy boarding school gruel. *(Calls off.)* My good man! *(To Charlie.)* I should have brought my whistle. I have a whistle that is audible only to the ears of old waiters. *(The Waiter at last arrives, played by Third Actor.)* Now, take out your little pad and your little pencil and see if you can get this straight: two Beefeater Gibsons. Repeat after me: two Beefeater Gibsons.

WAITER: *(An old man.)* How old is the boy?

HARDING: That, my good man, is none of your goddamned business.

WAITER: I'm sorry, sir, but I cannot serve the boy.

HARDING: Well I have some news for you. I have some very interesting news. This doesn't happen to be the only restaurant in New York. They've opened another on the corner. *(The Waiter goes off.)* Come on, Charlie. *(They exchange seats as the Waiter rips off the white tablecloth revealing an English print underneath.)*

CHARLIE: *(To audience.)* And we went to an English pub . . .

HARDING: *(Calling off.)* Heigh ho! Master of the hounds! Tallyho, and all that! We'd like something in the way of a stirrup cup! *(To Waiter, still played by Third Actor.)* Let's see what England can produce in the way of a cocktail!

WAITER: *(Irish accent.)* This isn't England.

HARDING: If there is one thing I can't tolerate, it's an impudent domestic. Come on, Charlie. *(They exchange seats again, as the Waiter reveals a red checkered tablecloth.)*

CHARLIE: *(To audience.)* The fifth place we went was Italian.

HARDING: *Buon giorno. Per favore, possiamo avere due cocktail americani, forti, forti. Molto gin, poco vermut.*

WAITER: *(Young; gay)* I don't understand Italian.

HARDING: Oh come off it! *Subito, subito.*

WAITER: I'm sorry, sir, this table is reserved.

HARDING: All right. Get us another table.

WAITER: All the tables are reserved.

HARDING: I get it. *Capeesh.* Well, the hell with you. *Vada all'inferno.* Onwards and upwards, Charlie. *(The Waiter goes off with the tablecloths. Charlie and Harding come downstage; street noises.)*

CHARLIE: I've got to make my train, Dad.

HARDING: Now?

CHARLIE: I do.

HARDING: I should have taken you to my club. The service there is excellent. But for some reason, I'm no longer a member . . . Well, come on. I'll walk you to Grand Central.

CHARLIE: That's O.K., Dad.

HARDING: No I want to. And I want to buy you a paper. A gentleman should have something to read on the train. *(A Newsman comes on with newspapers, once again played by the Third Actor.)* Kind sir, would you be good enough to favor me with one of your goddamned, no-good, ten-cent afternoon papers? *(The Newsman turns away.)* Is it asking too much, kind sir, for you to sell me one of your disgusting specimens of yellow journalism? *(The Newsman goes.)*

CHARLIE: I'm late, Dad.

HARDING: Now just wait a second, sonny. Just wait right there. I want to get a rise out of this chap. *(He goes off, calling after the Newsman.)* Oh sir! Scribe! Pawn of the Fifth Estate! *(He is off.)*

CHARLIE: *(Calling after him.)* Good-bye, Daddy . . . Good-bye. *(To audience.)* And that was the last time I saw my father.

(He goes off, as we hear party music, now the Fifties. Lively and reassuring, such as Bing Crosby singing "Dear Folks and Gentle People." Others come out, enjoying the party. Everyone has drinks. Behind, the background changes to a pleasant green, as seen though a picture window. Gee-Gee comes on, slightly drunk. He is played by the Third Actor. Peaches, played by the First Actress, approaches him.)

PEACHES: Are you all right?

GEE-GEE: *(Unconvincingly.)* Fine.

PEACHES: *(To audience.)* My husband and I have recently moved to one of the hill towns. I don't mean the real hill towns — Assisi or Perugia, perched on those three-thousand-foot crags — no, I mean the towns perched north of New York.

GEE-GEE: *(To audience; sardonically.)* They resemble the hill towns only in that the ailing, the disheartened, and the poor cannot ascend the steep moral paths that form their natural defenses.

PEACHES: *(To audience.)* Here life is comfortable and tranquil, and in nearly every house, there is love, graciousness, and high hopes. Here the schools are excellent, the roads are smooth, and —

(Archie, played by Second Actor, comes down to them.)

ARCHIE: Welcome, welcome.

GEE-GEE: Thank you, thank you.

ARCHIE: I'm interested in your names. *(To Peaches.)* Why do they call you Peaches?

PEACHES: Oh it's just a nickname. When I was little, I thought life was peaches and cream.

ARCHIE: I see. *(To Gee-Gee.)* And is it true that people call you Gee-Gee?

GEE-GEE: It is.

ARCHIE: Why?

GEE-GEE: I need another drink. *(He goes to the bar.)*

PEACHES: *(Quickly.)* It's from college. At college they called him Greek God. See? Gee-Gee. He was All-America twice.

ARCHIE: What college?

PEACHES: Wisconsin. But he went to Andover before that. He was Vice President of his class and captain of the hockey team. *(Gee-Gee returns with a drink.)*

ARCHIE: Say, Gee-Gee, did you know Chucky Ewing at Andover? He must have been there when you were. He went on to Yale and now works for Brown Brothers Harriman. He married Bunny Bean from Vassar and moved to Mamaroneck two years ago. They spend their summers in their family's house on Fisher's Island, and . . . *(He runs out of steam.)*

GEE-GEE: *(Looking at him vaguely.)* What?

ARCHIE: I said did you know Chucky —

GEE-GEE: God, it's stuffy in here. *(He takes off his tie.)*

PEACHES: *(Whispering.)* Oh sweetie. No.

GEE-GEE: Terribly stuffy. *(He kicks off his shoes.)*

PEACHES: Gee-Gee. Please. Not our first night here.

GEE-GEE: *(Taking off his shirt.)* I have to teach them, honey. They've got to learn.

PEACHES: *(To Archie.)* He's had a little too much to drink.

GEE-GEE: Like hell I have. I haven't had half enough. *(He chugalugs his drink; shouts.)* I'VE GOT TO TEACH THEM! *(Martha, Archie's wife, comes down to join him. She is played by the Third Actress.)*

MARTHA: What do you want to teach us, Gee-Gee?

GEE-GEE: *(Embracing her.)* You'll never know. You're all too goddamned stuffy.

ARCHIE: You're not teaching anybody anything. Gee-Gee, but the fact that you're rotten drunk.

GEE-GEE: What a goddamn bunch of stuffed shirts! Let's put a little vitality into the conversation, shall we? *(He starts a striptease, singing "Take it off, take it off, cried the boys from the rear . . .")*

PEACHES: *(To Martha; hopelessly.)* Oh dear. He did this in Scarsdale. He did it in Chappaqua.

MARTHA: But why?

PEACHES: I don't know. And he used to be so wonderful. *(Calls to Gee-Gee.)* Come back, Gee-Gee! Come back to me! Come back to the way you were! *(Gee-Gee is down to his boxer shorts.)*

ARCHIE: *(Going up to him.)* Get out of my house, Gee-Gee.

GEE-GEE: The pleasure's all mine, neighbor. *(He gives Archie a big kiss, then moons the room before he exits drunkenly. A long moment.)*

GUEST: *(Played by First Actor; to Archie, handing back his drink.)* Thanks for a lovely evening. *(He exits hurriedly with his wife, played by Second Actress.)*

PEACHES: *(Calling after him.)* Gee-Gee! Oh please! *(To the others, as she picks up his clothes.)* He doesn't hear me any more. He doesn't hear the children.

MARTHA: *(Helping her pick up.)* I'm sorry, Peaches.

PEACHES: I know you are. But you won't be around to say good-bye. Even the garbage man will be glad to see us go! . . . Oh come back, Gee-Gee! Come back to me! *(She hurries off, carrying his clothes. Pause.)*

ARCHIE: I wonder what he wanted to teach us?

MARTHA: *(Tentatively.)* I think . . . he wants to prepare us for something.

ARCHIE: Prepare us for what?

MARTHA: I don't know . . . Age. Sickness. Death.

ARCHIE: Jesus, Martha.

MARTHA: I mean, he seems to think we're all so rich and happy . . . Maybe he just wants to prepare us.

ARCHIE: Well I wish he could prepare us without taking off his clothes.

MARTHA: I wish he could, too. *(Archie goes off. Martha turns to audience.)* I don't know. Recently I've had this terrible feeling that I'm a character in a television situation comedy. I mean, I'm nice-looking, I'm well dressed, I have humorous and attractive children, but I have this terrible feeling that I'm in black-and-white and can be turned off by anybody. I just have this terrible feeling I can be turned off.

(She goes off, as we hear mysterious music. Ethan comes downstage with a book. He is played by the First Actor. He settles into a chair to read.)

ETHAN: *(To audience.)* It's late at night. I'm reading *Anna Karenina.* My wife Rachel is up in Seal Harbor with the kids while I've stayed down here to work. Our living room is comfortable, the book is interesting, and the neighborhood is quiet, what with so many people away. *(He reads, then puts down his book.)* Oh hell, I might as well admit it. Rachel's left me. She's left me twice before, but this is it. Hey, that's O.K.! You can cure yourself of a romantic, carnal, and disastrous marriage. But like any addict in the throes of a cure, you have to be careful of every step you take. *(The telephone rings.)* Like not answering the telephone. *(Indicating the phone.)* Because that's Rachel. Maybe she's repented or wants to tell me it's rained for five days, or one of the children has a passing fever — something . . . *(Shouting at phone.)* But I will not be tempted to resume a relationship that has been so miserable! *(The phone stops, he resumes reading. Cricket sounds. Then a dog barks.)* That's the Barstow's dog. He barks endlessly. *(The barking stops.)* That's funny. Why did he stop? *(He listens. A shadowy figure, in raincoat and hat, enters stealthily upstage. He is played by the Third Actor.)* Then I hear very close outside, a footstep and a cough. *(The figure coughs.)* I feel my flesh get hard — you know that feeling — and know I am being watched from the picture window. *(He jumps up. The figure goes.)* I flip on the outside carriage light and look out. But now the lawn is empty. *(Returns to his chair.)* The next night, I leave the outside light on, settle in with my book, and hear the dog bark once again. *(Barking; the Figure appears downstage.)* And there he is again! Now in the window above the piano . . . *(He yells.)* Hey, you! Get the hell out of here! *(He grabs the phone, dials O. The figure disappears.)* Rachel is gone! There's nothing to see! . . . Oh excuse me, operator. Give me the police. *(Toward off.)* Leave me alone! . . . Police? Ah, is that you, Stanley? Stanley, I want to report a prowler! . . . What? *(To audience.)* He seems to think I am trying to undermine real estate values. *(To phone.)* Yes . . . All right. Goodnight, Stanley. *(To audience.)* He said he was underpaid and overworked, and that if I wanted a guard around my house, I should vote to enlarge the police force. *(Lights change to daylight. We hear a train announcement: "The eight-eighteen for Grand Central is arriving on track two." Ethan puts on his jacket, adjusts his tie, and grabs his briefcase. Herb Marston, played by Third Actor, comes on downstage right, as if onto the station platform. He wears a hat and also carries a briefcase. He looks up the track, waiting for the train to arrive. Stepping onto the "platform" downstage left.; to audience.)* The next day I see my man. He is waiting on the platform for the eight-eighteen. It's Herb Marston, who lives in the big yellow house on Glenhollow Road. *(Ethan goes up to him.)* Hey! I don't mind you looking in my windows. Mr. Marston, but I wish you wouldn't trample on my wife's begonias! *(Marston checks his watch as Ethan turns to audience.)* That's what I planned to say. But I didn't. Because just as I was about to let fly — *(Herb's daughter, comes on with the New York Times. She is played by the Third Actress.)*

DAUGHTER: Here's your *Times*, Daddy. *(His wife comes on, carrying coffee in a paper bag. She is played by the Second Actress.)*

ESTHER: And coffee, for the train.

HERB: Thank you both. *(They embrace and go off.)*

ETHAN: *(To audience.)* So I couldn't. How could I? With his wife, and that sweet daughter, right there . . . And notice there was nothing irregular in his manner. He looked solvent and rested and moral — much more so than Chucky Ewing, down the platform, who is job hunting, or — *(Looks off.)* Uh oh. There's Grace Harris, otherwise known as Black Widow, probably off to another funeral . . . *(Grace approaches him, wearing a black coat and hat. She is played by the First Actress.)* . . . Hey, why is she giving me that sad, sad look?

GRACE: You poor, poor boy.

ETHAN: I'm not poor and I'm not a boy, Grace.

GRACE: I see the noose around your neck. *(She turns and goes off, funereally.)*

ETHAN: *(To audience.)* The noose! How did she know about the noose? Last night I dreamed about a hangman's noose. All night long, every time I closed my eyes, there it was swinging in front of me. Does she think I plan to hang myself? Is that why Marston stands in our flower garden, waiting for me to do it? O.K. Fine. Then I'll burn every rope in the house. *(The telephone rings again; he ignores it.)* And I'll stick to my cure! *(He takes up Anna Karenina, puts his finger on an arbitrary passage, reads:)* "And Anna saw that her only choice was to leap in front of the oncoming train. . ." *(He groans, sits on the couch, but now is uncomfortable. He reaches under the cushion and pulls out an old whiffle ball.)* What's this? . . . Oh my God, the kids' old whiffle ball . . . The games on the lawn . . . the sledding in winter . . . the bike trip . . . Oh my God! *(He kisses the whiffle ball reverently, then the telephone rings once more. He answers quickly.)* Yes! Oh my darling! *(To audience.)* It's been raining up there for a week. *(To phone.)*

I'll drive all night! I'll be there tomorrow! Oh, my love! *(To audience as he hurriedly puts on his jacket.)* And after that, so far as I know, Herb Marston no longer stands outside our house in the dark, though I see him often at the country club dances. *(He comes downstage. Street sounds.)* His daughter is to be married next month, and his wife has been cited by the United Fund for — *(Patsy comes on, played by Third Actress. She carries a paper bag.)*

PATSY: Yoo hoo! Ethan!

ETHAN: *(Crossing to her.)* Oh hello, Patsy.

PATSY: Could I ask you a rather peculiar question?

ETHAN: Shoot.

PATSY: What do Republicans drink? I mean, generally.

ETHAN: Republicans? Scotch, probably.

PATSY: *(Patting her bag.)* That's what I thought. Scotch.

ETHAN: What does Ed say?

PATSY: Ed's away . . . Thank you, Ethan. *(Ethan starts off.)* Oh. And how was your summer?

ETHAN: Fine. Everything was fine. Everyone is well and happy. *(He goes off tossing the whiffle ball. Patsy takes the scotch out of the bag, sets it up at her bar. Door chimes.)*

PATSY: *(Calling off.)* It's open!

FRED'S VOICE: Hello?

PATSY: *(Calling off.)* I'm in here. *(She drapes herself attractively somewhere. Fred comes on.)*

FRED: Good evening.

PATSY: Hello again . . . How about a drink?

FRED: A little Scotch maybe.

PATSY: Scotch? I believe I can produce scotch. *(Goes to bar.)* Yes, indeedy. Scotch.

FRED: What train does your husband come in on?

PATSY: *(Mixing him a drink.)* Him? Oh he's away. His business takes him all over the world.

FRED: What does he do?

PATSY: Him? Oh he manufactures plastic tongue depressors. They take him all over the world. *(She hands him a drink.)* You know, when you called, when you said you were stopping by, I was secretly hoping you might wear your uniform.

FRED: What uniform?

PATSY: Your general's uniform.

FRED: Oh I'm not a general.

PATSY: I heard someone call you "General" after church.

FRED: Oh that. That started in the locker room at the golf club. I happen to have political opinions. And I happen to express those opinions.

PATSY: You mean you know things that generals know?

FRED: I believe I do. For example, I know it's time to hang tough. If the Russians want trouble, I say throw a little nuclear hardware at 'em. Show 'em who's boss. I have the courage to say these things. So Chucky Ewing started calling me general. Never mind. Somebody has to keep watch around here.

PATSY: I couldn't agree more. *(She sits on the couch.)* I'm sorry your wife is sick.

FRED: Not sick. Just tired. From her volunteer work. She does a lot of collecting. It runs in her family. Her grandmother did smallpox. Her mother does mental health. My wife is TB. I told her I'd finish up her list. *(Sits next to her.)*

PATSY: So you called me.

FRED: So I called you.

PATSY: I'd better start looking for my checkbook.

FRED: *(Reaching for her.)* Not yet.

PATSY: *(Skittering away.)* Hey. At ease, General . . .

FRED: I can't be gone too long.,

PATSY: I want my favor first.

FRED: What favor?

PATSY: Guess.

FRED: I can't give you money. I'm not rich, you know.

PATSY: Oh I wouldn't think of taking money.

FRED: Then what is it?

PATSY: Something you wear.

FRED: My Dad's watch? My Sunday cuff links?

PATSY: Something else.

FRED: Ah hah! My Zippo lighter from the war!

PATSY: I won't tell you unless you promise to give it to me.

FRED: I never promise unless I can keep that promise.

PATSY: It's very small.

FRED: How small?

PATSY: Tiny. Weeny.

FRED: *(Seizing her in his arms.)* Please.

PATSY: I want a key to your bomb shelter.

FRED: Who told you about that?

PATSY: I saw it with my own eyes. I saw those bulldozers and trucks. I saw you plant grass seed over it. I saw your wife put that birdbath on top of it.

FRED: Is that the reason you came up to me after church?

PATSY: *(Marching her fingers up and down his rib cage.)* Creepy, creepy, creepy mouse . . .

FRED: That shelter was designed strictly for my family . . .

PATSY: Come to live in the general's house . . .

FRED: We've made some very tough decisions with that shelter. We've had to cut out cousins. We've had to let my Aunt Ida stay outside and burn . . .

PATSY: *(Seductively.)* . . . the rocket's red glare . . . the bombs bursting in air . . .

FRED: All right! *(He takes a small key on a chain from around his neck.)* If we hit them before they hit us, you might never have to use this. *(She takes it, drops it down the front of her dress.)*

PATSY: Thank you, General. Now for my checkbook. Suppose we take a little look upstairs.

(They go off as the lights change to dappled outdoor green. Maynard wheels on an outdoor grill. He is played by the Third Actor. His wife Zena, played by the Second Actress, glowers at him from a table.)

MAYNARD: *(To audience.)* What a splendid summer night! The light hits you like a blow. The air smells as if hundreds of wonderful girls had just wandered across the lawn. *(Cleaning the grill.)* In the summer I cook most of our dinners on a charcoal grill in the backyard. Tonight we had hamburgers, and I noticed my wife Zena didn't seem to have any appetite. The children ate heartily, of course, but perhaps they sensed a quarrel, because as soon as they were through, they slipped into the television room — to watch the quarrels there. *(He goes to clear the table.)*

ZENA: You're so inconsiderate. You never think of me.

MAYNARD: I'm sorry, darling. Wasn't the hamburger done?

ZENA: It wasn't the hamburger — I'm used to the garbage you cook. It's just that your whole attitude is so inconsiderate.

MAYNARD: What have I done, darling?

ZENA: What have you done? What have you done? You've ruined my life, that's what you've done!

MAYNARD: I don't see how I've ruined your life. I guess you're disappointed — lots of people are . . . *(They both glance at the audience.)* . . . but I don't think it's fair to blame it all on your marriage.

ZENA: Oh God.

MAYNARD: There are lots of things I wanted to do — wanted to climb the Matterhorn — but I wouldn't blame that fact that I haven't on anyone else.

ZENA: *(Laughing.)* You? Climb the Matterhorn? Ha. You couldn't even climb the Washington Monument.

MAYNARD: Sweetheart —

ZENA: You have ruined my life. *(She goes off with the plates as Jack comes on. He carries a cooking fork and wears an apron reading "Danger! Men Cooking!" Jack is played by the Second Actor.)*

JACK: *(To audience.)* As soon as I check into the hotel in Minneapolis, the telephone's ringing. She tells me the hot water heater isn't working. So I say why doesn't she call the plumber, and she cries. She cries over long-distance for about fifteen minutes. Now there's a very good jewelry store in Minneapolis, so I bought her a pair of earrings. Sapphires. Eight hundred dollars. I give them to her when I get home. We go over to the Barnstables for dinner, and later she tells me she's lost one. She doesn't know where. She won't even call the Barnstables to see if it's lying around on the floor. So then I say it's like throwing money into the fire, and she cries again. She says sapphires are cold stones — they express my inner coldness. She says there wasn't any love in those earrings — all I had to do was step into a jewelry store and buy them. So then I ask her does she expect me to make her jewelry — does she want me to go to night school and learn how to make one of those crummy silver bracelets? Hammered? You know. Every little hammer blow a sign of love and affection. Is that what she wants, for Chrissake? And that's another night I slept in the guest room . . . *(He goes off as Maynard comes on. He wheels the grill offstage.)*

MAYNARD: *(To audience.)* Now it's fall, and the children have gone away to school. *(Furtively, as Zena comes on with two plates.)* I think Zena is trying to poison me.

ZENA: Sit down and eat. We can at least try to watch *I've Got a Secret. (She turns on the "television." They sit side by side on the couch; he takes his plate.)*

MAYNARD: What's this?

ZENA: What does it look like? Ham, salad, and potatoes. *(Maynard takes a bite, spits it out.)*

MAYNARD: There's something wrong with the salad. *(He wipes out his mouth with his napkin.)*

ZENA: Ah yes. I was afraid that would happen. You left your lighter fluid in the pantry, and I mistook it for vinegar. *(She takes his plate and gets up.)*

MAYNARD: Where are you going?

ZENA: I thought I might try to take a bath.

MAYNARD: Why try, dear? Why not just do it?

ZENA: I'll try to ignore that. *(She goes off.)*

MAYNARD: *(To audience.)* Oh God, it could be just my imagination. Lord knows she irritates me these days. Even her manner of speaking offends me . . . "I must try to arrange the flowers." *(A la Dracula.)* "I must try to buy a hat." Is it me? Am I crazy? Or has the world gone mad? *(Maynard goes off as Burt, played by the First Actor, comes out, in a black sweater, dark gloves, and a cap. He is examining a wallet.)*

BURT: *(To audience.)* A few weeks ago, I lost my job. I'm broke and the bills are piling up, so tonight, after the Warburton's party, I sneaked back into their house, climbed the stairs, patted their cocker spaniel, entered their bedroom, and stole Bill Warburton's wallet out of his pants. *(Opens the wallet, counts the money.)* Nine hundred dollars! . . . But oh, I'm miserable! I never knew that the mind could open up so many chambers of such self reproach! Where is my innocence? Where are the trout streams of my youth? Where is the wet-leather smell of the loud waters and the keen woods after a smashing rain? *(Puts the money back in the wallet.)* At least this will pay the bills. *(He goes off, as Maynard comes back on.)*

MAYNARD: *(Quickly.)* Back to the poison. Two nights ago I came home, looked into the kitchen, and thought I saw . . . *(Zena comes on, carrying a can of pesticide.)* Oh!

ZENA: Oh. It's you.

MAYNARD: What were you doing?

ZENA: What does it look like I was doing?

MAYNARD: It looked like you were putting pesticide on the lamb chops.

ZENA: I know you don't grant me much intelligence, but I think I know better than that.

MAYNARD: But then what are you doing with the pesticide?

ZENA: I was trying to dust the roses! *(She goes off.)*

MAYNARD: *(To audience.)* I ate one of the lamb chops at dinner. I had to. It's a question of trust. I mean, we've been married for twenty years. Surely I know her well enough to think that she wouldn't . . . *(He belches.)* That night I spent an hour in the bathroom with acute indigestion. She seemed to be asleep when I came back to bed, but I did notice her eyes were open wide! *(He glances off, hissing like a vampire.)* So tonight I intend to watch. I will hide in the broom closet. *(He steps into the "closet," crouches down.)* Through the keyhole I can see most of the kitchen and observe her prepare the meal . . . *(Zena comes in, gets a drink, exits singing a song like "Whistle While You Work.")* We always keep the pesticide on the cellar stairs . . . Sure enough! There she is, taking it out! *(She goes off; he watches.)* O.K., she's stepping into the garden. She must be dusting the roses . . . But now she is coming back in . . . AND SHE DID NOT RETURN THE PESTICIDE TO ITS RIGHTFUL LOCATION! It is still with her!

... Now she is taking the meat out of the oven. She is spicing it . . . Her back is to me . . . I can't quite see . . . Is that salt and pepper she is sprinkling on the meat loaf, or is it nerve poison? . . . She's spooning out the vegetables, she's serving the meat . . . *(He steps out of the "closet.")* And here she comes with the evening meal. *(Zena comes in, carrying the meat loaf.)* Hiya.

ZENA: I think we should try to eat. *(She puts the meat loaf on the table in front of him.)*

MAYNARD: *(Shoving the meat loaf toward her.)* It's hot tonight, isn't it?

ZENA: *(Shoving it back.)* You think it's hot?

MAYNARD: *(Sliding it to her again.)* I do. Yes.

ZENA: Well. We can't expect to be comfortable, can we, if we go around hiding in broom closets! *(She shoots it into his lap.)*

MAYNARD: *(To audience.)* And somehow we got through another meal . . . *(Sound of thunder. They remain frozen at the table. Christina, played by First Actress, comes on in curlers, wearing a bathrobe. She carries a little notebook.)*

CHRISTINA: *(To audience.)* Lately my husband and I have had trouble getting to sleep. Burt is temporarily unemployed, so he relaxes by taking long walks around the neighborhood. As for me? Why I simply review what I've done during the course of the day. This morning, for example, I drove Burt to the early train so he could look for another job. Then I . . . *(Consults her notebook.)* Had the skis repaired. Booked a tennis court. Bought the wine and groceries because tonight was our turn to give the monthly dinner of the Société Gastronomique du Westchester Nord. Attended a League of Women Voters meeting on sewers. Went to a full-dress lunch for Bobsie Neil's aunt. Weeded the garden. Ironed a uniform for the part-time maid who helped with the dinner. Typed two and a half pages of my paper for the book club on the early novels of Henry James. Emptied the wastebaskets. Helped the sitter prepare the children's supper. Gave Ronny some batting practice. Put Lizzie's hair in pin curls. Got the cook. Met Burt at the five thirty-five. Took a bath. Dressed. Greeted our guests in French at half-past seven. Said *bon soir* to all at eleven. And that's about it. *(Puts her notebook away.)* Some people might say I am prideful for accomplishing all this. I don't think so. All I really am is a woman enjoying herself in a country that is prosperous and still young. *(Burt comes on, again in dark clothes.)* Coming to bed, darling?

BURT: I think I'll take a little walk.

CHRISTINA: *(Kisses him.)* Goodnight then, sweetheart. I have a big day tomorrow. *(She goes off. Burt puts on his cap, pulls on his black gloves.)*

BURT: *(To audience.)* Tonight I have to rob again. This time, it will be the

Maitlands, Maynard and Zena, over on Hobbyhorse Lane. They fight a lot, and then they drink a lot, so they should sleep very soundly. *(More thunder.)*

ZENA: Sounds like rain.

MAYNARD: Would you like to talk about the weather, darling?

ZENA: No, thank you. *(They sit.)*

BURT: *(To audience.)* Oh God! I keep thinking about my beginnings — how I was made by a riggish couple in a midtown hotel after a six-course dinner with wine. My mother told me time after time that if she hadn't had so many Old Fashioneds beforehand, I'd still be unborn on a star. *(Thunder. Zena gets up.)*

ZENA: Now I will try to do the dishes. *(She clears the table.)*

MAYNARD: I will try to help you, dear . . . *(He goes to the bar.)* Say, how about a glass of port?

ZENA: You plan to drink? After dinner?

MAYNARD: *(Taking a bottle of port.)* Want to join me?

ZENA: Well, I'll try. *(Maynard picks up the pesticide.)* What do you plan to do with that?

MAYNARD: *(Ambiguously.)* I thought I'd try to put it back. *(He goes off; she goes after him, worried, carrying the meat loaf and plates. Thunder.)*

BURT: *(To audience.)* I doubt if they can hear the thunder now their lights are out . . . *(The sudden sound of rain.)* But then suddenly I changed my mind. I wish I could say a kindly lion set me straight. Or the strains of distant music from a church. But it was no more than the rain! The rain on my head! The smell of it flying up to my nose! Goddammit, there are ways out of my trouble. I'm not trapped. It's no skin off my elbow how I have been given the gifts of life so long as I possess them, and I possess them now: the tie between the wet grass roots and the hair that grows out of my body, the thrill of my mortality that I know on summer nights, loving my children and looking down the front of my wife's dress. I'll return what I stole as soon as I can. And now I'll go home to bed. *(A Patrolman comes on with a flashlight; he is played by the Second Actor.)*

PATROLMAN: Mr. Hake! What are you doing out?

BURT: Just walking the dog, Stanley *(To audience.)* Even though I didn't own one. *(He calls off.)* Here, Toby! Here, Toby!

STANLEY: Good night, Mr. Hake. Sweet dreams.

BURT: You too, Stanley. *(He goes off calling and whistling.)* Good boy! Good dog! *(Stanley looks after him as the lights fade to black.)*

END OF ACT ONE

ACT TWO

Before the curtain: summery music.
At Rise: A summer seashore light. The second of waves and gulls. Virginia,
played by the First Actress, comes out and takes a dust cover off a couch. She
folds it as she speaks.

VIRGINIA: *(To audience.)* Each year we rent a house in the mountains or at the edge of the sea. I have never known the people we have rented from, but their ability to leave behind them a sense of physical and emotional presence is amazing. Someone was enormously happy here, and we rent their happiness as we rent their beach or their canoe. *(Paul comes on, in shirtsleeves, carrying his jacket, hat, and briefcase. He is tying his necktie. He is played by the Third Actor.)* Who, we wonder, is the lady in the portrait in the upstairs hallway? Whose was the Aqualung, the set of Virginia Woolf? Who hid the copy of *Fanny Hill* in the china closet? And who painted red enamel on the toenails of the claw-footed bathtub? *(She goes off as Paul comes downstage.)*

PAUL: *(Calling off.)* Mr. Kaziac! . . . Mr. Kaziac! Would you come up to the house a minute, please! *(To the audience as he ties his tie.)* There is a moment on Sunday when the tide of a summer day turns inexorably toward the evening train back to the city. You can swim, play tennis, or take a nap, but it doesn't make much difference. You are faced with the same apprehensiveness you felt in the army as a furlough came to an end . . . *(Kaziac comes on, in coveralls, carrying a shovel. He is played by the Second Actor.)* Ah. Mr. Kaziac. I wonder if I might speak to you a moment before I catch my train back to the city. *(He gestures for him to sit.)*

KAZIAC: *(Polish accent.)* Yes, sir?

PAUL: *(After insisting Kaziac sit.)* Last Friday night, on the way here from the station, I stopped to buy some rabbits for my children. I thought they might enjoy having some summer pets, particularly since I can't be with them during the week.

KAZIAC: Yes, sir.

PAUL: I put those rabbits down in that old chicken house. You may have noticed them when you were down there, cutting the grass.

KAZIAC: Yes, sir.

PAUL: Now it is Sunday, Mr. Kaziac, and those rabbits are dead. The children went down this morning to play with them and found them all dead. You may imagine their shock and disappointment.

KAZIAC: *(Getting up.)* I'll bury them, sir.

PAUL: I already have, Mr. Kaziac. I've buried them in the garden.

KAZIAC: The skunks will dig 'em up. You should of let me deal with them.

PAUL: You're a Communist, aren't you, Mr. Kaziac?

KAZIAC: No, sir.

PAUL: Yes, you are. You were a Communist in Poland, and you're a Communist here.

KAZIAC: Not a Communist, sir.

PAUL: I saw that newspaper you were reading. "Luxury Living Weakens U.S." Do you think luxury living has weakened me?

KAZIAC: Sir?

PAUL: Do you think you'll bury us, Mr. Kaziac? Just the way I buried those rabbits?

KAZIAC: *(Starting off.)* I go now.

PAUL: Mr. Kaziac. Those rabbits were poisoned. I found poison in the chicken house.

KAZIAC: Yes?

PAUL: Did you put that poison there, Mr. Kaziac?

KAZIAC: No.

PAUL: *(Coming close to him.)* Mr. Kaziac! I am serious! Don't you know how strong that poison is? Don't you know that children might have gotten into it? Don't you know it might have killed *them?* Did you do it? Oh Kaziac, listen: I have to work in the city Monday through Friday, but if you touch my children, if you harm them in any way — IN ANY WAY! — I swear I'll take that shovel and cut your head open! *(He indicates Kaziac is to leave. Kaziac looks at him, then goes off. Virginia comes back on, carrying his suitcase.)*

VIRGINIA: What was that all about?

PAUL: Never mind. Just establishing a firm understanding around here.

VIRGINIA: *(Helping him with his jacket.)* Well. Say good-bye to the children, and I'll bring the car around. *(She starts out, then stops.)* Oh. I found yet another list from the owners. They say don't go near the old chicken house. They put rat poison in it last fall. That must have killed those poor bunnies. *(She goes off. A long moment. Then Paul puts on his hat, takes his suitcase.)*

PAUL: *(To audience; brightly.)* No harm done. *(Sound of train pulling in; Paul steps on to a "railway platform." A Conductor comes on, played by First Actor. He places a step near the exit.)*

CONDUCTOR: All aboard!

PAUL: No harm.

CONDUCTOR: Sir? Were you speaking to me?

PAUL: *(Brightly, as he climbs aboard the "train.")* No harm at all.

(The Conductor follows after, hoisting up the step, as Wally, a young college boy, backs onto the stage with a football, as if to throw a long pass. He wears a sweatshirt and cut-offs, and is played by the Second Actor. Sounds of surf and gulls. Bright beach light.)

WALLY: *(Shouting off, to receiver.)* Off! Off! Way off! *(He is about to throw the pass. Claire comes on imperiously, played by the Third Actress.)*

CLAIRE: You there! Young man! *(He holds his pass, looks at her.)* Aren't you an Osgood?

WALLY: Excuse me?

CLAIRE: *(Scrutinizing him.)* You are an Osgood, aren't you? Let me see . . . You must be out of Sally Scott by Jack Osgood Junior.

WALLY: Actually I am.

CLAIRE: Of course you are. I recognized the nose . . . Well. Go, go, Play ball. *(Wally looks at her, then goes off perplexed, rubbing his nose. Claire turns to the audience.)* In the summer months, the northeastern coast seems to be transformed into a vast social clearing house. If you sit on the verandah at the beach club, listening to the heavy furniture of the North Atlantic, figures from your social past appear in the surf, thick as raisins in a cake. A wave takes form, boils, and breaks, revealing Consuelo Roosevelt and Mr. and Mrs. Dundas Vanderbilt, with the children of both marriages. Then a roller comes in from the right like a cavalry charge, bearing, on a rubber raft, Emerson Crane's second wife, and the Bishop of Pittsburgh in an inner tube. Soon a wave breaks at your feet with the noise of a slammed trunk lid, and — *(Her daughter Carol comes on, carrying a tennis racquet, played by the First Actress.)*

CAROL: Mother! The Whitneys want you to join them for lunch! They asked me, but I hate just tagging along. Maybe I'll bike into town.

CLAIRE: *(Vaguely.)* The ocean makes you think.

CAROL: *(Looking out.)* I suppose it does.

CLAIRE: It brings up your past. *(Looks at her.)* Now you've graduated from Farmington, I think it's time I told you that during the war I was in charge of a canteen at the Embarcadero. I gave myself to many lonely soldiers. *(She goes quickly upstage, assumes a pensive pose.)*

CAROL: *(Stunned; to audience.)* At first I thought it was a lie, but Mother had never lied. Yet if what she said was true, that means she has been a fraud. Her accent is a fraud, her tastes are fraudulent, and the seraphic look she assumes when she listens to music is simply the look of someone trying to recall an old telephone number. But what can I do? My father has long since gone, and I'm too young to make a life on my own. *(Pause.)* So I decided my mother had not said what she said. *(Hurrying after Claire.)* Mother! Mother! I've decided to join you and the Whitneys! *(They both go off as Rob comes on, played by Second Actor. He wears a bathrobe. It is now night.)*

ROB: *(To audience.)* Outside the window, we hear the percussive noise of the sea. It shakes the bluff where the house stands and sends its rhythm up through the plaster and the timbers of the place. We shake up a drink, send the children to bed, and make love in a strange room that smells of someone else's soap. In the middle of the night, the terrace door flies open with a crash, though there seems to be no wind. I go down to see . . . *(Nell, his wife, comes on in a bathrobe, half asleep. She is played by the Second Actress.)*

NELL: *(Half asleep.)* Oh why have they come back?

ROB: *(Putting his arm around her.)* No one's come back, darling. It was just the terrace door.

NELL: *(Still sleepily.)* Why have they come back? What have they lost?

ROB: Come on, sweetheart. Come back to bed. *(He puts his arm around her.)* It was nothing.

(He takes her off as Rick comes on, played by the First Actor. He wears a bathrobe and is drying his hair with a towel. Sounds of gulls and the sea.)

RICK: *(To audience.)* Whenever I swim, I try to avoid my old serviceable sidestroke. I practice the overhand stroke that seems to be obligatory these days. Nowadays the sidestroke is Lower Class. I saw it once in a swimming pool, and when I asked who the swimmer was, I was told he was the butler. When the ship sinks, when the plane ditches, I will try to reach the life raft with my overhand stroke and will at least drown stylishly, whereas if I use a Lower Class sidestroke, who knows? I might live forever. *(Charlotte, his mother, comes out, with a bowl of wildflowers, which she begins to arrange. She is played by the Second Actress.)*

CHARLOTTE: Look what I bought along the road.

RICK: They're pretty, Mother.

CHARLOTTE: Well I thought since I'm visiting, I should at least make some contribution to the domestic tranquillity.

RICK: Thank you, Mother.

CHARLOTTE: I so love flowers. I can't live without them. Should I suffer financial reverses and have to choose between flowers and groceries, I believe I would choose flowers.

RICK: Did you have a good lunch, Mother?

CHARLOTTE: The beach club has changed from the old days. Your father and I had lunch there years ago, when we visited the Pommeroys. Now it is very much changed.

RICK: How do you mean?

CHARLOTTE: They've let down the bars.

RICK: I don't understand.

CHARLOTTE: *(Brightly.)* They're letting in Jews.

RICK: Maybe we'd better change the subject.

CHARLOTTE: I don't see why. It's a fact of life.

RICK: My *wife* is Jewish, Mother!

CHARLOTTE: That's not the point. Her father is Italian. He bears a very distinguished northern Italian name.

RICK: Her mother was a Polish Jew. And you know it very well.

CHARLOTTE: Well I come from old Massachusetts stock, and I'm not ashamed of it.

RICK: Nobody's ashamed, Mother.

CHARLOTTE: You seem embarrassed of your roots. This morning I heard you say tomaytoe. Rather than tomahtoe.

RICK: It's just easier.

CHARLOTTE: Anyway, I like Jews.

RICK: Oh good, Mother. Good for you.

CHARLOTTE: They work terribly hard.

RICK: They do, they do.

CHARLOTTE: They work much harder than we do.

RICK: Some do, some don't.

CHARLOTTE: Your father said they're constantly doing business. They're up at dawn doing business, and stay at it straight through cocktails. That's why they're not terribly good at tennis.

RICK: Your logic eludes me, Mother.

CHARLOTTE: And they love the telephone. They talk on the telephone all the time. Your father knew a Jew who put a telephone in his bathroom.

RICK: Impossible.

CHARLOTTE: Now me, I hate the telephone. Always have. How can you talk to someone when you can't see them? For all I know, they could be making faces at you.

RICK: They probably are.

CHARLOTTE: I suppose the Jews don't care if people do that. They don't worry about the amenities.

RICK: Mother, stop it: we are more like the Jews than you'll ever imagine.

CHARLOTTE: How, pray tell?

RICK: Because both we and the Jews know how it feels to be exiles in our native land.

CHARLOTTE: Now *that* is probably the silliest thing you've said since I've arrived.

RICK: *(With a sigh.)* I think I'll take another swim.

CHARLOTTE: *(Taking flowers off.)* Do you suppose your dear Rachel would mind if I put these flowers in the dining room? If she does, I'll persuade her otherwise. Tactfully, though. I promise I'll be tactful.

RICK: I'm sure you will be, Mother. *(She goes off. Rick looks after her then exits another way, muttering.)* Sunday . . . She's leaving Sunday . . .

(John comes on immediately, repairing a pulley from his boat. He wears a windbreaker and is played by the Second Actor. Suddenly we hear a very loud recording of a song like the Beatles' "Sergeant Pepper's Lonely Hearts Club Band" coming from offstage.)

JOHN: *(Calling off)* Turn that down, please! *(The music gets louder.)* Would somebody please turn that thing DOWN!

(The music subsides. Janet comes out. She wears a man's shirt and shorts and is played by the Third Actress.)

JANET: You don't have to shout, Daddy.

JOHN: I'm afraid I do, since your friend Peter apparently has a hearing disability.

JANET: We happen to like music, Daddy. *(She goes off.)*

JOHN: *(Calling after her.)* I'm not sure that you do. You used to put four or five records on the changer back in Bedford and then walk out of the house. I never understood why. *(She comes back on, eating something.)* Once I went out to see if I could find you, and standing on the lawn, I thought I understood. You liked to hear music pouring out of the windows. You liked to come back to a house where music was playing. Was that it? Was I right?

JANET: Oh Daddy, I don't know. *(She starts off.)*

JOHN: Well now you're here, does it have to be that *loud?* Night and day, your friend Peter —

JANET: *(Interrupting.)* You don't like him, do you, Daddy?

JOHN: I like him fine.

JANET: I can tell you don't.

JOHN: I don't know him very well.

JANET: He's very sensitive.

JOHN: I should imagine. With that hair and beard, he reminds me of some minor apostle in a third-rate Passion Play.

JANET: He's the kindest person I've ever known.

JOHN: Let's talk about you, shall we, sweetheart? We didn't ask Peter to visit us this summer, we asked you. I want to know where you intend to live.

JANET: *(Sprawling somewhere.)* With him, Daddy. I told you.

JOHN: I understand that. But where? And on what?

JANET: We'll get a place in the East Village.

JOHN: The East Village?

JANET: We'll find something.

JOHN: Suppose I bought him off.

JANET: Bought him *off?*

JOHN: Gave him some money. Sent him abroad.

JANET: He's *been* abroad, Daddy! He spent a year in India.

john: Well perhaps he should be introduced to Western Europe.

JANET: If you sent him abroad, Daddy, you know what he'd do? He'd go right to East Berlin.

JOHN: East *Berlin?*

JANET: Yes! And he'd give his passport to some creative person so they could escape to the free world.

JOHN: Why doesn't he just paint "Peace" on his ass and jump off the Eiffel tower?

JANET: *(Starting out.)* I won't take this, Daddy.

JOHN: Sweetheart, come back. I'm sorry. *(She stops.)* I just want to know what you plan to do with your life? *(He tries to put his arm around her.)*

JANET: *(Breaking away.)* I don't know. Nobody my age knows. *(She sprawls somewhere else.)*

JOHN: Lots of people know, darling. I know at least fifty girls your age who know what they want to do. They want to be historians, editors, doctors, and mothers. They want to do something useful.

JANET: I plan to get a job.

JOHN: What kind of a job? You're not trained for anything.

JANET: I'll get a job in some office.

JOHN: Doing what?

JANET: Filing. Something. There are jobs.

JOHN: Oh my God, oh my God! After the sailing lessons and the skiing lessons, after the get-togethers and the cotillions, after the year in Florence, and the summer out West, you plan to end up as some filing clerk!

JANET: Daddy —

JOHN: Some filing clerk, whose principal excitement will be to go once or twice a year to a fourth-rate Chinese restaurant with your girlfriends, and get tipsy on two sweet Manhattans!

JANET: That does it, Daddy! That really does it! *(She goes off.)*

JOHN: *(Following her.)* Oh sweetheart, come home. Come home and stay and get your feet on the ground!

(He goes off as we hear sounds of a ferry arriving: bells and horns. Baxter comes on, played by First Actor. He wears seersucker trousers and a sweater slung over his shoulders.)

BAXTER: *(To audience.)* In the middle of the summer, for those of us who don't have to work on the mainland, the tennis courts get a little dusty, the golf courses lose their green, and even the sailing breezes don't seem as fresh. So on the first Monday in August, during the changing of the guard, I like to go down to meet the ferry and check out the new arrivals, just for something to do. *(Clarissa comes on, idly. She is played by the First Actress. He looks her over.)* This summer seemed to produce a particularly attractive crop. *(Clarissa stands waiting for someone.)* Now every woman has some key. And every man is fascinated by locks. So that's what I do in August — I become a locksmith. *(To Clarissa.)* Hello there.

CLARISSA: Hello.

(Mrs. Ryan, her mother-in-law, comes on, played by the Third Actress.)

MRS. RYAN: Clarissa, I've got the car!

BAXTER: *(Bowing politely.)* Hello, Mrs. Ryan.

MRS. RYAN: Ah, Baxter. This is my new daughter-in-law, Clarissa. She's taking the house for August.

BAXTER: And where's Larry?

CLARISSA: Larry is in France. He's —

MRS. RYAN: He's gone there for the government.

CLARISSA: He won't be back till the fall. And Mother Ryan's going, too.

MRS. RYAN: I don't think you need to tell Baxter our life story, Clarissa.

BAXTER: *(To Clarissa.)* So you'll be here by yourself?

MRS. RYAN: No! Clarissa will have houseguests right through Labor Day.

CLARISSA: But I —

MRS. RYAN: *(Taking Clarissa's arm.)* We should hurry, dear. I'm double parked. *(As they go off.)* Be careful of that man, Clarissa. He's been divorced twice and is known as a terrible roué.

CLARISSA: What's a roué? *(They are off.)*

BAXTER: *(To audience.)* I'd heard about her, actually. She comes from Chicago, and supposed to be as stupid as she is beautiful. *(Square dance music: Clarissa comes on. Baxter approaches her.)* Don't you like to dance?

CLARISSA: I love to dance. But that's not dancing. I don't believe in skipping and hopping. That's only for maids.

BAXTER: Maybe you'd like to go home.

CLARISSA: I can't. I came with the Hortons.

BAXTER: That's no reason why you have to go home with them.

CLARISSA: *(Considering it.)* That's very true.

BAXTER: *(Offering his arm.)* So let me do the honors. *(He leads her to a bench which becomes a car. He opens the door for her. She settles onto the seat, as he crosses around front and gets into the driver's seat. He starts the car. They drive. After a moment.)* What about your houseguests?

CLARISSA: What houseguests?

BAXTER: I thought you had houseguests all summer.

CLARISSA: Oh my mother-in-law just said that to ward off the men.

BAXTER: Then you're alone.

CLARISSA: I certainly am not. Wacky's there.

BAXTER: Wacky?

CLARISSA: My dog.

BAXTER: Ah. *(They drive.)* You're lovely, Clarissa.

CLARISSA: That's just my outward self. Nobody knows the real me.

BAXTER: *(To audience; as he drives.)* What was the key? Did she think of herself as an actress? A channel swimmer? An heiress? *(They drive.)*

CLARISSA: *(Looking out.)* Those stones on the point. They've grown a lot since I visited last year.

BAXTER: What?

CLARISSA: You can see, even in the moonlight. Those stones have grown.

BAXTER: Stones don't grow, Clarissa.

CLARISSA: Oh yes they do. Stones grow. There's a stone in our rose garden that's grown a foot.

BAXTER: *(Ironically.)* I didn't know stones grew.

CLARISSA: Well they do.

BAXTER: Ah. *(They drive.)* Where'd you go to school, Clarissa?

CLARISSA: I went to Miss Hall's School in Pittsfield, Massachusetts. I hear it's now gone belly up.

BAXTER: How about college?

CLARISSA: I didn't go to college.

BAXTER: No?

CLARISSA: I don't believe in college. I think college can be a waste of time and money. I mean, if you have thoughts, you have thoughts, and college professors get paid much too much trying to confuse those thoughts.

BAXTER: Ah. *(Pulling up the car.)* Well here we are.

CLARISSA: Yes. Here we are.

BAXTER: May I come in?

CLARISSA: No. You don't understand the kind of woman I am. Nobody does.

BAXTER: I'd like to find out. *(He leans over and tries to kiss her. Clarissa pushes him away and gets out of the car. She speaks through the "window.")*

CLARISSA: Now you've ruined everything. I know what you've been thinking. Most men do. Well, you needn't think it any longer. I'm going to write an airmail letter to Larry in France and tell him you tried to kiss me.

BAXTER: *(Quickly getting out of the car.)* I just want to know you better, Clarissa.

CLARISSA: Oh yes. Oh sure. Everyone thinks I'm dumb. Larry never lets me speak, and Mother Ryan says I'm stupid, and even my houseguests said I was kind of slow.

BAXTER: I think you're intelligent.

CLARISSA: You don't mean that.

BAXTER: I do. You have a wonderful intelligence. A wonderful mind.

CLARISSA: Nobody ever takes me seriously until they get their arms around me.

BAXTER: No, no. I imagine you have a lot of very interesting opinions.

CLARISSA: I do actually. For example, I think we're like cogs in a wheel. Do you think we're like cogs in a wheel?

BAXTER: Oh yes. Oh absolutely.

CLARISSA: Do you think women should work?

BAXTER: I'm interested in your opinion, Clarissa.

CLARISSA: My opinion is, I don't think married women should work. Unless they have a lot of money. So they can get a maid. But even then, I think it's a full-time job to take care of a man. I don't think that working or joining the church is going to change everything, or special diets, either. I eat what's reasonable. If ham is reasonable, I buy ham. If lamb is reasonable, I buy lamb. Don't you think that's intelligent?

BAXTER: I think that's very intelligent.

CLARISSA: But progressive education. I don't buy that. When we go to the Howards' for dinner, the children ride their bikes around the table all the time, and it's my opinion they get this way from progressive schools, and that children ought to be told what's nice and what isn't.

BAXTER: You're very intelligent, Clarissa.

CLARISSA: You really think so?

BAXTER: I do. I really do.

CLARISSA: Thank you, Baxter. *(He tries to kiss her again. She lets him.)*

BAXTER: You've got lovely hair, Clarissa.

CLARISSA: It isn't as pretty as it used to be. But I'm not going to dye it. I don't think women should dye their hair.

BAXTER: That's intelligent, too. I love your intelligence, Clarissa.

CLARISSA: Thank you very much. *(She starts to lead him off.)*

BAXTER: *(Over his shoulder to the audience as they go.)* And that was the key! It was as simple as that!

(Chaddy comes out immediately, played by the Third Actor.)

CHADDY: *(To audience.)* The branch of the family to which we belong was founded by a minister who was eulogized by Cotton Mather. We were ministers until the middle of the nineteenth century, and the harshness of our thought is preserved in books and sermons. Man is full of misery, they say, and all earthly beauty is lustful and corrupt. *(Mournful sea sounds: bell-buoys and foghorns. Lawrence comes on, carrying a wooden shingle. He is played by the Second Actor.)*

LAWRENCE: Look at this.

CHADDY: What?

LAWRENCE: This shingle. This shingle must be over two hundred years old.

CHADDY: And?

LAWRENCE: And? *And?* This house was built in the twenties. Grampa must have bought shingles from all the farms around here just to make it look venerable.

CHADDY: I guess he did.

LAWRENCE: I *know* he did. Look. You can still see the carpenter's chalk where this shingle was nailed into place. And if you look at the front door, which is a relatively new door, you'll see that the surface has been deeply scored, and white paint has been rubbed in to imitate rot.

CHADDY: O.K, Lawrence. O.K.

LAWRENCE: Imagine spending thousands of dollars to make a sound house look like a wreck. Imagine the frame of mind this implies. Imagine wanting to live so much in the past that you'll pay carpenter's wages to disfigure your front door.

CHADDY: Maybe we should hit a tennis ball, Lawrence. Let's hit a tennis ball.

LAWRENCE: You know why, don't you? You know why we retreat into the past.

CHADDY: No, why, Lawrence?

LAWRENCE: Because we, and our friends, and our part of the nation, can't cope with the present. That's why we have to have candles when we eat. That's why we fight over old furniture.

CHADDY: Who's fighting? We all agreed you could have the highboy, Lawrence. Since apparently it means so much to you.

LAWRENCE: Grampa left it to me. And you personally have resented it ever since.

CHADDY: Come out of it, Lawrence.

LAWRENCE: Come out of what?

CHADDY: This gloominess, buddy. Come out of it. You're spoiling your own good time and everyone else's. You've made everything tense and unpleasant all weekend. You think you know everything, but you don't, Lawrence. You don't know the half of it.

LAWRENCE: I'll tell you what I know. I know our sister is promiscuous. I know Dad is almost broke. I know Mother's an alcoholic. And . . . *(Tapping him with the shingle.)* I know you're a superficial fool.

CHADDY: *(Pushing him away.)* And you're a gloomy son of a bitch!

LAWRENCE: *(Shoving him.)* Get your fat face out of mine! *(They wrestle. Finally Chaddy pins Lawrence. Chaddy raises his fist. They freeze.)*

CHADDY: *(To audience.)* And I think I could have killed my brother then and there.

MRS. NUDD'S VOICE: *(From off.)* Boys!

CHADDY: *(To audience.)* But then my mother came and turned the hose on us. *(They jump up sputtering and step apart. Mrs. Nudd appears with a hose and nozzle.)*

MRS. NUDD: Boys! . . . Stop it!. . . Do something useful for the rest of the day! Do something with your children! Do something! *(She goes off imperiously. Pause.)*

LAWRENCE: That does it, you know. That really does it. This is my last summer here, I can tell you that! If it weren't for my kids, I'd leave right now! But after this weekend, you can count me out! And I'm taking my highboy with me! *(He strides off angrily. Immediately the lights brighten. We hear bird songs.)*

CHADDY: *(To audience.)* And then what do you know? Suddenly the sun came out. *(He stretches in the sun.)* What a morning! Jesus, what a morning! The wind is northerly, the weather is clear, and Mother's roses smell like strawberry jam! *(He looks where Lawrence has gone.)* Oh what can you do with a man like that? What can you do? How can you dissuade his eye in a crowd from seeking out the cheek with acne, the infirm hand: how can you teach him to respond to the inestimable greatness of the race, the harsh surface beauty of life? *(Looks out.)* The sea that morning was iridescent and dark. My wife and my sister were swimming now, and I saw their uncovered heads, black and gold in the dark water. I saw them come out and I saw that they were naked, unshy, beautiful, and full of grace, and I watched the naked women walk out of the sea. *(He closes his eyes dreamily. His sister Esther comes on in a bathrobe, drying her hair with a towel. She is played by the Third Actress. She comes behind him, puts her hands over his eyes.)*

ESTHER: Chaddy, don't you dare tell Mother, but you know what I did last week on my trip to New York?

CHADDY: What.

ESTHER: I auditioned for an off-Broadway play.

CHADDY: No!

ESTHER: I did! I walked into an office where there were four men. They were very circumspect, but they said I'd have to be nude.

CHADDY: Come on!

ESTHER: It's true! I'd be expected to simulate, or perform, copulation twice during the performance, and participate in a love pile at the end that involved the audience.

CHADDY: Good God! So you walked out?

ESTHER: Not at all. They asked me to take off my clothes, and I wasn't the least embarrassed. The only thing that worried me was that my feet might get dirty.

CHADDY: Jesus, Esther!

ESTHER: There I sat, naked, before these strangers, in front of a big photograph of Ethel Barrymore.

CHADDY: I can't believe this!

ESTHER: No, listen: I felt for the first time that I'd found myself, Chaddy. I felt like a new woman, a better woman. It was one of the most exciting experiences I have ever had.

CHADDY: Have you told Bill?

ESTHER: I'll cross that bridge if I get the part.

CHADDY: I'm disgusted, Esther.

ESTHER: Oh yes? Well, that's the trouble with this family. You're all so square and stuffy. You have no idea how wonderful and rich and strange life can be when you stop playing out those roles your parents designed for you. *(She goes off.)*

CHADDY: *(Following her.)* You'll never get the part, Esther! What about your stretch marks? *(He is off as the light changes to evening light. Nostalgic music. Mr. Nudd comes on, makes a drink. He is played by the First Actor. After a moment, Mrs. Nudd comes on, played by the First Actress.)*

MR. NUDD: Want a drink?

MRS. NUDD: It's a little early.

MR. NUDD: It's Labor Day.

MRS. NUDD: *(Immediately.)* Then please!

MR. NUDD: *(Making gin and tonics at the "bar.")* I just made another rule.

MRS. NUDD: What?

MR. NUDD: No grandchildren or dogs may enter this room for the next hour and a half.

MRS. NUDD: That is an excellent rule. *(He brings her a drink.)* Thank you, darling.

MR. NUDD: *(Looking off and out.)* Look at that light! Oh we're at our best in this light! We are at our very best. *(Their daughter Joan comes out warily. She is played by the Second Actress. She carries a letter.)*

JOAN: Are you two busy? Tell me the truth.

MR. NUDD: We're busy drinking.

MRS. NUDD: Of course we're not busy.

JOAN: I've got a proposition to make.

MR. NUDD: Uh oh.

JOAN: I've decided that I won't go back to town with you tomorrow. I've decided I'll stay here for a little while longer.

MRS. NUDD: Oh now . . .

JOAN: No, there's nothing for me to do in New York. I'm just a divorced woman rattling around. I wrote to Helen Parker asking her to stay with me, and she thinks it's a great idea. I have her letter right here. Read it. Read what she says. *(She hands Mrs. Nudd the letter.)*

MR. NUDD: Joan, dear. You can't stay here in the winter.

JOAN: Oh yes I can, yes I can, Daddy. We're willing to rough it. We'll take turns walking to the village for groceries.

MRS. NUDD: *(Handing the letter back.)* But darling. The house wasn't built to be lived in during the winter. The walls are thin. The water will be turned off.

JOAN: We don't care about water, Mummy — we'll get our water from the old ice pond.

MR. NUDD: Sweetheart, you'd last about a week. I'd have to come up and get you, and I don't want to close this house twice.

JOAN: I want to stay. I've planned it for so long!

MRS. NUDD: You're being ridiculous, Joan.

JOAN: I've never asked you for anything. You've always been so strict. You've never let me do what I want.

MR. NUDD: Be reasonable, darling. Please try and imagine . . .

JOAN: *(Exploding.)* Esther got everything she wanted. She went to Europe twice. She had that car in college. She had that fur coat. *(She sits on the floor.)* I want to stay, I want to stay, I want to stay!

MRS. NUDD: Joan, you're acting like a child.

JOAN: *(On the floor.)* I want to act like a child! Is there anything so terrible about wanting to act like a child for a little while? I don't have any joy in my life any more. When I'm unhappy, I try to remember a time when I was happy, but I can't remember a time any more.

MRS. NUDD: Joan, get up. Get up on your own two feet.

JOAN: I can't, I can't, it hurts to stand up — it hurts my legs.

MR. NUDD: Get up, Joanie. *(He stoops down, helps her up.)* Oh my baby. My little girl. *(He puts his arm around her, leads her in.)* Come inside, and I'll wash your face. *(He takes her in, looking over his shoulder at his wife.)*

MRS. NUDD: *(To audience.)* What makes the summer always an island? What makes it such a small island? And why do these good and gentle people who have surrounded me all my life seem like figures in a tragedy? What mistakes have we made? We have loved our neighbors, respected the force of modesty, held honor above gain . . . Where have we gone wrong?
(Chaddy comes out, with a checkerboard.)

CHADDY: Checkers, Mother?

MRS. NUDD: Now that's a good idea, Chaddy. Checkers. *(Chaddy gets himself a drink.)*

CHADDY: Do I look thirty-seven, Mother?

MRS. NUDD: Stop talking about your age, Chaddy. Do you realize that's all you've done, all Labor Day. Talk about your age.

CHADDY: I haven't talked about just that, Mother. I've talked about my problems at work. I've talked about the sailing races, I've talked about the kids' lousy schools . . .

MRS. NUDD: Ssshhh. Feel that refreshing breeze.
(Chaddy sets up the checkers on the floor in front of his mother. Esther comes on.)

ESTHER: "Feel that refreshing breeze" . . . Children drown, beautiful women are mangled in automobile accidents, cruise ships founder, and men die lingering deaths in mines and submarines, but you will find none of that here. Here it boils down to "feel that refreshing breeze."
(Mrs. Nudd laughs.)

SECOND ACTOR'S VOICE: *(Shouting; from off.)* Anyone seen my bathing suit?

CHADDY: Hey, Esther. Who are those strange people renting next door?

MRS. NUDD: They're not strange. They're cousins of the Ewings. Which makes it all the more surprising.

SECOND ACTOR'S VOICE: *(From off.)* I said, have you seen my bathing trunks?

SECOND ACTRESS'S VOICE: *(From off.)* They're kicking around underfoot somewhere.

SECOND ACTOR'S VOICE: I'm just talking about an innocent pair of bathing trunks! You make it sound as if they had been wandering around the house, drinking whiskey and breaking wind . . .

MRS. NUDD: *(With Esther conducting.)* Feel that refreshing breeze. *(Mr. Nudd comes back out.)* Everything all right with Joan?

MR. NUDD: It will be, it will be . . . I'm seriously thinking of lighting a fire.

ESTHER: Oh do that, Daddy. What a good idea. *(She steps over the checkerboard.)*

MRS. NUDD: Esther.

ESTHER: Oh. Excuse me, Mother.

MRS. NUDD: There's a box of candy somewhere.

ESTHER: It's stale, Mother.

MRS. NUDD: It's perfectly fine. Does anyone feel like candy?

CHADDY: Actually I think the kids ate it, Mother.

MRS. NUDD: Oh. *(Offstage voices are heard again.)*

SECOND ACTRESS'S VOICE: You goddamned fucked-up no good piece of shit! You can't make a nickel, you don't have a friend in the world, and in bed you stink!

SECOND ACTOR'S VOICE: Look who's talking about bed!

SECOND ACTRESS'S VOICE: Listen: when I come, when I really come, pictures fall off the walls!

MRS. NUDD, ESTHER, CHADDY, MR. NUDD: *(All together.)* Feel that refreshing breeze.

(Joan comes back out.)

JOAN: I apologize for my dumb idea.

MRS. NUDD: That's all right, darling.

JOAN: My shrink says it's good to express your feelings. But still I must have —

MR. NUDD: *(Interrupting.)* Joanie, Joanie, make yourself a drink. *(She does. Lawrence comes out.)*

LAWRENCE: Good Lord! You're all not drinking already!

MRS. NUDD: We are, Lawrence, dear. And I'll thank you not to make an issue of it.

MR. NUDD: Where's Ruth? Where's your sweet Jane, Chaddy?

ESTHER: Holding the fort.

CHADDY: Playing Capture the Flag with the kids.

MRS. NUDD: What fun.

LAWRENCE: By the way, I'm taking the highboy, Mother. I plan to strap it on my station wagon.

MRS. NUDD: So we have heard, dear. Since the weekend began.

ESTHER: Remember the day the pig fell in the well?

MRS. NUDD: That was your tennis summer, wasn't it, Esther? That was the summer you played tennis with Russell.

LAWRENCE: That wasn't all she played with Russell that summer.

ESTHER: Dry up, Lawrence! I mean it! . . . *(She looks out.)* When I get back to New York, I plan to go to work somewhere.

MRS. NUDD: *(As she plays checkers.)* Good for you, darling. Good for you.

MR. NUDD: *(Stepping out of the family circle; to audience.)* It had begun to blow outside, and the house creaked gently, like a hull when the wind takes up the sail. *(He surveys his family.)* The room with the people in it looked enduring and secure, though in the morning they would all be gone.

CHADDY: *(Making several jumps in checkers.)* Crown me, Mother. Crown me king.

MRS. NUDD: Oh Chaddy, you were always so good at games . . .

(Slow fade on all.)

THE END

OVERTIME

A Modern Sequel to The Merchant of Venice

To Nicholas Martin with great appreciation

ORIGINAL PRODUCTION

Overtime was produced by Manhattan Theatre Club, Stage II (Lynne Meadow, Artistic Director; Barry Grove, Managing Director) in New York City, on March 5, 1996. It was directed by Nicholas Martin; the set design was by John Lee Beatty; the costume design was by Michael Krass; the lighting design was by Brian MacDevitt; the sound design was by Aural Fixation and the production stage manager was Ed Fitzgerald. The cast was as follows:

PORTIA	Joan McMurtrey
BASSANIO	Jere Shea
NERISSA	Marissa Chibas
GRATIANO	Michael Potts
JESSICA	Jill Tasker
LORENZO	Willis Sparks
ANTONIO	Rocco Sisto
SHYLOCK	Nicholas Kepros
SALERIO	Robert Stanton

Overtime received its premiere at the Old Globe Theatre (Jack O'Brien, Artistic Director) in San Diego, California, in July, 1995. It was directed by Nicholas Martin; the set design was by Robert Morgan; the costume design was by Michael Krass; the lighting design was by Kenneth Posner; the sound design was by Jeff Ladman and the production stage manager was Raoul Machado. The cast was as follows:

PORTIA	Joan McMurtrey
BASSANIO	Bo Foxworth
NERISSA	Angela Lanza
GRATIANO	Sterling Mazur
JESSICA	Wendy Kaplan
LORENZO	David Aaron Baker
ANTONIO	Tom Lacey
SHYLOCK	Nicholas Kepros
SALERIO	David Leddingham.

AUTHOR'S NOTE

The Greeks usually presented what they called a satyr play immediately after their tragedies. It would be a ribald, comic take-off on the dark and serious work that had preceded it. I wrote *Overtime* in the same sort of vein; I saw it as a kind of satirical response to Shakespeare's *The Merchant of Venice*. Shakespeare's play was one of his first I ever read, and over the years I've seen a number of productions. In an earlier life, I taught it many times as well. And I have to say I've always loved it. Its language is gorgeous, its plot suspenseful and full of surprises, its theme surprisingly modern. The basic polarity—the contrast between the commercial world of Venice and the romantic idyll of suburban Belmont—seemed beautifully worked out and strikingly up-to-date.

On the other hand, the play is also brutally anti-Semitic. Shakespeare's treatment of Shylock has to be confronted and dealt with, but I thought I could do that, too. John Gross has written an excellent book entitled *Shylock*, which explores the way the character has been presented since Elizabethan times, and having read that, I more than ever wanted to take a swing at the subject. I have written other plays which, for better or worse, bounce off a classical backboard, and I thought I knew how to do it in such a way that the result wouldn't seem simply a parody or a cartoon.

I had another reason for writing *Overtime*. I had noticed—and a number of secondary school teachers had told me—that there are very few contemporary plays with sizable casts that are suitable for American high school students to perform. I thought, as I began to write *Overtime*, that maybe I could write a funny play with a lot of youthful parts that young people would enjoy playing and that at the same time would send them scurrying to their copies of *The Merchant of Venice*. In my most elaborate fantasies, I saw *Overtime* as a play that would help reinvigorate drama in high schools, spark an interest in Shakespeare, and squelch anti-Semitism in America forever.

What I didn't realize was that not many people these days have read *The Merchant of Venice*, and many of those who have are not particularly attached to it. I had gone and written a satyr play which evoked a work which the audience either wasn't familiar with, or didn't care about, or, worse, didn't want to be reminded of.

We opened *Overtime* at the Old Globe Theatre in San Diego, which prides itself on its excellent productions of the Shakespeare canon, and has created over the years a core audience that is fairly sophisticated in this area. As a result, my play seemed to work pretty well there. I can't say people were giving us standing ovations, but I think they appreciated the play and had a good time at it. We were successful enough to move east and settle under the aegis of the Manhattan Theatre Club, but here we discovered a somewhat different response. New York audiences tend to have a larger Jewish component, and anti-Semitism to them is not something to joke about. If they didn't know *The Merchant of Venice,* they certainly knew *about* it, and I'm afraid to them and the critics, I came off simply as a wise guy, playing with fire. In any case, most of the reviews were scathing, and I felt like someone who has told a bad joke at a large party and offended everyone in sight. The play ran out its run in its small theater but certainly didn't extend, and it hasn't had any life to speak of since. On the good side, it was lovingly directed by Nicholas Martin, and the actors were all fine, especially Joan McMurtry who played the tough role of Portia without making her seem either smug or silly.

CHARACTERS

PORTIA, Wasp, youngish
BASSANIO, Irish American, young
NERISSA, Latina, young
GRATIANO, African American, young
JESSICA, Jewish, young
LORENZO, Wasp, young
ANTONIO, Italian American, older
SHYLOCK, Jewish, older
SALERIO, youngish

SETTING

The grounds of Portia's estate in Belmont outside Venice.

The set should suggest the garden of one of those old summer estates in the Berkshires, gone pretty much to seed. A few pieces of old metal summer furniture are scattered on the lawn in front of mossy, worn steps leading up to the house. Antique wrought-iron lamps might provide additional light.

The play progresses through sunset into a starry, moonlit night.

OVERTIME

ACT ONE

At rise: Elizabethan music.
Early evening. Summer.
Portia stands on the steps, holding several documents. Bassanio, Nerissa,
Gratiano, Jessica, Lorenzo, and Antonio are grouped decorously below her.
Everyone wears light contemporary summer clothes.

PORTIA: Antonio.
    (Antonio approaches her.)
    I have better news in store for you
    Than you expect.
    (She hands him a letter.)
    Unseal this letter soon.
    There you shall find three of your argosies
    Are richly come to harbor suddenly.
    (General enthusiasm.)
ANTONIO: *(Taking the letter.)*
    I am dumb.
    (He walks aside to open it.)
BASSANIO: *(Grinning up to Portia.)* Were you the doctor, and I knew you not?
PORTIA: I was.
    (Congenial laughter.)
GRATIANO: *(To Nerissa.)* Were you the clerk that is to make me cuckold?
NERISSA: Aye, but the clerk that never means to do it
    Unless he live until he be a man.
    (More laughter and enthusiasm.)
BASSANIO: *(Arm around Portia.)* Sweet Doctor, you shall be my bedfellow.
JESSICA: *(Aside to Lorenzo.)* I don't get it. What are they talking about?
LORENZO: *(To Jessica.)* I'm not sure. But I don't think it's important.
ANTONIO: *(To Portia, after reading his letter.)* Sweet lady, you have given me
    life and living;
    For here I read for certain that my ships
    Are safely come to road.
    (General enthusiasm.)
LORENZO: *(Low to Jessica.)* "Road" means "harbor." Which means his ships
    have come in.

JESSICA: *(Low to Lorenzo.)* I know that. So when does the fun start?

LORENZO: Sssh. She's got more exposition.

PORTIA: *(Seeing Lorenzo; producing another document.)* How now, Lorenzo?
My clerk hath some good comforts too for you.
(She hands the document to Nerissa.)

NERISSA: Ay, and I'll give them him without a fee.
(Laughter as she hands Lorenzo the document.)
There do I give to you and Jessica,
From the rich Jew, a special deed of gift,
After his death, of all he dies possessed of.

JESSICA: Cool!

LORENZO: Fair ladies, you drop manna in the way
Of starved people.

PORTIA: And yet I am sure you are not satisfied
Of these events at full. Let us go in;
And we will answer all things faithfully.

GRATIANO: *(Coming down to Lorenzo, indicating the ring on his finger.)*
Well, while I live I'll fear no other thing
So sore as keeping safe Nerissa's ring.
(The three couples kiss as Salerio comes on. He is dressed more formally, wearing a business suit and tie. He stands to one side and watches as the group starts in.)

PORTIA: Oh wait!
(The group stops.)
Just one more thing.
(The group waits.)
Tonight I happen to have planned a little party!
(Cheers from all. The formal Elizabethan music modulates into the sound of a society dance band, coming from within. The lights brighten up as the group hurries off.)

SALERIO: *(Calling to Portia.)* Portia . . . Portia! . . . Portia! *(Portia is ushering her guests inside. She finally notices him.)* May I speak to you for a moment?
(The others by now have gone in.)

PORTIA: Can't it wait, Salerio?

SALERIO: It's rather important.

PORTIA: Could you make it snappy? I should get the ball rolling.

SALERIO: *(Taking her aside.)* That's what I want to speak to you about.

PORTIA: *(Indicating the noise within.)* What? This party?

SALERIO: It's the first I've heard of it.

PORTIA: This? Oh this is just a little post-trial celebration.

SALERIO: I see.

PORTIA: Just a little get-together, that's all.

SALERIO: I see.

PORTIA: Call it a wedding reception, if you want. I mean, as you may have noticed, a number of people are pairing off, myself included. So I thought we should commemorate things with a small social gathering.

SALERIO: Portia: as you well know, your father appointed me your financial advisor before he died.

PORTIA: Yes. Right. And?

SALERIO: Since his death, I have tried to do my best on your behalf. I have managed your investments, filed your taxes, and paid your parking tickets.

PORTIA: I appreciate that, Salerio. Now may I please go?

SALERIO: All I have asked in return is that you consult me before you commit yourself to any major expenditure.

PORTIA: Which I have done, Salerio.

SALERIO: I don't recall any mention of this party.

PORTIA: This? Oh well, this is strictly spur-of-the-moment.

SALERIO: *(Producing a small notebook.)* Could you tell me how many you've invited? Just for the record.

PORTIA: How many? Oh that's easy. Just the people you saw, plus a few more of my absolutely closest friends.

SALERIO: *(Pen poised.)* How many? Just so I'll know.

PORTIA: Oh gosh. Fifty, at the most. Not counting my class from law school.

SALERIO: *(As he writes.)* Are you serving drinks?

PORTIA: *(Kiddingly.)* No, Salerio. I thought we'd settle for Kool Aid . . . Of course I'm serving drinks. And champagne, all around!

SALERIO: *(Writing.)* French or Italian?

PORTIA: You know me and champagne.

SALERIO: *(Writing.)* Dom Perignon, 1978.

PORTIA: *(Mock romantically.)* You remembered.

SALERIO: Hors d'oevres?

PORTIA: No.

SALERIO: No?

PORTIA: No, actually I've asked Cipriani's to send over a small supper.

SALERIO: *(Again writing.)* You've asked Venice's finest four-star restaurant to provide dinner for at least a hundred people.

PORTIA: Just something simple, Salerio. Insalata verdi. Saltimboca. Zabbaglioni. Oh, and decaf cappuccino. *(The music becomes louder.)*

SALERIO: *(As he writes.)* I believe I hear music.

PORTIA: People obviously want to dance. So I brought in one of those silly little bands from the Piazza San Marco.

SALERIO: They don't sound terribly Italian.

PORTIA: I know. That's because I beefed them up with Peter Duchin.

SALERIO: *(Writing.)* You have imported Peter Duchin and his entire orchestra.

PORTIA: They agreed to fly Business Class.

SALERIO: *(Sardonically.)* Oh good. Oh good. *(Finishes writing, closes notebook.)* Thank you, Portia.

PORTIA: Now may I go?

SALERIO: This is an expensive party, Portia.

PORTIA: What's wrong with that?

SALERIO: Nothing at all. Except that you can't afford it.

PORTIA: What do you mean? I'm known throughout Venice as a lady richly left.

SALERIO: I'm afraid those riches left have somewhat diminished over time, Portia. Controlling stock in the Pullman corporation? A major position in Studebaker? We live in a very different world.

PORTIA: You should have told me this before.

SALERIO: I tell you this, Portia, at least once a week. But you never listen. You never listened to your father, either. That's why he hoped you'd marry a rich man.

PORTIA: Which I just did.

SALERIO: Forgive me, Portia, but you did not. You married a man who pretended he was rich. You married a boy who bankrupted his best friend so he could show up in an Armani suit and a second-hand Alfa Romeo.

PORTIA: Oh stop being such a wet blanket, Salerio! Honestly! No wonder I don't listen to you. You're always putting me down. When I organized the Belmont Women's Invitational Tennis tournament, you did everything you could to discourage me from entering.

SALERIO: You had no serve, Portia.

PORTIA: I got to the semifinals without one! And when I decided to go to law school, you told me it was a major mistake.

SALERIO: Which it was. You gave so many parties that you flunked out.

PORTIA: At least I tried! And tonight I'm trying again. Trying to bring a number of different people together at the end of a very tricky day. We are celebrating a whole new Venice, Salerio! Now come in and raise a glass!

SALERIO: I don't drink, Portia.

PORTIA: You could at least wish me well.

SALERIO: *(After a pause.)* Good luck, Portia.

PORTIA: Thank you. *(She shakes his hand.)* And now I'd better rejoin the happy throng.

SALERIO: *(Holding onto her hand.)* May I kiss the bride?

PORTIA: What?

SALERIO: I believe a kiss is customary at wedding receptions.

PORTIA: I know it is, but . . .

SALERIO: Or don't people kiss their accountants?

PORTIA: Of course they do, Salerio. *(Jokingly.)* Except at tax time.

SALERIO: *(Insistently.)* It's not tax time now.

PORTIA: It's just that tonight's first kiss belongs to my husband.

SALERIO: Why?

PORTIA: Personal reasons.

SALERIO: Oh?

PORTIA: If you must know, our marriage hasn't been consummated yet.

SALERIO: What? Why not?

PORTIA: Because we haven't had time, Salerio. We only met last week. And the minute we were married, Shylock called in his bond, and we had to rush to the rescue. So there was simply no time to go to bed.

SALERIO: I see. *(Aside.)* Then there may be a small window of opportunity for a dark horse candidate.

PORTIA: I didn't hear you.

SALERIO: Never mind. That was an aside.

PORTIA: Oh. Sorry.

SALERIO: *(Starting off)* I'd better do something about your fast-dwindling fortune.

PORTIA: I'm sure you'll find a solution. You always do.

SALERIO: If I do, may I have that kiss?

PORTIA: Why, Salerio. I didn't know you cared.

SALERIO: I didn't either, Portia. All these years I've thought you were way beyond reach. But I have to say that your present financial picture has made you seem . . . somewhat more accessible. *(He turns and goes. Music and party sounds come up. Portia starts for the house as Lorenzo comes out, still reading Shylock's will.)*

PORTIA: Hi.

LORENZO: Hello.

PORTIA: I have a faint cold fear thrills through my veins

That this could be my final party.

LORENZO: *(Looking up from his reading.)* Huh?

PORTIA: Never mind. Have fun. *(She hurries into the house. Lorenzo perches somewhere and reads the will. Jessica comes out. Dance music is heard.)*

JESSICA: Yoo hoo! *(He glances at her and returns to his reading. Posing sexily.)* Lorenzo, don't you want to dance?

LORENZO: *(Vaguely.)* In a minute.

JESSICA: *(Dancing around.)* I love to dance.

LORENZO: *(Reading.)* Let me just finish reading your father's will. *(The music comes up a little.)*

JESSICA: Listen to those wonderful old tunes! They were designed to be danced to. Don't they make you want to sweep me off my feet?

LORENZO: *(Studying the will.)* I'm trying to concentrate, Jessica.

JESSICA: *(Still dancing.)* How often do people get a chance to dance these days? I mean, really *dance*. Together. The old way. Come on! What did they used to say? "Let's cut a rug!"

LORENZO: *(Indicating the will.)* I don't believe this.

JESSICA: What?

LORENZO: Shylock's will. He's leaving us everything.

JESSICA: I believe Portia already pointed that out.

LORENZO: No, but look what it entails. *(He shows her.)* His house in the ghetto. That's for openers. Along with several other pieces of prime real estate on the Rialto. And your mother's jewels — everything you didn't already swipe. Plus a number of good paintings — there's a Rothko here, and a Rauschenberg! And finally a long list of first-rate blue chip stocks, including McDonald's and Motorola.

JESSICA: I suppose he puts it all in your name.

LORENZO: Not at all.

JESSICA: You sure? He's furious at me for running off with a gentile.

LORENZO: *(Shows her.)* Look. Read. "For my dear Jessica and Lorenzo." See? You come first.

JESSICA: There must be a hitch.

LORENZO: There doesn't seem to be.

JESSICA: Look for a pound of flesh. In small print.

LORENZO: Nothing like that here.

JESSICA: Yes well, he had to do it, Lorenzo. The court laid down the law.

LORENZO: What court? That was no court. He goes in on a civil suit and comes out branded a criminal. Who was the judge? Where was the jury?

JESSICA: I don't understand these legal things.

LORENZO: I'll bet Shylock does. Yet he's going along with the whole thing. He's even endorsing it. Look. There's a personal note at the end. *(Reads.)* "Enjoy yourselves. Love, Dad."

JESSICA: *(Looking over his shoulder.)* It sure looks like his writing.

LORENZO: "Enjoy yourselves." . . . Gosh . . . If it were my father, it would be all tied up in trust. But yours is saying "Live it up!"

JESSICA: It's just a will, remember? He could change it tomorrow.

LORENZO: But he writes "Love." It's hard to change that. Love. From Shylock? I mean, wow. And "Dad"? He wants me to call him Dad!

JESSICA: I know what this is. It's his wedding present.

LORENZO: But we're not married.

JESSICA: He knows we plan to be.

LORENZO: Then he must approve of it.

JESSICA: He knows he can't prevent it.

LORENZO: Even though I stole you away?

JESSICA: Hold it right there. You didn't steal me, Lorenzo. I left. Of my own free will.

LORENZO: OK. OK.

JESSICA: And I'm glad I did. You don't know what it was like living in that house. I was strictly a second-class citizen. My brothers got all the attention. They got the bar mitzvahs and the college educations and a guaranteed piece of his business after they graduated.

LORENZO: You didn't want to go to college.

JESSICA: I still don't. I hear it's more of the same at college. Guys hogging the limelight in the front row. Women huddled in back, taking neat little notes, hoping for approval. Same old story, same old world.

LORENZO: I thought you were your father's favorite.

JESSICA: Oh sure. As long as I stayed in the kitchen, braising the brisket. Once I got the meal on the table, could I join the conversation? Fat chance. My job was to shut up and carry in the kugel. Then do the dishes. Clean the house. Sit upstairs at the synagogue. Find myself a nice Jewish boy so I could spend the rest of my life doing more of the same.

LORENZO: I'm amazed. I always thought Jews were wonderful to their women.

JESSICA: That's because you always see them buying us stuff. They feel guilty about the way they treat us at home, so they pile on the gifts when they take us out. Then they feel guilty about that, so they brand us Jewish princesses! *(Putting on lipstick.)* That's why we've had to become feminists.

LORENZO: Jessica, my love, no offense, but I don't quite remember you marching through the Piazza San Marco on behalf of the sisterhood.

JESSICA: I didn't have to. I saw another way.

LORENZO: What way?

JESSICA: *(Snapping closed her compact.)* Portia's way.

LORENZO: Portia's way?

JESSICA: Ever since I saw her picture in the Style section of the *Sunday Times*, dancing in a white dress in that tent out on this lawn, surrounded by men, all bowing and scraping and waiting to cut in, I realized that rich gentile women have been liberated for centuries. I mean, there she was, the Snow Queen, ruling the roost.

LORENZO: I was there.

JESSICA: I know. I read the guest list. That's why I set my sights on you. That's why I stood around at all those intercollegiate hockey games, freezing my ass off, waving and squealing until you asked me out. I wanted a Wasp boy and I got one! And now I expect you to treat me in a thoroughly Waspy way — pulling out my chair, sending me flowers on Christmas and Easter, and dancing with me on demand. *(She makes him assume the ballroom dancing position.)* Starting here, starting now. *(They dance.)*

LORENZO: *(As they dance.)* How come you never told me all this stuff before?

JESSICA: You never gave me the chance. Ever since I left home, you've kept me flat on my back in that motel room in Genoa.

LORENZO: You'll have to admit we Wasps are great lovers.

JESSICA: I hear you're better dancers. So come ON. Make some moves, please! Or I'll tell everyone you're anti-Semitic.

LORENZO: *(Breaking away from her.)* That's the one thing I'm not!

JESSICA: Oh hell, you probably are, and don't even know it. My father says your whole crowd is permanently prejudiced.

LORENZO: Then why in God's name did he leave us all he is possessed of?

JESSICA: Maybe he wants to make us feel guilty.

LORENZO: Then it worked, goddammit. I feel fundamentally shitty about this whole damn thing! *(Portia comes out with Bassanio; Bassanio carries a slice of pizza in a napkin and a couple of cans of beer.)*

PORTIA: Anybody hungry?

BASSANIO: *(With his mouth full.)* Food's here.

PORTIA: *(To Bassanio, who's drinking beer.)* I wish you'd use a glass.

BASSANIO: *(Tossing the extra beer can to Lorenzo.)* Glass breaks.

PORTIA: *(To Lorenzo and Jessica.)* Cipriani's sent over a spectacular wedding cake.

BASSANIO: Time to chow down, gang.

LORENZO: *(Tossing back the beer.)* Maybe later.

PORTIA: *(To Jessica.)* What's the matter with him?

JESSICA: He's decided to feel guilty.

PORTIA: Guilty? About what?

JESSICA: Daddy.

BASSANIO: Guilty about Shylock?

PORTIA: Oh now honestly.

LORENZO: We treated him terribly.

BASSANIO: What about how he treated us?

PORTIA: Exactly.

BASSANIO: He took us to court, for Chrissake!

LORENZO: He just wanted his bond, that's all!

BASSANIO: Hey. Which just happened to be a pound of flesh!

PORTIA: Which, I might add, he planned to cut from an area rather close to Antonio's heart!

BASSANIO: There you are.

PORTIA: He was literally sharpening his knife, Lorenzo! On the sole of his shoe!

JESSICA: Jesus, Lorenzo. Where've you been?

LORENZO: Maybe he was just kidding.

BASSANIO: What? Kidding? Shylock?

PORTIA: Some joke.

LORENZO: I'm serious. Maybe he was just playing games. *(To Bassanio.)* The way you did when you pretended to be rich. *(To Portia.)* Or you, Portia. When you pretended to be that lawyer. *(To Jessica.)* Or you, Jessica. When you dressed as a man in order to run away with me. We all play these hokey games, all the time. Why shouldn't Shylock?

JESSICA: Because he's not the type, that's why.

PORTIA: Jewish people don't behave that way, Lorenzo. They take life terribly seriously. It comes from their mothers.

JESSICA: I'm Jewish, and I don't take life seriously.

PORTIA: I know you don't, sweetie. That's why you've made such a successful crossover.

JESSICA: *(Hugging her.)* Thank you, Portia.

BASSANIO: If you want my opinion, Shylock got off easy.

LORENZO: We took his money. We forced him to convert.

BASSANIO: We did him a favor, Lorenzo! We let him into the One True Church!

PORTIA: No, now wait, Bassanio. Not so fast. I want Lorenzo to feel totally comfortable here. *(To Lorenzo.)* So. Let's review the bidding. First, Shylock is in fine shape. We purposely left him with part of his fortune, so he'd be able to bounce back financially. So the money thing is fine. As for making him turn Christian, that's no big deal. I've been a Christian all my life, and it really doesn't mean very much.

BASSANIO: Right. Show up at Mass Christmas and Easter. Take a lap around the beads when you've fucked up. That's about it, man.

LORENZO: Maybe Shylock takes religion more seriously than we do.

JESSICA: I hate religion! Religion does nothing but cause wars. Look at the Crusades! Look at Bosnia!

LORENZO: That's superficial crap, Jessica. No wonder Shylock didn't let you talk at the dinner table.

JESSICA: *(To the others.)* Hear that? Hear what he said to me?

PORTIA: You really are feeling guilty, aren't you, Lorenzo?

JESSICA: Guilt is a totally debilitating emotion.

LORENZO: Guilt is the beginning of wisdom.

JESSICA: Talk to my shrink. She'll tell you about guilt.

LORENZO: Civilization is founded on guilt!

PORTIA: No, now stop that, you two! I mean it! Nothing can destroy a party quicker than a squabbling couple. *(Lorenzo and Jessica settle down.)* Now. Tell you what. If the Christian thing really bothers you, Lorenzo, I'll call the Archbishop of Venice first thing in the morning. He was an old friend of my father's. I'm sure he can have Shylock thoroughly excommunicated.

BASSANIO: *(Arm around Portia.)* Know what I like about this babe? She's always coming up with a fair solution.

PORTIA: That's because I happen to believe that the quality of mercy is not strained, darling.

BASSANIO: *(Kissing her.)* May I quote you on that?

PORTIA: Would that make you feel better, Lorenzo? If we finessed the Christian thing?

LORENZO: I dunno. I still feel we're papering things over. We humiliated Shylock in front of the entire Venetian community, and now we're doing our old Wasp number: Pull a string or two. Abra Cadabra! Wasn't there, didn't happen.

JESSICA: Oh God in heaven!

PORTIA: All right, then. How about this? Suppose we invited him over.

BASSANIO: Who? Shylock?

JESSICA: WHAT? Invite him here?

BASSANIO: Invite Shylock? To our wedding reception?

PORTIA: I am asking Lorenzo a question, Bassanio. *(To Lorenzo.)* Would that do it, Lorenzo?

LORENZO: It might.

PORTIA: Jessica, how about you?

JESSICA: He'd never come, thank God.

PORTIA: What if I wrote him a nice little note?

BASSANIO: Are we talking about Shylock here? Are we talking about the basic bad guy of Venice?

PORTIA: Those battles are over, darling. I like to believe we're moving toward a new and different Venice. Now get me a pen and a piece of that little blue note paper, would you, sweetheart? *(Bassanio goes off reluctantly.)*

JESSICA: Daddy hates goyim, Portia.

PORTIA: I don't recognize that word, Jessica. And I don't want it used in my house.

JESSICA: He hates parties, then!

PORTIA: Maybe no one's ever bothered to make an effort. *(Bassanio comes out with the paper and a pen. He gives them to Portia.)* Thank you, dreamboat. *(She writes a note as she talks.)* Are you with me on this one, Lorenzo?

LORENZO: Sure. Give it a try.

PORTIA: Jessica?

JESSICA: He'll just say no.

PORTIA: Any other objections? Bassanio?

BASSANIO: Hell, we'll never get to bed.

PORTIA: Now, now. Hold your horses. Where's Nerissa?

LORENZO: I think she was planning to consummate her marriage with Gratiano.

PORTIA: Now that's what I call jumping the gun. *(Calls off.)* What ho! Nerissa! *(Nerissa stumbles on, followed by Gratiano. Both are adjusting their clothes.)* Nerissa, darling. I wonder if you would deliver this note to Shylock. Would you do that for me, sweetie? I'm sure Gratiano will go with you.

NERISSA: Are you serious?

PORTIA: I am. Nerissa. And I'll tell you why at a more appropriate time.

NERISSA: *(Buttoning her blouse.)* But we were just about to consummate our marriage.

GRATIANO: *(Tucking in his shirt.)* We were kind of looking forward to it.

BASSANIO: Tell me about it.

PORTIA: I'm sorry. Shylock comes first.

GRATIANO: I'll bet the guy's totally knocked out, losing that trial and all.

PORTIA: Well then Nerissa will just have to pound on his door a little harder. Now do me this favor, you two! Please.

NERISSA: I don't even know where he lives.

JESSICA: Don't ask me for directions. It's too traumatic for me even to *think* about going back to that house.

PORTIA: Bassanio, you must know the way, seeing as how you and Shylock were somewhat involved financially.

BASSANIO: Hey lay off, baby! Don't rub it in.

PORTIA: I'm just asking you to give them travel instructions, sweetheart.

BASSANIO: *(Grumpily to Gratiano and Nerissa.)* OK. Here's what you do. *(He shakes out a large tourist map of Venice.)* You cross the Grand Canal to the Ghetto Vecchio, and then take your first left after the Synagogue, and then . . . *(We can't hear the rest.)*

PORTIA: *(To Lorenzo.)* Meanwhile, Lorenzo and Jessica, do you think now you're ready to join the party?

LORENZO: OK.

JESSICA: Thank God.

PORTIA: *(Taking them by the arm.)* Let's go then. Because I have a little surprise for both of you.

LORENZO: A surprise? What surprise?

JESSICA: Didn't yon cause enough surprises at the trial?

PORTIA: I love surprises. I love springing things on people and seeing their expressions. I love all that. Coming, Bassanio? *(She ushers Lorenzo and Jessica offstage.)*

BASSANIO: *(Aside to Gratiano.)* I've got a big surprise for her, once I get her to bed!

GRATIANO: *(Giving him the high five.)* I hear you, friend! *(Bassanio hurries out after Portia. Pause.)* Shit.

NERISSA: What?

GRATIANO: Having to hump all the way back into town.

NERISSA: Let's start, so we can get it over with. *(They start off.)*

GRATIANO: She's kind of a bossy bitch, isn't she?

NERISSA: *(Stopping.)* What did you say?

GRATIANO: I said she was kind of a —

NERISSA: Don't you dare call her that!

GRATIANO: What would you call her then?

NERISSA: I'd call her simply a control-freak.

GRATIANO: She likes to be quarterback, coach, and umpire all at the same time!

NERISSA: That's because she's an only child.

GRATIANO: Yeah?

NERISSA: Her mother died when she was born, and her father spoiled her rotten.

GRATIANO: *(Imitating Portia.)* "I love surprises. I love all that."

NERISSA: *(Giggling.)* That's her.

GRATIANO: As long as she's doing the surprising. Right?

NERISSA: That's enough, please.

GRATIANO: *(Still imitating.)* "I'll tell you why at a more appropriate time."

NERISSA: *(Still laughing.)* Sssshh. She'll hear you.

GRATIANO: Sorry. Shouldn't make trouble for the maid.

NERISSA: *(Stopping laughing.)* What did you say?

GRATIANO: I said I didn't want to get you in trouble.

NERISSA: You said "the maid."

GRATIANO: So?

NERISSA: I am not the maid.

GRATIANO: I thought you were.

NERISSA: Why did you think I was the maid?

GRATIANO: Do this, do that. I just figured.

NERISSA: You figured wrong.

GRATIANO: So let's break.

NERISSA: *(Holding her ground.)* I am definitely not a maid. What I am is her best friend. Or her sister, really. They adopted me after her mother died. I give her constant support and companionship.

GRATIANO: Gotcha.

NERISSA: A maid gets paid. With me, no money exchanges hands. Ever. I have been with Portia all my life, day and night, winter and summer, totally at her beck and call, and never asked for a nickel.

GRATIANO: OK.

NERISSA: Maids get their own rooms and their own televisions. Maids get summer vacations and social security. Maids get to sit in parks and interact with other maids. I don't. I am committed . . . *(Pause.)* Caught . . . *(Pause.)* Trapped! . . . in a totally subordinate role. *(She explodes.)* I mean, God! When you think about it. She sets up that damn game show for her suitors, and guess who has to run from casket to casket playing Vanna White. She decides to play lawyer against Shylock, guess who's sent to do the major research at the law school library. She decides to marry your boss, guess who has to roll out the red —

GRATIANO: Hold it.

NERISSA: What?

GRATIANO: Bassanio is not my boss.

NERISSA: I thought you were his assistant.

GRATIANO: Nerissa, baby: he and I are not even in the same line of work. If we were, I'd be *his* boss. I'm starting my own construction business. What does he do? Nothing. Except borrow money. And spend it on himself. So he can marry a rich girl.

NERISSA: Sorry.

GRATIANO: It bugs me. Folks see a black man, they immediately think he works for the white guy. If he works at all.

NERISSA: I said I was sorry.

GRATIANO: Bassanio and I are friends. Period. Buddies. I met him at summer camp. And no, I was not there on the Fresh Air Fund. I was the shop instructor. He was my junior counselor. I put him in charge of sandpaper.

NERISSA: I was wrong, all right.

GRATIANO: Now go on with what you were saying.

NERISSA: We don't know each other very well, do we?

GRATIANO: We sure don't.

NERISSA: Portia and Bassanio decide to get married, and we automatically fall into line.

GRATIANO: We moved kind of fast.

NERISSA: I mean, what am I? An afterthought? An echo?

GRATIANO: Try carbon copy.

NERISSA: I am suddenly very tired of following that woman around, wearing her clothes, imitating the way she talks . . .

GRATIANO: *(Sounding more black.)* What's wrong with flowin' with our own language, baby? Know what I'm sayin'?

NERISSA: Eso mismo! Exactamente!

GRATIANO: Whoa! You Spanish?

NERISSA: They said my birth parents were Spanish speaking.

GRATIANO: That covers a lot of ground.

NERISSA: That's just the problem. I could be anything. Cubana, Mexicana, Puerto Riquena. Que importa? Nobody cares. But in my solitude, I have my secret dreams. I feel the noble blood of Montezuma coursing through my veins, mixing with the turbulent passions of the Spanish conquistadors.

GRATIANO: Sounds cool.

NERISSA: It does, doesn't it? Even in translation. You see? Whatever I am, I have our language, the Spanish language, the magnificent language of Cervantes, Calderon de la Barca, and Gloria Estefan.

GRATIANO: Say it, baby!

NERISSA: What about you? I imagine that deep inside you resonate with the rich rhythms of your African roots, amplified by the slave experience and the long struggle upward for civil rights.

GRATIANO: Easy. You're sort of slipping into stereotype there.

NERISSA: You're right. I felt that. See? It just proves my point. We really know very little about each other. And yet we promised to spend our lives together, just because those two gringos are doing it.

GRATIANO: You getting cold feet?

NERISSA: It might not be a bad idea to slow down . . . Maybe we should continue this discussion on our way into the inner city.

GRATIANO: Now you've lost me, baby. After what you said, how come you still willing to step 'n' fetch it for Portia?

NERISSA: She pays the bills, my man. So vamonos. I imagine you've got a pink Cadillac waiting in the driveway.

GRATIANO: Actually it's a forest-green Volvo station wagon.

NERISSA: See how I just assumed? Oh, Gratiano. You and I have a long way to go!

GRATIANO: We better hurry.

NERISSA: No, no. Just the opposite. Let's take our own sweet time. *(She takes his arm.)*

GRATIANO: Portia — *la bruja!*

NERISSA: You got it. Portia the witch! *(They go off slowly and proudly. Music and party sounds. Antonio comes on, looking at his watch. After a moment, Portia comes on.)*

PORTIA: Antonio! You're not leaving?

ANTONIO: Thought I might quietly duck out.

PORTIA: The night is young!

ANTONIO: Not for old bachelors like myself.

PORTIA: You won't even stay for the cutting of the cake?

ANTONIO: I'm a little wrung out, Portia. You forget that not very long ago, I was sitting in the courtroom, baring my chest, while Shylock came at me with a knife, eager to carve himself a pound of my flesh.

PORTIA: Boy, that was a scary moment, wasn't it?

ANTONIO: It ended happily, anyway. Thanks to you.

PORTIA: Thank God I remembered something from law school.

ANTONIO: You saved the day, and I'll always be indebted to you. Thank you, dear lady.

PORTIA: I should be thanking you, Antonio. For giving me Bassanio.

ANTONIO: I don't think I gave him to you, Portia.

PORTIA: You lent him that money.

ANTONIO: Which Shylock lent to me.

PORTIA: You put up your bond.

ANTONIO: I tried to be a good friend.

PORTIA: More than a friend, Antonio. He's told me. You've been a big brother to him. Best seats at the ballgame. Box at the opera . . .

ANTONIO: The ballgames took. The opera didn't.

PORTIA: The point is, you gave him a leg up in life. Tomorrow I'm going to make him sit down and write you a good long thank-you note for everything you've done.

ANTONIO: I won't rush to the mailbox. *(Holds out his hand.)* Anyway, *la comedia e finita. Buona sera, signora.*

PORTIA: I hope you'll continue to come around.

ANTONIO: Come around?

PORTIA: Christmas. Thanksgiving. Birthdays. When we have children, I want you to be a godfather.

ANTONIO: *(Imitating Brando.)* Just because I'm Italian don't mean I'm Mafia, lady.

PORTIA: No, now seriously, Antonio. I want you to feel part of our family. You can be what the French call *un ami de maison.*

ANTONIO: A friend of the household . . . No thanks, Portia.

PORTIA: No, now this is important to me. I'm not big on the idea of the nuclear family. I want all sorts of different people to come and go around here. I'm a huge fan of Chekhov.

ANTONIO: Still, no. Bassanio has his life. I have mine.

PORTIA: Are you saying that marriage and friendship don't mix?

ANTONIO: Some marriages. Some friendships.

PORTIA: That's just about the silliest thing I've heard all day.

ANTONIO: Portia, when I was in that courtroom, baring my heart to Shylock's knife, I learned something.

PORTIA: Learned something?

ANTONIO: There I was, being impossibly noble, giving up my fortune, and ready to give up my life . . . for what? For Bassanio. For that boy.

PORTIA: I thought you were a very good sport, Antonio. We all did.

ANTONIO: I thought I was, too, at the start. But as the trial wore on, I realized something. Do you know what I said to the assembled multitude, right before you showed up to save the day?

PORTIA: What did you say?

ANTONIO: I said . . . I can quote it exactly . . .
I am a tainted wether of the flock,
Meetest for death."

PORTIA: You said that? At the trial?

ANTONIO: I did. And I went on to say
The weakest kind of fruit
Drops earliest to the ground, and so let me.

PORTIA: All of which means?

ANTONIO: All of which means I didn't like myself very much.

PORTIA: Why?

ANTONIO: Why? Because I realized — *(Pause.)* I don't think I'm ready to tell you, Portia. I'm not sure you'd like me either. *(Pause.)* But I *will* tell you this. I can't spend the rest of my life hovering on the fringes of your family. Forgive me, but I can't. I can't turn myself into some sort of polite appendage, dragging up the extra chair for a meal, walking the dog, baby-sitting in a pinch . . .

PORTIA: Antonio. . .

ANTONIO: Nope. Can't do it, Portia. Telephoning too much, leaving querulous messages on the answering machine. Offering to make the drinks when you entertain, getting tolerant nods from your guests, who whisper "Who was that?" when I leave the room. No ma'am. Sorry. Can't. I can't end up as some pale, moony satellite, circling endlessly around middle class life. I'd rather fade quietly out of the picture. And keep my dignity, if nothing else. Good night, Portia. Or rather, good-bye. *(He starts off.)*

PORTIA: Have you said good-bye to Bassanio?

ANTONIO: No.

PORTIA: Don't you think you should?

ANTONIO: Say it for me, would you?

PORTIA: He'd be devastated if you just disappeared.

ANTONIO: He's been avoiding me since we got here.

PORTIA: He's just busy, that's all. He's the groom.

ANTONIO: You think that's it?

PORTIA: I think you need to clear the air.

ANTONIO: Someday, maybe.

PORTIA: Now. Before you go. Oh, Antonio, look. I'm not sure what's bothering you, but I *am* sure we've moved beyond that stupid trial. It's high time we were more open and direct with one other. Otherwise we might as well all go back to square one, running around in disguises, keeping secrets from each other, and doing all those dumb things that got us into trouble in the first place.

ANTONIO: You have a point.

PORTIA: If you leave now, I know that you'll feel resentful, and Bassanio'll feel guilty, and I'll have lost a good friend.

ANTONIO: That makes sense . . .

PORTIA: You didn't stake him to all that cash, you didn't put your life on the *line*, for God's sake — just to feel ignored after he's married.

ANTONIO: True enough.

PORTIA: Bassanio should learn that there are such things as loyalty and gratitude. Now go back in there and tell him exactly how you feel, point blank. Then maybe you'll stay on, and we can all have a much more pleasant evening.

ANTONIO: You think he'd listen?

PORTIA: *(Taking his arm.)* Of course. Come on. We'll track him down right now.

ANTONIO: Portia, would you mind if I stopped at the bar first? Just to gird up my loins. This might be tougher than you think.

PORTIA: Fine. Stoke up, then let loose. Meanwhile, I'll check on a little surprise I've got cooked up for Lorenzo and Jessica. *(Portia goes on into the house. Antonio starts off. Bassanio comes on, guzzling another can of beer. He sees Lorenzo coming on from another way. He also carries a beer.)*

BASSANIO: Lorenzo! *(To Antonio, casually, as he walks past him.)* How's it going? *(Antonio looks after him, then goes slowly off. Bassanio goes to Lorenzo.)* I've been looking all over for you. Where've you been, buddy?

LORENZO: Just getting some air.

BASSANIO: Hey, you're my best man. You're supposed to stay right by my side all through this shit.

LORENZO: Sorry. How can I help?

BASSANIO: Come in and catch a piece of the Red Sox game. We'll grab a few brewskies and slouch on the couch.

LORENZO: I can't go in there, Bassanio.

BASSANIO: What's the matter?

LORENZO: There's a priest in there. He keeps eyeing me and making weird little signs of the cross.

BASSANIO: Oh right.

LORENZO: You know about him?

BASSANIO: Oh sure. He's the surprise Portia was talking about.

LORENZO: He's the surprise?

BASSANIO: Shit. Spilled the beans. Oh well, what the hell? She wants him to marry you and Jessica.

LORENZO: Tonight? Jesus, Bassanio! I feel a little manipulated here.

BASSANIO: Your turn, man. I did it. Gratiano did it. Hold your nose and jump, buddy.

LORENZO: I'm not sure I'm ready for it. I'm serious.

BASSANIO: What's the problem?

LORENZO: I can't tell you.

BASSANIO: Can't *tell* me? Can't tell *me?* The guy who did the major planning when you stole Jessica away from Shylock for that dirty weekend in Genoa? Talk to me, man.

LORENZO: I can't, Bassanio. If I were a Catholic, I couldn't even confess it to the most dissolute priest in the diocese.

BASSANIO: Hold it. Are you saying something here?

LORENZO: I guess I am.

BASSANIO: I sense it. I sense you're saying something here.

LORENZO: I am, Bassanio.

BASSANIO: You're saying you're gay, aren't you?

LORENZO: No.

BASSANIO: You sure?

LORENZO: As sure as anyone can be in these ambiguous times.

BASSANIO: Sure you're not interested in me?

LORENZO: Positive.

BASSANIO: I've been working out a lot lately. I've got a terrific body.

LORENZO: If that were my problem, Bassanio, I swear I'd embrace it — and you — with immediate relish.

BASSANIO: Don't even think about it.

LORENZO: I won't. I promise.

BASSANIO: So then what? Is it almost as bad as being gay? Have you committed murder or something?

LORENZO: No.

BASSANIO: Do you want to kill someone? Do you harbor murderous thoughts?

LORENZO: No.

BASSANIO: Do you want to kill me? Are you jealous of my body?

LORENZO: I swear that's not it, Bassanio.

BASSANIO: Then what? Talk it out, man. Rape? Incest? Nowadays we reveal these things. We have talk shows, we have support groups. And here you won't tell your best friend. It hurts, buddy. It hurts a lot. It makes me feel we have nothing more to say to each other, unless the Red Sox win the pennant. *(He starts out.)*

LORENZO: OK, Bassanio! I'll tell you. Though you'll probably haul off and deck me when I do.

BASSANIO: *(Coming back.)* Deck you? What kind of a friend do you think I am?

LORENZO: I'll know after I tell you.

BASSANIO: Go ahead, then. Shoot. I'm ready.

LORENZO: *(Takes a deep breath.)* The reason I don't want to marry Jessica is . . .

BASSANIO: Grunt it out, man.

LORENZO: The reason I don't want to marry Jessica is I think I'm basically anti-Semitic.

BASSANIO: WHAT?

LORENZO: I'm anti-Semitic, Bassanio.

BASSANIO: That's what I thought you said. *(He hauls off and decks him.)*

LORENZO: *(Sprawling; rubbing his jaw.)* Thanks. I needed that.

BASSANIO: *(Helping him up.)* I had to do it, Lorenzo. Now that I've seen *Schindler's List.*

LORENZO: I understand.

BASSANIO: It was a blow struck against prejudice and bias wherever they may occur.

LORENZO: I appreciate that.

BASSANIO: Lord knows, coming from Irish immigrants who were rejected by the Boston Brahmins, I had every right to strike it.

LORENZO: You did, you did.

BASSANIO: God. Anti-Semitism. Jesus. I thought we were over all that. I thought all that shit had been thoroughly flushed down the Grand Canal.

LORENZO: I thought so, too.

BASSANIO: And from you particularly! With your relationship with Jessica! And all those sympathetic things you said about Shylock!

LORENZO: That's the thing, Bassanio. I keep thinking about Shylock. And all the other Jews I've met recently.

BASSANIO: Venice has a sizable Jewish community.

LORENZO: I know it does. And ever since I started dating Jessica, I've tried to reach out to it. I subscribe to *Commentary* and the *Venice Voice.* I hang out at delicatessens and kosher restaurants. When I go to the movies, I applaud the Jewish names when they roll the credits. When I watch sit-coms, I laugh at the Jewish jokes. When I need a doctor —

BASSANIO: HOLD IT! There's something creepy about what you're saying here.

LORENZO: I know that. I'm singling out Jewish culture. Take it one step further, I'd sound like a Nazi.

BASSANIO: That's it, you son of a bitch! *(Raises his fist again.)*

LORENZO: No wait, Bassanio. There's an essential difference between Hitler and me.

BASSANIO: Explain it quickly.

LORENZO: The difference is that I have no hate, or anger, or resentment towards the Jewish people. In fact, the only feelings I have are admiration and envy.

BASSANIO: Admiration and envy?

LORENZO: I want to BE Jewish, Bassanio.

BASSANIO: You want to be Jewish?

LORENZO: I'd LOVE to be. In fact, I'm beginning to realize that's why I went for Jessica. That's why I'm hung up on Shylock. That's why I asked for the complete works of Wendy Wasserstein last Christmas.

BASSANIO: But why does that make you anti-Semitic?

LORENZO: Let's take it step by step. You know why I took that trip to Israel last year?

BASSANIO: To get it on with Jewish women?

LORENZO: To get circumcised, Bassanio.

BASSANIO: What?

LORENZO: And it hurt like hell!

BASSANIO: Jesus. I can imagine.

LORENZO: But I'll tell you what hurts more, Bassanio. Knowing that I'll never make the grade. No matter what steps I take to join the Jewish community, I'm still beyond the pale. I'm living in a ghetto, Bassanio, self-imposed, but a ghetto nonetheless. And I'm filled with the lonely sense that some-where else in the world, there's a big, wonderful party going on — no, not a party, this is a party — but somewhere else there's a big, wonder-fully serious seminar going on, composed primarily of Jews, with good food, warm feelings, highly intelligent conversation, and very little empha-sis on liquor. And the sad truth is I'll never be invited.

BASSANIO: You poor guy.

LORENZO: *(Taking a big swallow of his drink.)* I am poor, Bassanio. In spirit. I admit it. OK, I may stand to inherit a sizable income from Shylock, but I am destitute where it counts — namely, in the essential area of ethnic identity. Take you, for example. When you feel low, you can at least retreat to the quaint comforts of the Church of Rome and the boozy exuber-ance of the Irish pub. Gratiano has the deep beat of the blues to sustain him. Antonio falls back on pasta and Verdi. And the Jews! Oh God, the Jews! They call on four thousand years of an astonishing history, seared by suffering, highlighted by displays of excellence in every vocation, con-tinually underscored by the sonorous poetry of the Old Testament and the folksy verities of the Yiddish idiom. But what cultural net lies under *me?* Where do I turn in my hour of need? A pallid, conformist Episco-palianism? The bland bourgeois life of the suburban country club? The shallow pieties of Barbara Bush? Oh God, Bassanio, I wish I were Jewish!

BASSANIO: But why does that make you anti-Semitic?

LORENZO: I'm trying to tell you, Bassanio. Can you at least see why I ran off with Jessica?

BASSANIO: Because she's Jewish.

LORENZO: Exactly. I figured that if I married her, at least my children would grow up enjoying the warm attentions of a Jewish mother. And as they grew older, I thought that through Jewish connections, they might have an easier time getting jobs with movie producers in Hollywood.

BASSANIO: Then let that happen, man!

LORENZO: I can't, Bassanio! I'm not sure I love her. I may only love her Jewishness. I may be stereotyping her and the whole magnificent tradition she is heiress to. Oh God, to think this way, to group people this way, to refuse to allow for individual differences, is a crime against nature and society. But I can't help doing it! *That's* why I'm anti-Semitic, Bassanio! You see? I'm the *ultimate* anti-Semite! Oh hell, I'm hopeless! I probably should slink off Hemingway-like to Harry's Bar and hunker down with a bottle in some private booth. Rather than marrying into Jessica's tradition, I should simply embrace my own —by drinking myself to death immediately! *(He downs his drink.)*

BASSANIO: *(Restraining him.)* No, Lorenzo. No. Hang in there, buddy. Better a living bigot than a dead drunk.

LORENZO: But what can I do? These thoughts overwhelm me.

BASSANIO: Have you shared them with Jessica herself?

LORENZO: I don't dare. She hates anti-Semitism in all its forms. She wrote a three-page paper on it in high school.

BASSANIO: No, hey, lookit, buddy. Go in there, cut her off from the herd, sit her down in some corner, and tell her your problem. Remember: it's not Wasp to Jew, it's Lorenzo to Jessica. OK?

LORENZO: OK. I'll try. *(Embracing him.)* God, what a good friend you are, Bassanio. You really know how to handle us self-hating Wasps. *(Starts out, then returns.)* I'm glad you hit me, too. It shows you've still held onto that rough and ready temperament you inherited from the shanty Irish who helped build our urban infrastructure.

BASSANIO: Just go, buddy. Just go. *(Lorenzo goes in. Bassanio remains.)* Ya-ta-ta, ya-ta-ta, talk, talk talk. *(He starts doing push ups. Party sounds within. Portia comes out.)*

PORTIA: Hello, young lover.

BASSANIO: *(Going to her.)* When do we go to bed, babe?

PORTIA: Tomorrow and tomorrow and tomorrow.

BASSANIO: *(Going to embrace her.)* 'Tis a consummation devoutly to be wished.

PORTIA: Hey. Slow down. We have to cut the cake and say good-bye to our guests.

BASSANIO: *(Looking off)* Looks like they're hanging in.

PORTIA: That's because everyone's having a spectacular time. Which reminds me. Your pal Antonio is at the bar. He wants to talk to you.

BASSANIO: Can't it wait?

PORTIA: Go to him, sweetheart. He adores you.

BASSANIO: He always wants to talk about opera.

PORTIA: Then listen to him. You'll learn something.

BASSANIO: For you, I'll do it . . . *(He serenades her with a few bars from the tune the band is playing, then starts off, calling:)* Hey, Antonio! Long time no see, buddy! *(He is off. Portia looks after him fondly, takes up the tune. She doesn't notice Salerio, who comes on, carrying a leather loose-leaf folder. He gets caught up in the romance, tries to dance, stumbles, and falls.)*

PORTIA: *(Noticing him.)* Are you all right?

SALERIO: *(Getting up; huffily.)* Perfectly fine . . . Are we now in a musical comedy?

PORTIA: It certainly feels like one.

SALERIO: I find most musicals flat, stale, and unprofitable.

PORTIA: I'm too happy to argue . . . Have you solved my financial difficulties?

SALERIO: I've done what I could.

PORTIA: Thank you. Because this party is becoming a huge success. You should look at it as my own, personal investment in a new Venice.

SALERIO: If it's all so successful, why are you out here alone?

PORTIA: What's wrong with being alone?

SALERIO: At your own wedding reception?

PORTIA: Actually, it's a great pleasure, Salerio. Notice I'm not tearing around, picking up plates and emptying ashtrays. I'm just sitting back and watching the whole thing purr.

SALERIO: Your new Venice.

PORTIA: Exactly. I imagine God feels the same, on a good day.

SALERIO: I heard an amusing joke down at the Rialto.

PORTIA: Tell me.

SALERIO: Do you know what the ostrich said when he came upon a flock of his fellows, all with their heads buried in the sand and their tails waving in the breeze?

PORTIA: No. What did the ostrich say?

SALERIO: He said, "Where is everybody?" *(Portia laughs.)*

PORTIA: Very good, Salerio. You made a funny. See? Even you are loosening up. Now come in and dance.

SALERIO: You didn't answer the question.

PORTIA: Where is everybody? All right. Let's see. Gratiano and Nerissa are probably scurrying back from town, with Shylock in tow.

SALERIO: Shylock?

PORTIA: I'm hoping he'll show up and make the evening complete.

SALERIO: He'd make the evening something else.

PORTIA: To continue: Lorenzo and Jessica are probably off in a corner with a priest, working out the details of a delightfully interdenominational marriage. With luck, Shylock will arrive in time to give the bride away.

SALERIO: With luck . . . And Bassanio?

PORTIA: Bassanio is at the bar, having a heart to heart conversation with his old pal Antonio. So all's well with the world.

SALERIO: All's well that ends well. *(Gratiano and Nerissa come back on; Both are talking at once. Nerissa might now wear a Spanish shawl.)*

NERISSA: *(Slight Latino accent.)* . . . What do you mean? My people have suffered just as much as yours! Look what the Spaniards did to the native populations! They eradicated entire civilizations!

GRATIANO: They didn't put you in chains and throw you into slave ships!

NERISSA: That's because we preferred to die proud and free!

PORTIA: Hello.

GRATIANO: *(To Nerissa.)* Whereas we were strong enough to cross the water and create a new civilization of our own!

NERISSA: What civilization?

PORTIA: Hello!

GRATIANO: *(Ignoring Portia.)* What civilization? This civilization right here! Black music, from the spiritual on up through rock and roll! The natural poetry of our street language! The grace and agility of our leading athletes! Hell, everything vibrant and alive in contemporary culture comes straight from us!

PORTIA: *(Finally getting through.)* I'd like to have the floor now, please. *(Nerissa and Gratiano stop arguing, look at her.)*

NERISSA: May I help you?

PORTIA: I believe I sent you two on a little errand.

GRATIANO: Oh. Right. Shylock.

PORTIA: Is he joining us or not?

NERISSA: He wasn't there.

GRATIANO: He had gone to work.

PORTIA: At this hour?

GRATIANO: I guess he needs the cash, since you cleaned him out.

PORTIA: Hmmm. Well. Fall off a horse, get right back up. Good for Shylock.

NERISSA: We left your note under his door.

GRATIANO: I doubt if he'll bother to read it.

PORTIA: Thank you anyway. You did what you could. And now. Gratiano, I imagine you'd like to retire with Nerissa to the nearest bedchamber.

GRATIANO: Why do you say that?

PORTIA: Well I mean . . .

GRATIANO: Just because I'm a black man, you think I'm only interested in sex.

PORTIA: No, no. I simply meant —

GRATIANO: You see me as an animal, don't you? When I'm not shuffling off, running errands for you, you think I'm just a big dick with a small brain.

PORTIA: I didn't mean that at all! I simply —

GRATIANO: Yeah well give me a call when you're ready to regard me as human being! *(Starts off.)*

NERISSA: *(Calling after him.)* Where are you going?

GRATIANO: There's a jazz joint off the Piazza San Marco where the brothers are making the sweetest sounds north of Nigeria. *(Becomes more and more black in his dialect.)* I'll hang out there till the white folks come in and steal the tunes for theyselves! *(He goes off angrily.)*

PORTIA: Go after him, Nerissa! Quickly!

NERISSA: Stop ordering me around!

PORTIA: What?

NERISSA: You're always doing it! Nerissa, bring out the caskets! Nerissa, play a law clerk! Nerissa, fall in love immediately!

PORTIA: Nerissa . . . Sweetheart . . .

NERISSA: *Madre Maria! Se arabo! (With a stronger Spanish accent)* Why have I been following jou around all these years? Trying to look like jou. Dress like jou. *Be* like jou. As if the only valid image of womanhood came from your stack of old Yay Crew catalogues!
(She starts out, bumping into Bassanio who is coming in. She shoves him aside.)
Nunca mas! Bruha! Te quisiera arancar la lengua!
(To Salerio.) Y tu! Que tu haces alli? Te estoy vigilando!
(Bassanio comes on as Nerissa starts off still talking.) Todos ustedes son iquales y no me importa tres pitos lo que piensan de mi, porque este casa me tiene hasta les tetas y me voy porque yo no aquanto mas y se acabo!
(She continues talking on into the wings. Pause.)

BASSANIO: What got into her?

PORTIA: I'm not sure . . .

SALERIO: *(To Portia.)* Am I witnessing a preview of your new Venice?

PORTIA: You are witnessing a temporary setback.

BASSANIO: Portia, I gotta tell you something.

PORTIA: What, sweetheart?

BASSANIO: I just hit Antonio.

PORTIA: You hit Antonio?

BASSANIO: Knocked him down. *(To Salerio.)* I have a violent streak because of my Irish heritage.

SALERIO: I see.

PORTIA: But why did you hit him, sweetheart? He's your great old friend.

BASSANIO: He said he harbors strong feelings toward me.

PORTIA: But that's a compliment, darling!

BASSANIO: Like hell it is! The guy's gay!

PORTIA: But what if he is?

BASSANIO: I hate gays! *(To Salerio.)* Being a devout Roman Catholic, I'm right with the Pope on this one.

SALERIO: I see.

PORTIA: Bassanio, I want you to go in there and apologize to that man right now.

BASSANIO: But he kissed me!

PORTIA: Men do that all the time these days!

BASSANIO: But he said he loved me! Men don't say that!

PORTIA: Why didn't you simply reply that you loved *me? (Pause.)*

BASSANIO: You're right. I should have. *(To Salerio.)* Why didn't I? Jesus!

SALERIO: I don't know.

BASSANIO: *(To Salerio.)* I have an Irish tendency to overreact. Which comes from three hundred years of English occupation. *(Slyly indicates Portia.)*

SALERIO: I see.

PORTIA: Where is Antonio now?

BASSANIO: Over at a friend's house. He wanted to listen to *La Traviata* as recorded by Maria Callas in Lisbon in 1958.

SALERIO: *(To Portia.)* You seem to have lost Antonio to Italian opera.

PORTIA: I know. It's infuriating. The most attractive men in Venice all run off to the opera. *(Lorenzo and Jessica come in.)*

LORENZO: Portia, may we speak to you a moment?

PORTIA: I don't want to hear.

JESSICA: We've decided to break up.

PORTIA: Knew it.

LORENZO: We talked it over and realized it would never work. I want to be Jewish. She wants to be Wasp.

JESSICA: No I don't. I've decided Wasps are dated and decadent.

LORENZO: *(To Portia.)* You can see why we have to call things off.

PORTIA: But I had this priest ready and waiting.

JESSICA: Don't worry about him.

LORENZO: He just ran off with the piano player.

JESSICA: That's why the music stopped.

PORTIA: I didn't notice.

SALERIO: I noticed.

PORTIA: I'll bet you noticed.

JESSICA: Anyway I'm going to move in with Tommy Woo.

PORTIA: Who?

JESSICA: No, Woo. Tommy Woo.

BASSANIO: Maybe she means the Who's Tommy.

JESSICA: I do not. I mean Tommy Woo. *(Pointing off.)* Know who that is, standing over there? Tommy Woo, that's who. *(Waves.)* Yoo hoo! Mr. Woo!

PORTIA: *(Looking off.)* That . . . waiter?

LORENZO: She met him when he was serving the saltimboca.

PORTIA: But he's . . . Chinese, Jessica.

JESSICA: That's all right. He's got his Green Card.

PORTIA: But you're a Jewish princess, Jessica. You've been raised to expect an elaborate life. Can a Chinese waiter make you happy?

JESSICA: That just goes to show how prejudiced you are, Portia! Being a waiter is just a summer job for Tommy. He goes to Harvard and majors in advanced electronics. I'm convinced he's the coming thing.

PORTIA: *(To Lorenzo.)* What does this do to you?

LORENZO: Tommy Woo? I wish I knew.

BASSANIO: *(Teasing him.)* Boo hoo.

LORENZO: Fuck you.

PORTIA: Poor Lorenzo.

LORENZO: I guess it was inevitable. They say Jews are addicted to Chinese food.

BASSANIO: *(Confidentially.)* There you go, stereotyping people again. *(Lorenzo slaps himself)*

PORTIA: Won't Tommy Woo come out and join us?

JESSICA: He's shy, coming as he does from such a different culture. But you wait. His day is dawning, and I plan to be right by his side . . . *(To others.)* No more dancing for me! I'm into Kung Foo with Tommy Woo! *(Jessica hurries off.)*

BASSANIO: *(Arm around Lorenzo.)* Sorry, buddy. That's a rough one.

LORENZO: Say, how about shooting some hoops out by the garage? Just to subdue my testosterone level.

BASSANIO: A little mano a mano? I'm psyched! My stuff's in the car! West Side rules! First to seven by two! *(They start off jostling each other.)*

PORTIA: But we haven't even cut the cake!

BASSANIO: Oh. *(Returning.)* The cake's gone, Portia.

PORTIA: Gone?

BASSANIO: Dog ate it.

PORTIA: Oh no.

LORENZO: Come on, Bassanio! I'll kick your white ass! *(They spar around Portia.)*

BASSANIO: No trashin', man! You are on your knees! You are pleading for mercy! You are dead! *(They rush off pushing and shoving each other. Long pause.)*

SALERIO: Portia . . .

PORTIA: Don't say a word.

SALERIO: I'm afraid I have to, Portia.

PORTIA: More bad news?

SALERIO: I've had to declare bankruptcy on your behalf.

PORTIA: Bankruptcy?

SALERIO: This party was the last straw.

PORTIA: I thought you said you took care of things.

SALERIO: I said I did what I could. Bankruptcy was your best bet.

PORTIA: Does it mean much? Bankruptcy? You read about people declaring it all the time, and then riding around in Rolls-Royces.

SALERIO: In your case, Portia, bankruptcy means that they plan to foreclose on your estate.

PORTIA: Foreclose?

SALERIO: I'm afraid so.

PORTIA: When?

SALERIO: As soon as they can.

PORTIA: The whole thing?

SALERIO: You'll be lucky to keep a pillowcase.

PORTIA: Oh boy. Gosh. Hmmm. Gee. Let me just pull myself together here. *(She takes a deep breath.)* Well, it was fun while it lasted. I'll just have to go to work, that's all. I'll get a job in a bookstore and improve my mind.

SALERIO: Nowadays it would be a video store, Portia. You can improve your mind by explaining to teenagers the artistic merits of *Lethal Weapon Three*.

PORTIA: Some accountant you turned out to be.

SALERIO: I got the best deal I could.

PORTIA: And left me flat broke.

SALERIO: Not quite, Portia. *(Indicating his loose-leaf folder.)* Before I declared bankruptcy, I took everything I could liquidate and invested it in Switzerland.

PORTIA: Switzerland?

SALERIO: *(Opening his folder; showing her.)* Good, solid, untouchable Swiss bonds, at six and a half percent interest, tax free. You will still have a small income.

PORTIA: *(Looking over his shoulder.)* That's something, at least.

SALERIO: Of course you'll have to establish residence to collect it.

PORTIA: In Switzerland?

SALERIO: In Switzerland. I bought you a small condominium on Lake Geneva. *(Shows her.)* Two bedrooms, sizable living room, and eat-in kitchen.

PORTIA: In Switzerland.

SALERIO: In Switzerland.

PORTIA: I don't know anyone in Switzerland.

SALERIO: You'd know me.

PORTIA: You'd go there, too?

SALERIO: *(Showing her.)* I bought the adjoining apartment.

PORTIA: Oh.

SALERIO: They have a common balcony, Portia. We could sit there, side by side, every evening, watching the sun settle comfortably over the Alps. And after we've been there eighteen months, we could apply for a permit from the co-op board to knock down the wall between us.

PORTIA: I don't love you, Salerio.

SALERIO: You'd learn to, Portia. Listen. The Swiss offer major tax advantages for married couples. The deduction at death, for example, is better than Florida's.

PORTIA: I'm already married.

SALERIO: Are you?

PORTIA: Whenever he tires of that goddamn game.

SALERIO: They say basketball today, golf tomorrow.

PORTIA: *(Sitting down on the steps; starting to cry.)* Oh dear.
(He quickly spreads out a pocket handkerchief; sits down beside her.)

SALERIO: I love you, Portia.

PORTIA: I don't think so.

SALERIO: The way I love good wine.

PORTIA: You don't drink.

SALERIO: I'm a closet drinker. I'll sip you privately and appreciatively all the days of your life.

PORTIA: Is that enough?

SALERIO: Would you prefer to be guzzled like a can of Coke? And tossed aside when done?

PORTIA: No . . .

SALERIO: Portia, you asked me to resolve your financial difficulties. I've responded as best I know how. I am offering you a comfortable home, a modest income, and congenial companionship in a picturesque natural setting till death do us part. Isn't that better, in the long run, than being ignored and homeless in Venice?

PORTIA: Maybe . . .

SALERIO: Then let me collect on that kiss. *(He leans over to kiss her. As she is about to respond, an Older Man comes in, He is attractive and fit, wearing an elegant black tuxedo.)*

SHYLOCK: Excuse me.

PORTIA: *(Getting up; peering at him.)* Yes? May I help you?

SHYLOCK: Where is everybody?

PORTIA: *(Recognizing him.)* Shylock? *(Salerio gets up slowly.)* *(Quick curtain.)*

END OF ACT ONE

ACT TWO

As we were: Portia greets Shylock; Salerio stands by.

PORTIA: Shylock?

SHYLOCK: *(Bowing.)* Portia.

PORTIA: I didn't recognize you.

SHYLOCK: These days I hardly recognize myself. *(Looks at her.)* You look different, too, Portia.

PORTIA: Oh well. The last time you saw me I was disguised as an impossibly self-righteous lawyer from Padua. Remember?

SHYLOCK: How could I forget? You threw the book at me.

PORTIA: I suppose I did. Are you here to exact your revenge?

SHYLOCK: It's a little late in the day for that.

PORTIA: Thank God. I've got enough to worry about.

SHYLOCK: Let's consider the whole thing water over the dam.

PORTIA: Or under the bridge, since this is Venice.

SHYLOCK: Right. Polluted water under the Bridge of Sighs.

PORTIA: Exactly! What a good way to put it, Shylock! *(Salerio coughs.)*

PORTIA: Oh. This is Salerio, my accountant.

SALERIO: And travelling companion.

SHYLOCK: How do you do?

SALERIO: *(Shaking hands.)* I believe we've met before, Shylock.

SHYLOCK: Oh yes. Many a time and oft on the Rialto. I also saw you at the trial. Weren't you prowling around in back?

PORTIA: He always prowls around in back.

SALERIO: I'm an accountant. I like to account for things.

PORTIA: How about a drink, Shylock?

SHYLOCK: No thanks.

PORTIA: You're sure? A nightcap or something? Champagne? Maybe a brandy?

SHYLOCK: Got any fruit juice?

PORTIA: Fruit juice? Hmmm. Let me think . . . There's Bloody Mary Mix. I know we have that.

SHYLOCK: No thanks. I've got a nervous stomach.

PORTIA: Now wait. *(She thinks.)* Ah hah! Orange juice! Salerio, would you run into the house and get Shylock a big glass of that freshly squeezed orange juice in the ice box? Would you do that for me, please?

SALERIO: *(Bowing.)* Certainly, Portia. *(He starts off.)*

SHYLOCK: *(Calling after him.)* And something to eat, maybe?

PORTIA: Food? Hmmm. Food. *(Salerio waits.)*

SHYLOCK: *(Apologetically.)* Jews like to eat.

PORTIA: I'm not too good about food. *(To Salerio.)* I suppose the caterers have left.

SALERIO: *(Glancing off)* Seems so.

SHYLOCK: Just a pretzel will do.

PORTIA: *(To Salerio.)* Tell you what: I think there's an old box of Bremner Wafers in the cupboard over the dishwasher. Put them on a tray.

SALERIO: Certainly, Portia.

PORTIA: Oh, and bring out one of those little bistro chairs.

SALERIO: Certainly, Portia. *(Salerio goes off.)*

SHYLOCK: Friend of the family?

PORTIA: Sort of. Do you like him?

SHYLOCK: Do you?

PORTIA: He's good for me, Shylock. He tells me the bottom line.

SHYLOCK: He makes me nervous.

PORTIA: *(Whispering.)* Me, too . . . *(Salerio returns with a chair.)* Thank you, Salerio.

SALERIO: You're welcome, Portia. *(He goes off.)*

PORTIA: Well. Sit down, Shylock. Please.

SHYLOCK: *(Looking around.)* I thought there was a party here.

PORTIA: *(Cleaning up.)* There was, Shylock. There was definitely a party here. But now it seems to be somewhat in disarray.

SHYLOCK: Why?

PORTIA: Oh well. One thing after another. But don't tell me that's why you're here, Shylock. Just to party it up.

SHYLOCK: I thought since I've been forced to join the club, I might as well make use of my membership.

PORTIA: I don't believe that for one minute.

SHYLOCK: Actually I was intrigued by the note I found under my door.

PORTIA: Oh God. My dumb note.

SHYLOCK: *(Taking it out of his pocket.)* I liked it. *(Reads.)* "Come help us celebrate a new Venice. Regrets only. Portia." *(Looks at her.)* A new Venice . . . I'm interested in that.

PORTIA: So was I. Several centuries ago.

SHYLOCK: No longer?

PORTIA: I've grown up since. "Regrets only" — that's me now. *(Pause.)*

SHYLOCK: I also came to find my daughter.

PORTIA: Ah. Jessica.

238 A. R. GURNEY

SHYLOCK: Is she around?

PORTIA: No, she's not, Shylock. Not at the moment, I'm sorry to say.

SHYLOCK: She's off with Lorenzo?

PORTIA: No, actually *not* with Lorenzo, Shylock. She seems to have broken up with Lorenzo.

SHYLOCK: She just ran off with him.

PORTIA: I know she did, Shylock. But now she's just run off with someone else.

SHYLOCK: *Oy.*

PORTIA: No, now he looked like a very nice man.

SHYLOCK: What's his name?

PORTIA: I can't quite remember the name, Shylock. It's a tricky name, actually. It's a Chinese name. He's Chinese.

SHYLOCK: *Oy.*

PORTIA: No, now stop that. He goes to Harvard.

SHYLOCK: I should genuflect?

PORTIA: Lots of people do these days.

SHYLOCK: What's his line, this Chinese gentleman?

PORTIA: Line? He works, Shylock. He was working here. Actually, he's a waiter.

SHYLOCK: A waiter?

PORTIA: No, now that's just a summer job, Shylock. Apparently he's doing well at Harvard. He'll be very good for Jessica.

SHYLOCK: From your mouth . . . So. How about you? Where's that fellow of yours? The boy who borrowed the money?

PORTIA: Bassanio? Oh well, he's off, too. Playing basketball with Lorenzo.

SHYLOCK: Isn't this your wedding night?

PORTIA: It is, Shylock. It was supposed to be. But they felt they needed a little male bonding.

SHYLOCK: *Oy.*

PORTIA: And Antonio has come out of the closet, and Nerissa has decided she's been exploited, and Gratiano is immersing himself in African-American culture.

SHYLOCK: *Oy veh.*

PORTIA: It's all falling apart, Shylock, if you must know. It's an absolute mess. And the worst thing about it is, it's all my fault.

SHYLOCK: Why your fault?

PORTIA: Because I was the Queen Bee around here. I was rich, I had pull, I could have done something really significant for Venice and the world. Instead, what did I do? Played games. Bossed people around. Made everyone dance to my tune. Look what I did to you! I got the court to impose that huge fine and force you to become Christian.

SHYLOCK: People have always done that to Jews. We survive.

PORTIA: Some don't. Look at the Spanish Inquisition.

SHYLOCK: Excuse me, dear lady, but I've looked already.

PORTIA: You must hate us very much.

SHYLOCK: I'll tell you frankly, Portia: I did. I used to. And we Jews are supposed to never, never forget. But I have to say there are times when it slips my mind.

PORTIA: Really?

SHYLOCK: Especially on a lovely night like this. When there's moonlight and stars. And I'm talking to a pretty girl.

PORTIA: Why, Shylock! Are you flirting with me?

SHYLOCK: If the shoe fits, I can get it for you wholesale.

PORTIA: Yes well, don't bother. I'm not worth it. I'm a superficial woman, Shylock. That's what *I've* learned tonight. Oh God, when I think about it! Even inviting you here tonight was a dumb thing to do! Trying to pull things together with a party! What a silly cow I am! What a fatuous, frivolous dope!

SHYLOCK: Now, now.

PORTIA: I'm shallow. Shylock. I've always suspected it, and now I'm sure. I've had things too easy for too long. I've tried to be deep, really, but it doesn't work. I've read Dostoyevsky and Beckett. I've even read books *about* Dostoyevsky and Beckett. But I just can't look at life the way they do. I'm hopelessly one-dimensional. If this were a movie, I'd be played by Doris Day!

SHYLOCK: An admirable actress.

PORTIA: Not for these times, let me tell you. Oh look: the least I can do is apologize. For the whole thing. On behalf of our whole gang.

SHYLOCK: I went a little overboard myself. *(Salerio comes in with a glass of orange juice and a box of Bremner wafers.)*

SALERIO: Here are the refreshments you requested.

SHYLOCK: *(Taking the orange juice.)* Thank you very much.

PORTIA: *(Taking the cracker box; to Salerio.)* I thought I mentioned a tray.

SALERIO: I couldn't locate one.

PORTIA: There was a little silver one right there!

SALERIO: The caterer must have taken it.

PORTIA: There. You see, Shylock? The whole social fabric is ripping apart. Even Cipriani's is corrupt.

SHYLOCK: Never mind. There are too many trays in the world.

PORTIA: Do you know, I've always felt that. Too many trays! *(To Salerio.)* This man is very wise. *(To Shylock; offering him the box.)* Cracker, Shylock?

SHYLOCK: Thank you. *(He reaches deep into the box, finally retrieves one. Portia turns the box upside down, realizes it is empty, angrily glares at Salerio, puts the box away somewhere. Shylock sits down.)* So. Well. What next? *(He eats his cracker.)*

PORTIA: I wish I knew.

SALERIO: I believe I can answer that question, Shylock. Portia and I are moving to Switzerland.

PORTIA: Thinking about it.

SHYLOCK: What's in Switzerland?

SALERIO: Peace. Civility. Coherence.

PORTIA: Fabulous skiing, too, Shylock. We could spend our lives going gently downhill.

SALERIO: It's the last oasis of order in this desert of a century.

SHYLOCK: Switzerland. Well.

PORTIA: Everyone has a private Switzerland to retreat to, Shylock. I'd just be visiting mine more permanently.

SHYLOCK: You're giving up on Venice?

PORTIA: Venice is giving up on me. I'm deeply in debt. They're foreclosing any minute.

SHYLOCK: I heard.

PORTIA: So I should get out while the getting's good. To Switzerland.

SHYLOCK: Not many Jews in Switzerland.

PORTIA: Not many anything in Switzerland.

SALERIO: There are plenty of Swiss.

PORTIA: Do you know any Swiss, Shylock?

SHYLOCK: Just a family named Robinson. *(Portia laughs.)* They changed it from Rubinstein.

PORTIA: *(Laughs more.)* That's funny. You're marvelous, Shylock! *(To Salerio.)* I adore this man! *(To Shylock.)* You'll have to visit us in Switzerland. I'll give you a small dinner party.

SHYLOCK: Actually I prefer Venice.

SALERIO: You *like* Venice?

SHYLOCK: I've been many places, but I like it here.

PORTIA: I suppose because it's a democracy.

SHYLOCK: That's part of it.

SALERIO: Democracy? Forgive me, Shylock, but Venice is no democracy. It is an oligarchy and always has been. Government by the rich, for the rich, and dedicated to the proposition that they get even richer.

SHYLOCK: Sometimes it seems that way.

SALERIO: Switzerland's the democracy. The oldest one on earth.

SHYLOCK: Oh yes? Three hundred years of democracy. And what have they produced? The cuckoo clock.

PORTIA: *(Laughing.)* Another goodie, Shylock.

SALERIO: Oh no. He stole that one from a movie.

PORTIA: Did you, Shylock? You rascal you!

SALERIO: *The Third Man*, screenplay by Graham Greene, directed by Carol Reed.

SHYLOCK: All right, I'll admit it. *(To Portia.)* But only because I'm trying to convince you to stay in Venice.

PORTIA: I wish I could.

SHYLOCK: Think of the possibilities here in Venice. A great commercial center, facing half east, half west. A haven for oppressed people. Energy, variety — more *life* per square inch than anywhere else in the world! The future lies with Venice.

PORTIA: How can you root for Venice, Shylock? After what Venice did to you?

SHYLOCK: Because in Venice you have the constant feeling that most of its citizens — even the most prejudiced — are yearning to make things better.

PORTIA: That's what I want! A new Venice!

SALERIO: Oh come on, you two. Nowadays Venice is simply about money. Ask any accountant. Money is our drug of choice, and we're thoroughly addicted to it. People who have it are frantic to make more, and people who don't are desperate to get hooked. That's really why you got into trouble, Shylock. You were seen as the ultimate drug dealer.

PORTIA: Oh please.

SALERIO: It's true. Shylock has long been better at making money than any of us. Oh I know, I know, he became good at it because we wouldn't let him do anything else. So he's been practicing since the Middle Ages and now he's got it down pat. What's more, he doesn't make any bones about it. He doesn't constantly claim he's saving the world or improving society or even providing jobs. He is simply making money. That's really why we resent him. And envy him. And punish him when we can.

PORTIA: I read somewhere that last year Shylock gave away more money to Venetian culture than anyone else in the area. For example, the entire Teatro Venezia is supported primarily by Shylock's money.

SALERIO: Exactly. That makes us all the more resentful. We spend our days dealing for the drug of money, pumping it into our veins, or stashing it away for future use, while our main man here is blithely tossing it away on some hopelessly not-for-profit enterprise. It's infuriating.

SHYLOCK: I'm getting embarrassed here.

PORTIA: Of course you are, poor man. I apologize, Shylock. We've been very rude, talking about you while you're right here in front of us. But you'll be rid of us any minute. Soon Salerio and I will be sitting on some balcony in Switzerland, saying whatever we want, with nobody listening to any of it.

SHYLOCK: I thought you had a husband to worry about.

PORTIA: Ooops. Right. Well, I do and I don't, Shylock. For reasons we needn't go into, he and I are not quite totally married yet. Which may be a good thing. I'm beginning to think he might be a little young for me. I might have to throw him back.

SHYLOCK: After all you went through?

PORTIA: I'm afraid it was just sexual attraction.

SHYLOCK: Nothing wrong with that.

PORTIA: There is when there's nothing else.

SALERIO: I couldn't agree more. I'll go purchase our airline tickets. Swissair, First Class to Geneva, all right with you?

PORTIA: I guess.

SALERIO: I'll need your credit card.

PORTIA: It's upstairs on my dressing table.

SALERIO: Thank you. *(Shakes hands with Shylock.)* Good-bye, Shylock. I'm sorry Venice is not what you'd like it to be.

SHYLOCK: It never will be if its citizens retreat to Switzerland.

SALERIO: Better Switzerland than chaos. *(He goes off)*

SHYLOCK: *(Looking after him.)* Strange gentleman.

PORTIA: Do you like him more?

SHYLOCK: Do you?

PORTIA: I'm trying to. *(Pause.)* Well. I'll go pack.

SHYLOCK: What's your hurry?

PORTIA: I don't want to be here when the real estate agents start bringing people around. Peeking into closets. Criticizing the wallpaper. I'd hate all that.

SHYLOCK: I understand.

PORTIA: I've also got to figure out what to take with me.

SHYLOCK: I remember from my wife Leah, God rest her soul — there's no talking to a woman when she's planning what to wear.

PORTIA: Exactly. So please excuse me. *(Stopping.)* Oh. You're welcome to stay, by the way. There's a pool out back if you want to take a dip. Don't worry about a bathing suit. Nobody cares.

SHYLOCK: They might if they saw me.

PORTIA: Well then, you could watch television in the library. Or there's a ping pong table in the game room if you can drum up someone to play. *(Indicating the bar.)* There's plenty of liquor, of course, and if you're still hungry —

SHYLOCK: Portia.

PORTIA: Yes?

SHYLOCK: I bought the place.

PORTIA: You bought what place?

SHYLOCK: This place. Your estate. Belmont. I bought it.

PORTIA: When?

SHYLOCK: Tonight. Before I came.

PORTIA: How?

SHYLOCK: With money.

PORTIA: I thought we cleaned you out.

SHYLOCK: I made telephone calls.

PORTIA: Oh.

SHYLOCK: I suppose now you'll bring up the International Jewish Conspiracy.

PORTIA: I don't even know what that is.

SHYLOCK: Neither do I. This was just a rich cousin in Crakow. *(Pause.)*

PORTIA: Wow. Hmmm. I'm kind of thrown for a loop here, Shylock.

SHYLOCK: I'll take good care of it, Portia.

PORTIA: Are you going to chop down the cherry trees?

SHYLOCK: What cherry trees?

PORTIA: I just meant this seems like a different play.

SHYLOCK: Yes.

PORTIA: Why did you buy it, Shylock?

SHYLOCK: I couldn't let a good thing go.

PORTIA: I suppose you plan to subdivide it.

SHYLOCK: Subdivide it?

PORTIA: Isn't that what people do when they buy old estates? Subdivide them and put in parking lots and Wal-Marts and stuff?

SHYLOCK: Hadn't thought of that. I just wanted it. For my daughter.

PORTIA: Oh. Right. Jessica.

SHYLOCK: She's a Jewish princess. She likes castles.

PORTIA: You're very thoughtful to give her one.

SHYLOCK: Maybe this will bring her back.

PORTIA: All the more reason for me to get packing. *(Starts in again.)*

SHYLOCK: You could stay on, if you'd like, Portia. As long as you want. There's plenty of room. As you well know.

PORTIA: No, no. One thing about us Wasps. We know when to leave. Thank you, good-bye, and move out smartly, that's us. Well. Hmmm. The least I can do is give you a quick tour of the premises. Come on. I'll show you around. *(She takes his arm; they start off.)* Now promise me you won't peek in the closets or criticize the wallpaper . . . Do you like Ralph Lauren and Laura Ashley?

SHYLOCK: Love him, hate her.

PORTIA: *(Laughing.)* I don't know why, Shylock, but I really get a kick out of you! *(They are off. A moment. Then Lorenzo comes on, bouncing a basketball, followed by Bassanio. They are both in T-shirts and shorts, sweaty, and drinking beer.)*

BASSANIO: Come on. Another game.

LORENZO: I'm bushed, Bassanio.

BASSANIO: Scared I'll win? Chicken! Pawk, pawk!

LORENZO: Winning . . . losing . . . I don't know. Suddenly I'm tired of competition. Maybe it has something to do with my obsession with Judaism. "Do no vain boasting as the gentiles do."

BASSANIO: O.K. We'll switch to a scoreless game. There's an all-night batting cage out by the Lido. Come on. A hundred balls apiece. *(Practices his swing.)*

LORENZO: Isn't this supposed to be your wedding night?

BASSANIO: Jesus, Mary and Joseph! It completely slipped my mind!
(Gratiano comes on from town. He now wears khakis, a work shirt, and working boots.)

GRATIANO: You guys hear the news? Shylock just bought this place!

LORENZO: Shylock ?

GRATIANO: They had it on CNN.

BASSANIO: Did they say who won the Red Sox game?

LORENZO: Forget the Red Sox, Bassanio! Think of Shylock! There's your real winner!

BASSANIO: Oh. Right.

GRATIANO: Hello! This could make me! I came out to give him my card. He might want to do some remodeling.

LORENZO: The place sure could use it.

BASSANIO: Hey, you could turn that old billiard room into a world-class fitness center. Take down the English hunting prints, put up a few mirrors . . . *(All three begin to pose and grunt.)*

LORENZO: *(Breaking out of it.)* Hey, where's Nerissa, man?

GRATIANO: Last time I saw her, she was in a late-night Spanish restaurant, savoring the salty glories of a frozen margarita. *(Shows them his finger.)* She also took her ring back.

LORENZO: I'm sorry.

GRATIANO: No, that's OK. A million years ago, Africa and South America were a single continent. But now there's an ocean between us . . . What about Jessica?

LORENZO: I imagine she's learning how to use chopsticks.

GRATIANO: *(To Bassanio.)* And Portia?

BASSANIO: Who?

GRATIANO: Your wife, man!

BASSANIO: Christ! I keep forgetting!

GRATIANO: *(To Lorenzo, indicating Bassanio.)* I think Freud has something to tell us here.

BASSANIO: Who's Freud?

LORENZO: Freud was a brilliant Jewish doctor who says we forget what we want to forget.

BASSANIO: I don't remember reading that at Saint Mary's School of the Parochial Sorrows.

GRATIANO: He is supposed to have opened the door onto our real feelings.

BASSANIO: Do you think Freud would say that I've been shooting baskets with you because I subconsciously want to avoid going to bed with Portia?

LORENZO: He might.

BASSANIO: Do you think he might also say that I hit Antonio because I'm refusing to acknowledge my own latent homosexual tendencies?

GRATIANO: He might say that, too.

BASSANIO: Oh boy! Freud, huh? He might even say I'm too immature to take on the commitments of a heterosexual relationship and am totally in denial of my feminine side.

GRATIANO: That's the way Freud might sum it up.

BASSANIO: *(Grimly.)* Then I know where I belong.

LORENZO: With Antonio?

BASSANIO: No. In the Marine Corps . . . I'm enlisting right now.

LORENZO: I'll walk you to your Alfa Romeo. *(He claps him on the back and they start off. Shylock comes on. Gratiano peels off to deal with him.)*

GRATIANO: Shylock, sir . . . My card.

SHYLOCK: *(Taking it; reads.)* "Construction and renovation." Well. *(Looks at him.)* Portia just recommended you.

GRATIANO: I'm ready to go.

SHYLOCK: Any other references?

GRATIANO: I'm just starting out.

SHYLOCK: This is not a small job. The place needs a major overhaul.

GRATIANO: I know.

SHYLOCK: The roof leaks. The sills are rotting. The wiring is downright dangerous.

GRATIANO: I noticed.

SHYLOCK: Well. Write up your proposal and I'll see.

GRATIANO: Fair enough. *(Starts off)*

SHYLOCK: Gratiano *(Gratiano stops.)* Before you go, sit down.

GRATIANO: I prefer to stand, thanks.

SHYLOCK: Mind if I sit? I'm tired.

GRATIANO: Suit yourself. *(Shylock sits. A pause.)*

SHYLOCK: Gratiano, the world is moving very fast these days.

GRATIANO: Yes.

SHYLOCK: The present is very different from the past. Property is changing hands. Lovers are changing partners. Enemies are becoming friends.

GRATIANO: I'm aware of that.

SHYLOCK: When I talk to people these days, Gratiano, I try very hard not to bring up the past. I don't like beating dead dogs. What's over is over. As Nixon said, "mistakes were made" — God! Talk about change! Here I am quoting Nixon!

GRATIANO: Why not? You're the Establishment now, Shylock.

SHYLOCK: Who knows what's Establishment? Time will tell. Or possibly Newsweek. *(His little joke.)*

GRATIANO: What are you getting at, Shylock?

SHYLOCK: I'm getting at *you,* Gratiano. Try as I might, I can't forget one thing. And that's what you said to me at the trial. Do you remember that? When they deprived me not only of my livelihood but even of my religion? When my whole identity had been publicly stripped away? When I was being forcibly led to — what did they call it? — "the baptismal font"? Do you remember what you said to me as I was being dragged out the door?

GRATIANO: Vaguely.

SHYLOCK: I don't remember it vaguely. I remember it word for word. This is what you said:

In christening shalt thou have two godfathers.

Had I been judge, thou shouldst have had ten more,
To bring thee to the gallows, not the font.

Do you remember saying that, Gratiano?

GRATIANO: Yes.

SHYLOCK: Now it was a complicated speech, but it seemed to say you wanted me hung, rather than baptized.

GRATIANO: Yes.

SHYLOCK: You wanted me dead, didn't you?

GRATIANO: I did.

SHYLOCK: Why? You, of all people. Haven't we Jews been more your friends than any of the others? Haven't we worked with you, suffered with you, occasionally died with you, and on your behalf?

GRATIANO: Yes.

SHYLOCK: Then why did you, more than any of the others, want me dead?

GRATIANO: May I answer a question with a question?

SHYLOCK: A good Jewish habit. Go ahead.

GRATIANO: Why did you want to kill Antonio? *(Pause.)*

SHYLOCK: You're right. I did, didn't I?

GRATIANO: You wanted to cut out his heart.

SHYLOCK: I did. I did.

GRATIANO: Why?

SHYLOCK: Because he undercut my business every chance he got.

GRATIANO: But isn't that what you're supposed to do in the business world? Isn't that what I'll try to do to another contractor, by submitting a lower bid. Isn't that part of the deal?

SHYLOCK: Yes. That's part of the deal. *(Pause.)* But it is NOT part of the deal to insult a man while you're doing it. To humiliate him. To make vile jokes about him behind his back and sometimes to his face. To spit on him. To exclude him from the very community he is helping to create. To treat him — and by extension, all his people — as if they were less than human, even as you embrace the definition of humanity you've inherited from him. I mean, hath not a Jew eyes, organs, dimensions — *(Stops.)* I'm sorry. I sound like a broken record. *(Gets something out of his pocket.)* I need a Mylanta Plus. Want one?

GRATIANO: Actually I do, thanks. *(They each chew an antacid.)*

SHYLOCK: These discussions go right to my gut.

GRATIANO: I know the feeling.

SHYLOCK: Anyway, that's me and Antonio. How about me and you? Did I ever treat you the way Antonio treated me?

GRATIANO: No.

SHYLOCK: But you hated me.

GRATIANO: I did.

SHYLOCK: Do you still?

GRATIANO: I do.

SHYLOCK: Again may I ask why?

GRATIANO: Because I can't get around it.

SHYLOCK: What can't you get around?

GRATIANO: That you've made it and I haven't. Yesterday you were the most vilified man in Venice. Now here you are, sitting on fifty acres of the loveliest land west of the Adriatic. And where am I? In hock up to my elbows, barely in business after two years of trying. How come you and not me? Is it a question of suffering? Have you suffered more than we? Has your suffering earned you special privileges? We've had our holocausts, too, you know. Slave ships and whippings and lynchings and forcibly severed families and the grim horrors of our own ghettos. Haven't these torments steeled us for the struggle? Haven't they made us wise? You'd think so. Yet why are we still where we are? Why are so many of our brothers shooting each other in the street, and so many of our sisters breeding themselves into despair? Why can't we pull ourselves out and up? Is it our culture, then? Are we culturally deprived? I don't think so. OK. maybe we're not People of the Book — but remember, it was once against the law for us to read. As individuals, I think we've achieved as much as you — maybe more, since we've had less time and less base to build on. But as a people, why are we still behind? Do your books give the answer to that, Shylock? Maybe the Good Book does. *(Suggests a black preacher.)* Maybe it's God. Maybe God has chosen you and not us. But why? Our religion is as dedicated as yours. Our spirituals are as powerful as your psalms, our prayers as deep and sincere. How could God, if he's worth his salt, turn his countenance from his most devoted congregation? *(Swings back into his own voice.)* So what's our trouble then? You know the answer as well as I. It's taking me too long a speech to be able to say it. It's our skin, Shylock. Our black skin. Wrong! Not black. Because we're not really black, and you know it. We are beige, we are burnt umber, we are the color of fine old furniture. We are only designated black by the sallow, the pink, and the pale. That was the excuse for putting us into slavery years ago, and that's what keeps us still enslaved today. Wherever we go, whatever we do, our fate is painted indelibly on our face. So yes, Shylock. We are fellow sufferers, and because of that, you've been more our friend than any of the others. So the more you rise beyond us, the more you stand as a living reminder of how *we've* been chosen, simply by how we look, to stay behind. I hate you for *that*, Shylock.

SHYLOCK: Why should I work with a man who hates me?

GRATIANO: Because I need the job.

SHYLOCK: Put in your bid, and I'll take a look at it.

GRATIANO: Will you look at it seriously?

SHYLOCK: If it's the lowest.

GRATIANO: I guarantee it will be.

SHYLOCK: Because you're nonunion?

GRATIANO: Because they won't let us in.

SHYLOCK: I know the feeling.

GRATIANO: You did once. I wonder if you do now.

(Portia comes out.)

PORTIA: Am I interrupting something?

SHYLOCK: Yes, thank God.

PORTIA: There's someone here who wants to see you.

SHYLOCK: *(To Gratiano.)* Oh well. Who ever got along with his contractor anyway? Go work up your numbers. We'll talk again.

GRATIANO: *(Ironically; giving the black-power salute.)* Shalom!

(He goes off.)

PORTIA: *(Toward off.)* Come on out! *(To Shylock.)* Look what the cat dragged in. *(She brings Jessica on, who is nervous and guilty.)*

SHYLOCK: Oh my God . . . If you have tears, prepare to shed them now. *(Jessica tries to leave.)*

PORTIA: *(Arm around Jessica.)* Now, now my father said the same thing when I flunked out of law school. *(To Shylock.)* Are we going to have a family fight?

SHYLOCK: Not at all.

PORTIA: Good. Then I'll get back to my packing. *(She goes. Pause.)*

JESSICA: Hello, Daddy. *(Pause.)*

SHYLOCK: *(Finally.)* Welcome home, Princess.

JESSICA: Thanks, Dad.

SHYLOCK: I bought you a present.

JESSICA: I don't want a present, Dad.

SHYLOCK: You might want this one. *(Indicates.)* Look around. It's yours. Your castle, Princess. Fifty-four acres. Pool, gardens, partial view of the Adriatic . . .

JESSICA: Dad . . .

SHYLOCK: And I'm fixing it up for you, darling. Modern kitchen. All new appliances.

JESSICA: I don't want it, Dad.

SHYLOCK: Don't want it?

JESSICA: I just want to talk.

SHYLOCK: Talk?

JESSICA: Without being interrupted. The way I never could at the dinner table.

SHYLOCK: All right, darling. Talk. Talk. Talk.

JESSICA: First, I want to apologize for running away.

SHYLOCK: Oh well. Sometimes people run off in order to come back. Your cousin Sophie in Odessa brought home a Cossack. . .

JESSICA: Dad . . .

SHYLOCK: I'm the one who should apologize, sweetheart. With our own children, we make all the mistakes. Out of love, Jessie. Always out of love.

JESSICA: Dad, please!

SHYLOCK: Forgive me, sweetheart. Go ahead. Talk.

JESSICA: I also want to tell you —

SHYLOCK: You're no longer with Lorenzo. You've found a Chinaman. A father knows.

JESSICA: Dad . . .

SHYLOCK: Good businessmen, the Chinese. Jews of Asia. Wave of the future.

JESSICA: Daddy . . .

SHYLOCK: Let me meet the man. Bring on the Chink.

JESSICA: Please don't call him that, Dad! You, of all people, making ethnic slurs.

SHYLOCK: Sorry, darling. I'm just nervous. Continue with the talking.

JESSICA: I'm not with him anymore, Dad. We had major cultural differences. I wanted to discuss Tiananmen Square. He wanted to study for his Graduate Record Exam. *(Sits at his feet.)* I guess I don't understand men, Dad.

SHYLOCK: You'll find the right one, sweetheart. When your mother died, I thought my life was over . . . But who knows? *(Glances toward the house.)* Suddenly it can be a whole new ballgame.

JESSICA: You feel that, too?

SHYLOCK: I do, darling. Now finish the talking.

JESSICA: Maybe I don't have to. *(Calling off.)* Come on out. I think he's ready for it.

SHYLOCK: Ready for what, darling? *(Nerissa comes out, lookin especially Latin with large earrings, elaborate hairdo, and exotic clothes.)*

NERISSA: *Come esta, Senor.*

JESSICA: *(Taking Nerissa's arm.)* This is Nerissa, Dad. We've decided to be together.

SHYLOCK: *Oy.*

JESSICA: And please don't say oy. It sounds so Jewish.

SHYLOCK: I'm sorry. *(To Nerissa; awkwardly.)* Welcome . . . Sit down . . . Have a glass of tea.

NERISSA: *Disculpeme usted, Señor, pero Jessica y yo tenemos que conocer mejor como majeres antes de poder enrollarnos en lo que es el mundo complicado del hombre.*

SHYLOCK: Can't she speak English?

JESSICA: She doesn't want to. She says the key to her identity lies in her native tongue.

SHYLOCK: Then how can you understand her? You flunked Spanish in high school.

JESSICA: Oh Dad. Don't you know that women communicate on a level deeper than language.

SHYLOCK: *Oy* — I mean, *yo comprendo.*

JESSICA: I now realize that when I ran away from home, I was simply rebelling against how men treat women all over the world.

SHYLOCK: Men change, darling. Times change, too. Communicate any way you want. English, Spanish, Yiddish, who cares, as long as you come home, you and Nerissa both.

NERISSA: *Estas loco? Ni hablar. Ni pensar. Ni imaginar. De ninguna manera. No podrza yo hacer eso. Olvidelo. Francamente no me de la gana. Ast es!*

SHYLOCK: What did she say?

JESSICA: She said no.

NERISSA: *Necesito buscar mis raices; ella necita cortar las sayas.*

JESSICA: She says she needs to discover her roots, and I need to sever mine.

NERISSA: *(Dancing up to Shylock.) Oye Pappy! Pensamos comenzar en el verdadero comienzo . . . (Turning to Jessica.) . . . o sea, en la isla Espanola, donde el mismisimo Cristobal Colón acaba de llegar! (They embrace and giggle excitedly.)*

JESSICA: *(To Shylock.)* She wants to begin at the beginning — namely, on the island of Hispaniola, where Columbus first discovered the New World.

SHYLOCK: She's leaving Venice for Haiti?

JESSICA: So am I, Dad. I'm trying to move beyond my own rights, or women's rights, to human rights in general.

SHYLOCK: I suppose Haiti's a good place to begin. *(Nerissa nudges Jessica.)*

JESSICA: But here's the real reason I came back, Dad. I wanted to give you this. *(Hands him a ring.)*

SHYLOCK: *(Looking at it.)* Your mother's ring . . . I heard you hocked it in Genoa. For a pet monkey.

JESSICA: I was an asshole, all right?

SHYLOCK: I'll make a deal with you. I won't say oy if you won't say that word, yes?

JESSICA: What word? Asshole?

SHYLOCK: *Oy.*

JESSICA: It's a deal, Dad. *(She kisses him.)* So long, Daddy. Take care. *(She starts out with Nerissa.)*

SHYLOCK: *(Calling after her.)* Come back soon, darling! I'll give you your own special contest right in this house, just like Portia's. Suitors will come from far and wide, and you'll have the pick of the pack. Who knows? Maybe you'll end up marrying some nice Jewish dermatologist.

JESSICA: *Oy.*

NERISSA: *Adios, Venezia! (Jessica and Nerissa go, Nerissa speaking a torrent of Spanish, Jessica, nodding energetically, Shylock waving longingly after them. Portia comes to the doorway.)*

PORTIA: Is the coast clear?

SHYLOCK: I believe so.

PORTIA: Good. Because you have another visitor, Shylock. *(Calls off.)* He'll see you now. *(To Shylock.)* I feel like a receptionist in a dentist's office. *(Antonio comes out hesitantly. He is now dressed more elegantly.)*

SHYLOCK: Antonio!

ANTONIO: You sent for me, Shylock?

SHYLOCK: I did not.

ANTONIO: You didn't?

PORTIA: Actually, I did. I left a message on his machine saying you wanted to do business with him.

SHYLOCK: Do *business?*

ANTONIO: What business?

SHYLOCK: Portia, have you forgotten that for years Antonio and I have been mortal enemies?

ANTONIO: *(Turning to leave.)* I see that I'm here under totally false pretenses.

PORTIA: *(Holding him.)* No, now wait. You're two of my favorite people. And both marvelous businessmen. So before I go, I think you should make at least *some* attempt to get together.

(She goes in. Long pause.)

ANTONIO: I hear you've bounced back.

SHYLOCK: When you hit us, do we not bounce?

ANTONIO: They say you've bought Belmont.

SHYLOCK: No one else seemed to want it.

ANTONIO: I couldn't afford the heating bills.

SHYLOCK: Why not? I'm told three of your ships came in.

ANTONIO: Ah yes. Loaded with Japanese goods. And one's gone out again, half empty. My balance of trade is a little shaky these days.

SHYLOCK: You sound like me. I'm in hock up to my elbows after buying this thing . . . Why don't we pool what we have left.

ANTONIO: I'd have to pass on that.

SHYLOCK: Still anti-Semitic, eh?

ANTONIO: Not at all. There's another reason. Read tomorrow's *Venice Voice.* I'm a gay white male, bursting out of the closet, both guns blazing.

SHYLOCK: So?

ANTONIO: So it wouldn't work. In international commerce, being gay is a major liability. The Russians imprison us, the Chinese torture us, the Arabs castrate us — even in Venice, there are Christians who want to damn us into outer darkness.

SHYLOCK: This is the religion you made me convert to?

ANTONIO: I'm afraid it is. We preach love thy neighbor as ourself. But if he's not *like* ourself, we have a tendency to beat him up. *(Lorenzo comes on, sees Shylock.)*

LORENZO: Hi! It's so great to finally meet you. *(Shylock looks at him blankly.)* I'm Lorenzo. Your ex-future-son-in-law.

SHYLOCK: Ah.

LORENZO: There's so much we have to talk about.

SHYLOCK: Some other time, please. I am telling this gentleman we should turn our swords into stock shares.

LORENZO: God, what rich Biblical imagery! Do it, gentlemen!

ANTONIO: I can't. I've lived a tormented life for too long. I now need the reassuring support of my own particular subculture.

SHYLOCK: *(To Lorenzo.)* What did he say?

LORENZO: I'm not sure, Shylock. But I *am* sure that whenever we gentiles get hung up, Jews are always willing to go the extra mile.

SHYLOCK: Antonio, let me tell you a short, short story.

LORENZO: *(To Antonio.)* Here comes a wonderfully appropriate Jewish anecdote.

SHYLOCK: *(To Lorenzo.)* Please. *(To Antonio, patiently.)* Before I married my wife Leah — God rest her soul — I was seriously dating another girl. But we split up. Because of a personal problem she had struggled with all her life.

ANTONIO: She was gay?

SHYLOCK: She was left-handed.

ANTONIO: You dropped her for that?

SHYLOCK: She dropped *me*. For not noticing.

ANTONIO: What's your point, Shylock?

SHYLOCK: My point is, now I notice. So shut up with this mishegas about who's gay already. Let's work together. Times are changing so fast that soon no one will care whether you're a southpaw or a fruit.

LORENZO: *(Quickly.)* Gay, Shylock. The word is a gay.

SHYLOCK: *(Hitting himself on the head.)* I'm learning, I'm learning.

ANTONIO: Suppose we did go into business together, Shylock. What could I possibly bring to it that you don't?

SHYLOCK: Good taste, for one thing.

ANTONIO: Good taste?

SHYLOCK: I've got none. I've had to confine my inventory primarily to Venetian blinds.

ANTONIO: You think I've got good taste, Shylock? Me? An aging Italian homosexual? My living room looks like a Neapolitan whorehouse.

SHYLOCK: I wouldn't know, of course.

ANTONIO: You're like everybody else, Shylock. You think we all like decorating rooms and musical comedy.

SHYLOCK: Give me some credit, please. I know you all like grand opera.

ANTONIO: I like opera, Shylock, because I think Guiseppe Verdi has more balls than any composer around. But I am also a champion bowler and a major fan of the Venice Vikings.

SHYLOCK: Good! Then you can talk football scores with clients at power breakfasts while I'm reading the chess column in the *Times*.

ANTONIO: Oh hell, Shylock. You win. Let's give it a try.

LORENZO: Then shake hands, gentlemen! *(He brings them together. They shake hands.)* God, this is a moving moment! I can't help but think of the Middle East Peace Process. *(Antonio tries to kiss Shylock.)*

SHYLOCK: No kissing, please. Not till we've made our first million.
(Salerio comes on, dressed in snow boots, a ski parka, and woolen hat for Switzerland.)

SALERIO: Will someone please get Portia? We've got a plane to catch.

LORENZO: Plane? Where to?

SHYLOCK: Salerio's taking Portia off to Switzerland.

LORENZO: What? Why?

SHYLOCK: Ask Portia.

LORENZO: I sure will! *(He rushes into the house.)*

ANTONIO: I can't see Venice without Portia.

SALERIO: I prefer to see Portia without Venice.

(Portia comes on in a nifty traveling outfit, carrying a bag and a pair of figure skates.)

PORTIA: *(To Shylock and Antonio.)* Have you two gotten together?

SHYLOCK: It looks that way.

PORTIA: Good. At least I've done the state some service before I say good-bye.

(Lorenzo returns, carrying a large load of bags.)

LORENZO: How come you're going to Switzerland?

PORTIA: I'll tell you at a more appropriate time. I believe there are a few more bags. *(Lorenzo goes in for more bags. Portia turns to the others.)* Now please. I don't want hear anything more about what's happened since I was inside. The world changes every time I turn around, and I'm too shallow and superficial to take it in . . .

SALERIO: *(Producing two first-class plane tickets.)* Our transportation is waiting.

PORTIA: Fine. So. Now for a series of brisk good-byes. *(Goes to Shylock, holding out her hand.)* Shylock, you first. *(Gratiano enters, in his working clothes but wearing a native African cap.)*

GRATIANO: Behold the bridegroom cometh!

(Bassanio marches on, in a Marine Corps dress uniform.)

BASSANIO: Hup, two, three, four . . . Companeee . . . Halt!

PORTIA: Good God, look at you!

GRATIANO: He looks like the doorman at the Ritz.

PORTIA: Nonsense. *(To Antonio.)* Isn't he gorgeous?

ANTONIO: Oh he doth hang upon the cheek of night
Like a rich jewel in an Ethiope's ear.

GRATIANO: Watch it, pal.

BASSANIO: Portia, I've come to say good-bye. They're shipping me out on the next tide.

PORTIA: Where to, darling?

BASSANIO: I had a choice. It was either the Halls of Montezuma or the Shores of Tripoli.

PORTIA: Which did you take?

BASSANIO: Montezuma.

SHYLOCK: Mexico over Libya? *(To Antonio.)* As a Venetian waiter would say . . .

SHYLOCK: and ANTONIO: *(Together.)* "Good choice!"

BASSANIO: *(Kissing Portia.)* I'll send you a postcard, Portia.

PORTIA: Send it care of American Express in Geneva, sweetie. That's where I guess I'll be.

BASSANIO: Switzerland? OK. When I'm more mature, I'll come there and win you again.

PORTIA: I wouldn't, darling. It's hugely expensive. Service *compris* at twenty percent.

BASSANIO: How about it, Shylock?

SHYLOCK: Neither a borrower nor a lender be,
For borrowing—

BASSANIO: Maybe Antonio will help me out.

ANTONIO: What? After you slugged me? Sorry, kid. From here on in, you're on your own.

BASSANIO: That wasn't me who hit you, Antonio. That was the child in me.

ANTONIO: Tell it to the Marines.

BASSANIO: Oh shit. Do you think I'll ever grow up, Antonio?

ANTONIO: Now they've discovered America, I hear you don't have to . . . Come on. I'll see you off.

GRATIANO: *(Calling after him.)* Call me a gondola, buddy.

BASSANIO: *(As they go.)* You're a gondola, buddy.
(He and Antonio are off.)

PORTIA: *(Looking after Bassanio.)* He looks more attractive than ever in uniform.

SALERIO: I suggest we leave, Portia. Before you fall all over again.

PORTIA: *(Snapping out of it.)* Right.
(Lorenzo brings out more of Portia's baggage: a great jumble of skis, fishing rods, surfboard, tennis racquets, etc.)

LORENZO: Here's the last of the carry-on stuff.

SALERIO: Luckily I ordered a truck.

PORTIA: *(To Shylock.)* See how well he knows me? We'll get along fine in Switzerland. *(Again holds out her hand to Shylock.)* So. Shylock . . .

LORENZO: Wait. May I put my oar in here? I want to make a speech.

PORTIA: Make it a short one, Lorenzo. We're in overtime now, and the clock is spinning away.

LORENZO: O.K. Here goes . . . Portia: You may not have heard, but I recently lost my girl to another woman.

PORTIA: How sad.

LORENZO: No. It's fine. I loved her Jewishness, not her womanhood. She sensed that and moved on.

PORTIA: At least you're being a good sport about it.

LORENZO: So are you, Portia. So are you being a good sport about your problems. We are both good sports, which is why I'm making this speech.

SALERIO: *(Picking up some bags.)* Is that it?

LORENZO: No, now wait. If you leave, Portia, it means the end of us Wasps in Venice. So maybe, before we wave good-bye, we should ask ourselves what we have given to the greater Venetian community.

PORTIA: I wish I knew.

SHYLOCK: *(To Gratiano.)* What's a Wasp? I don't even know what one is.

GRATIANO: You will, my Jewish brother. You will.

LORENZO: *(With urgency.)* Listen, Portia. How about the way we deal with money? Frugality? Simplicity? A penny saved? That's us, isn't it? Sure it is! We hate to borrow and we always pay our bills promptly, don't we, Portia?

PORTIA: Maybe that's why we're broke today.

LORENZO: OK, then, wait, what about this fitness kick? Fresh air and green vegetables? Exercise? That's basically Wasp, isn't it, Portia?

PORTIA: I hate sitting around, I'll say that.

LORENZO: There you are! And, um, hold it, hey, the environment! Nature! Conservation! The Sierra Club is riddled with Wasps.

PORTIA: Let one in, you let us all in.

LORENZO: Sure! So we've contributed. And we're still trying. We're making an effort! That's it! That's what it really boils down to. Making an effort. Hanging in. Being tough. We believe in a straight back and a firm jaw and —

SHYLOCK: Excuse me.

LORENZO: Yes, Shylock. Feel free to interrupt. Wasps don't normally do that, but Jews do. So fine. Please.

SHYLOCK: I'm just having difficulty following the argument.

LORENZO: Argument? There's no argument. Wasps don't like to argue. I'm just asking Portia to be my wife, that's all.

PORTIA: Lorenzo!

SALERIO: What?

SHYLOCK: Wouldn't that be putting your wagons in a circle?

LORENZO: Why not? Portia, we'd be a great team, you and I. We'd play mixed doubles every Sunday, and win, too, because of our love of games. And we'd sing Cole Porter around the piano, and know most of the words, and have discreet sex on nonschool nights. We'd produce big blue-eyed children with corny nicknames, who'd say things are yummy, Mummy, any time you want. What do you say, Portia? What do you say?

PORTIA: But you don't love me, Lorenzo.

LORENZO: No, I don't. But I'll be a good sport about it. And I know you will be, too.

PORTIA: Lorenzo, sweetie, know what you're doing? You're stereotyping us.

LORENZO: What?

PORTIA: You're stereotyping all Wasps everywhere.

LORENZO: Good God, I am, aren't I? I've just stereotyped my own people! Christ, I'm a mess! The only thing that can save me is the love of a good woman!

PORTIA: Maybe you should ask Jessica for a rematch.

LORENZO: Maybe I will . . . *(Suddenly.)* Or maybe I'll get a dog!
(He runs off.)

GRATIANO: I'd better keep an eye on him.

PORTIA: Go on, Gratiano.

GRATIANO: *(Starts out, stops, turns.)* I'd propose to you myself, Portia, but I'm a lousy lover.

PORTIA: I don't believe that for one minute.

GRATIANO: *(Slyly; à la Fats Waller.)* One never knows, do one.
(He goes off after Lorenzo.)

SALERIO: *(Again checking his watch.)* We'll miss our flight, Portia.

PORTIA: Oh hell, let's take a later one. More and more I hate to leave all this delicious confusion.

SALERIO: I'm afraid you have to, Portia.

SHYLOCK: What's the hurry?

SALERIO: There's a warrant out for your arrest.

PORTIA: Arrest? On what grounds?

SALERIO: For what you did at the trial: Impersonating an attorney. Practicing law without a license. Manipulating a judgment with a clear conflict of interest. They say it was typical of how you and your crowd have run this town since its inception.

PORTIA: They have a point.

SALERIO: So I suggest we leave before they haul you in.

SHYLOCK: Wait. I'm the injured party here. The warrant won't hold up if I don't press charges.

SALERIO: I pressed them myself. As a concerned citizen in a class action.

PORTIA: You, Salerio? How could you?

SALERIO: Because I'll stop at nothing to take you away! We accountants are capable of wild, demonic passions once we move beyond the balance sheet. *(Takes Portia's arm.)* Give a hand with the luggage, Shylock.

SHYLOCK: Not so fast, Salerio. Unless you immediately go down to city hall and withdraw your complaint, I will announce to the world who you really are.

SALERIO: Who I really am?

SHYLOCK: There's something about you that made me nervous. When Jews get nervous, they call the Anti-Defamation League. That's what I did when I was inside. They faxed me your résumé. *(Takes out a fax.)*

SALERIO: They've got nothing on me.

SHYLOCK: *(Putting on his reading glasses.)* Oh no? What about your ethnic identity?

PORTIA: Isn't Salerio a native Venetian?

SHYLOCK: He is not. He is a native Serbian. *(Reading.)* His original name was Salerovitch.

PORTIA: Serbian!

SHYLOCK: And I am afraid he has inherited from that unfortunate country an instinct to disrupt any multicultural community that tries to arise.

SALERIO: *(Serbian accent.)* Ah hah! So we Serbs are the villains *du jour*, eh? Last week it was Sadam Hussein. Next week, someone else. Sorry, Shylock. I'll ride that one out in Switzerland.

SHYLOCK: *(Reading from his list.)* Point two. The Antidefamation League told me who your uncle was.

SALERIO: They had no right! That's private and personal!

PORTIA: Who was his uncle?

SHYLOCK: His uncle was a man named Iago.

SALERIO: Oh no. Oh no.

PORTIA: Iago? We read about him in boarding school! The devil figure! A master at destroying the precarious trust on which all human relationships are built! He's related to that Iago?

SHYLOCK: His uncle on his mother's side.

PORTIA: I am appalled.

SALERIO: Thank you, Shylock, for proving that we still live in a world of bias and prejudice. You, of all people, have just defamed a man . . . *(The accent returns.)* Simply because of where he was born and the fact that he had a crazy uncle. *(He subdues the accent.)* So much for your new Venice.

SHYLOCK: *(To Portia.)* He's right. *(Tears up the fax.)* Strike everything I said from the record. We cannot judge the man on these grounds.

PORTIA: You can't, because you're Jewish, Shylock, and live by a higher moral code. As for me, I'm a superficial Wasp, and I feel perfectly comfortable in revealing that he has a disgusting personal habit!

SALERIO: What disgusting personal habit?

PORTIA: Salerio, I hereby announce to the world and to your HMO that you are a secret smoker!

SALERIO: That is a lie!

PORTIA: I have Polaroids to prove it!

SALERIO: *(Aside.)* Fuck.

SHYLOCK: Please! There are ladies present!

SALERIO: That was an aside, Shylock!

SHYLOCK: Excuse me.

SALERIO: *(With the accent again.)* Yes, well, I'll go quietly. *(Glancing at Portia.)* Unlike some people, I know when the game's over.

SHYLOCK: *(Holding out his hand.)* You might return the lady's credit card. *(Salerio reaches into his pocket, hands Shylock the card.)*

SALERIO: Gladly. It's about to expire anyway.

(He goes off noisily tapping a cigarette out of a fresh pack.)

SHYLOCK: *(Looking at the credit card.)* He was right. This is about to run out.

PORTIA: An image of my life.

SHYLOCK: Now, now.

PORTIA: Thank you anyway, Shylock. You saved the day.

SHYLOCK: I have to say I'm still not satisfied, Portia. I put on a dress shirt, I get out my tuxedo, I expected a party.

PORTIA: *(Sitting on a suitcase.)* I'll never give another party. Ever. I'm thinking of becoming a nun. *(Pause.)* Except I never liked their shoes.

SHYLOCK: Portia: remember when I said that the great thing about Venice was that everyone wanted to make things better?

PORTIA: How could I forget?

SHYLOCK: I was thinking especially of you.

PORTIA: Me? How come?

SHYLOCK: The party you tried to give. You could have just jumped into bed with your sexy boyfriend. But first you wanted to celebrate something. And you wanted everybody in on it. Even me. It was a wonderful idea.

PORTIA: It was dumb from the word go.

SHYLOCK: No, no. All evening long, you've been groping towards a true democracy.

PORTIA: I may have groped, but I sure missed the brass ring.

SHYLOCK: Grope again.

PORTIA: Now? It's a little late, isn't it? People have all gone home. They're locking their doors and turning on their burglar alarms.

SHYLOCK: Call them out again.

PORTIA: What? I don't understand you, Shylock. Here you are, a man who has been thoroughly victimized by the Venetian establishment, now urging a trivial Venetian lady — a lady who helped victimize you, I might add — to throw a party in the middle of the night.

SHYLOCK: I'm being very selfish, Portia.

PORTIA: How do you mean?

SHYLOCK: I believe in the social contract. When that goes, we Jews are the first to suffer. That's why women like you are so important. You keep the whole game going, even in overtime.

PORTIA: Are you serious?

SHYLOCK: Where would the world be without women like you to bring us together? Penelope! Eleanor of Acquitaine! Kitty Carlisle Hart! You're the backbone of civilization, Portia.

PORTIA: Why . . . thank you, Shylock.

SHYLOCK: No, seriously. Everything seems to be separating out these days. The Piazza San Marco has been supplanted by a suburban Mall. The Campanile by a television tower. The Teatro Venezia by a multiplex cinema. We travel alone, exercise in front of mirrors, and eat on the run. What opportunities do we have to rub up against each other in a real way? Give another party, Portia. With you greeting people at the door, maybe the spirit of democracy has a chance to shine.

PORTIA: You make me sound like the Statue of Liberty.

SHYLOCK: I hope so. Now please. I bought this place, show me how to use it.

PORTIA: Tell you what. I'll organize a shindig if you'll pay the bill.

SHYLOCK: It's a deal.

PORTIA: We'll call it an open house.

SHYLOCK: Good idea! Then my daughter might show up.

(They start out.)

PORTIA: We'll need more liquor.

SHYLOCK: And food, please.

PORTIA: Food is tricky. Same with music. Everyone wants something different these days.

SHYLOCK: Give people a choice.

PORTIA: All right, Shylock. It sounds like a very peculiar get-together, but you asked for it. *(Taking his arm.)* By the way, do you like to dance?

SHYLOCK: With you, I'll try anything.

PORTIA: I'll put on some CDs. Before the night is over, I'll bet you and I are doing some pretty funky steps.

SHYLOCK: *Oy. (They go in, as Lorenzo comes on with Gratiano.)*

LORENZO: *(Watching Portia and Shylock go.)* She's going to marry Shylock.

GRATIANO: Portia and Shylock? Not in a million years.

LORENZO: *(Arm around Gratiano.)* You wait. As sure as summer follows spring, Sweet Portia will be wearing Shylock's ring!

(Both laugh as music comes up and the lights go to black. Note: the curtain call should be considered a continuation of the play as the community of the cast reassembles and dances in all sorts of styles and combinations before taking its bows.)

THE END